Beyond Comfort Zones in Multiculturalism

Critical Studies in Education and Culture Series

Education Still under Siege: Second Edition
Stanley Aronowitz and Henry A. Giroux

Media Education and the (Re)Production of Culture
David Sholle and Stan Denski

Critical Pedagogy: An Introduction
Barry Kanpol

Coming Out in College: The Struggle for a Queer Identity
Robert A. Rhoads

Education and the Postmodern Condition
Michael Peters, editor

Critical Multiculturalism: Uncommon Voices in a Common Struggle
Barry Kanpol and Peter McLaren, editors

Beyond Liberation and Excellence: Reconstructing the Public Discourse on Education
David E. Purpel and Svi Shapiro

Schooling in a "Total Institution": Critical Perspectives on Prison Education
Howard S. Davidson, editor

Simulation, Spectacle, and the Ironies of Education Reform
Guy Senese with Ralph Page

Repositioning Feminism and Education: Perspectives on Educating for Social Change
*Janice Jipson, Petra Munro, Susan Victor, Karen Froude Jones, and
Gretchen Freed-Rowland*

Culture, Politics, and Irish School Dropouts: Constructing Political Identities
G. Honor Fagan

Anti-Racism, Feminism, and Critical Approaches to Education
Roxana Ng, Pat Staton, and Joyce Scane

Beyond Comfort Zones in Multiculturalism

CONFRONTING THE POLITICS OF PRIVILEGE

Edited by
Sandra Jackson
and
José Solís

Critical Studies in Education and Culture Series
Edited by Henry A. Giroux and Paulo Freire

BERGIN & GARVEY
Westport, Connecticut • London

Library of Congress Cataloging-in-Publication Data

Beyond comfort zones in multiculturalism : confronting the politics of
    privilege / edited by Sandra Jackson and José Solís.
        p.   cm. —   (Critical studies in education and culture series,
    ISSN 1064–8615)
      Includes bibliographical references and index.
      ISBN 0–89789–415–4 (alk. paper)
        1. Multicultural education—United States.   2. Multiculturalism—
    United States.   I. Jackson, Sandra.   II. Solís, José.
      III. Series.
      LC1099.3.B494   1995
      370.19'6—dc20   95–6950

British Library Cataloguing in Publication Data is available.

Library of Congress Catalog Card Number: 95–6950

ISBN: 0–89789–415–4
ISSN: 1064–8615

First published in 1995

Bergin & Garvey, 88 Post Road West, Westport, CT 06881
An imprint of Greenwood Publishing Group, Inc.

Printed in the United States of America

The paper used in this book complies with the
Permanent Paper Standard issued by the National
Information Standards Organization (Z39.48–1984).

10 9 8 7 6 5 4 3 2 1

This book is dedicated to those
whose insistence upon their liberation
gives meaning to the principle of
educating for freedom.

Contents

Contents

Acknowledgments

This book is the result of much direct and indirect effort by many people whose support was given for its development and production. The idea for the book arose from our concern with the persistence of land based issues characterizing the realities of certain groups of people of color and the impact that this issue has for their understanding of multiculturalism.

Within this context, we would like to extend our sincerest and heartfelt appreciation for the voices of the contributors who, despite their heavy schedules and other assignments, offer us in these pages eloquent chapters and serious challenges for us all. These authors have committed their lives to struggling and educating in an effort to contribute to the liberation of their peoples and land.

In editing this book, communication with many people in many places became a formidable task for us. This burden was lightened thanks to the secretarial support offered by Lisa Silverman and Lisa McDonald at DePaul University's School of Education. On the production side of publication, we would like to express our gratitude to Mervin Méndez and María Vázquez for their help in reading and putting the text into shape; to Tom Roser of DePaul University's LA&S Computer Skills Center; to the University Research Council at DePaul University for granting us support so that we could finalize the work; and to David Pellaur, chair of the Philosophy Department at DePaul for use of his scanner. We would especially like to thank our editor Lynn Flint and our production manager Katie Chase at Greenwood Publishing Group for their support and invaluable assistance in preparing the manuscript for publication.

For us it is with the utmost respect and hope that the book achieves broad appeal and educational value that we extend our appreciation to Henry Giroux and Paulo Freire for including it in their series at Bergin & Garvey.

Finally, we would like to recognize the endless hours of support given to the project by our spouses, Fassile Demise and Martha González. They were both reaffirming and critical in helping us forge the character of the book.

Series Foreword

Henry A. Giroux

Within the last decade, the debate over the meaning and purpose of education has occupied the center of political and social life in the United States. Dominated largely by an aggressive and ongoing attempt by various sectors of the Right, including "fundamentalists," nationalists, and political conservatives, the debate over educational policy has been organized around a set of values and practices that take as their paradigmatic model the laws and ideology of the marketplace and the imperatives of a newly emerging cultural traditionalism. In the first in-stance, schooling is being redefined through a corporate ideology that stresses the primacy of choice over community, competition over cooperation, and excellence over equity. At stake here is the imperative to organize public schooling around the related practices of competition, reprivatization, standardization, and individ-ualism.

In the second instance, the New Right has waged a cultural war against schools as part of a wider attempt to contest the emergence of new public cultures and social movements that have begun to demand that schools take seriously the imperatives of living in a multiracial and multicultural democracy. The contours of this cultural offensive are evident in the call by the Right for standardized testing, the rejection of multiculturalism, and the development of curricula around what is euphemistically called a "common culture." In this perspective, the notion of a common culture serves as a referent to denounce any attempt by subordinate groups to challenge the narrow ideological and political parameters by which such a culture both defines and expresses itself. It is not too surprising that the theoretical and political distance between defining schools around a common culture and denouncing cultural difference as the enemy of democratic life is relatively short indeed.

This debate is important not simply because it makes visible the role that schools play as sites of political and cultural contestation, but because it is within this debate that the notion of the United States as an open and democratic society is being questioned and redefined. Moreover, this debate provides a challenge to progressive educators both in and outside of the United States to address a number of conditions central to a postmodern world. First, public schools cannot be seen as either objective or neutral. As institutions actively involved in constructing political subjects and presupposing a vision of the future, they must be dealt with in terms that are simultaneously historical, critical, and transformative. Second, the relationship between knowledge and power in schools places undue emphasis on disciplinary structures and on individual achievement as the primary unit of value. Critical educators need a language that emphasizes how social identities are constructed within unequal relations of power in the schools and how schooling can be organized through interdisciplinary approaches to learning and cultural differences that address the dialectical and multifaceted experiences of everyday life. Third, the existing cultural transformation of American society into a multiracial and multicultural society structured in multiple relations of domination demands that we address how schooling can become sites for cultural democracy rather than channeling colonies reproducing new forms of nativism and racism. Finally, critical educators need a new language that takes seriously the relationship between democracy and the establishment of those teaching and learning conditions that enable forms of self- and social determination in students and teachers. This suggests not only new forms of self-definition for human agency, it also points to redistributing power within the school and between the school and the larger society.

Critical Studies in Education and Culture is intended as both a critique and as a positive response to these concerns and the debates from which they emerge. Each volume is intended to address the meaning of schooling as a form of cultural politics and cultural work as a pedagogical practice that serves to deepen and extend the possibilities of democratic public life. Broadly conceived, some central considerations present themselves as defining concerns of the Series. Within the last decade, a number of new theoretical discourses and vocabularies have emerged that challenge the narrow disciplinary boundaries and theoretical parameters that construct the traditional relationship among knowledge, power, and schooling. The emerging discourses of feminism, postcolonialism, literary studies, cultural studies, and postmodernism have broadened our understanding of how schools work as sites of containment and possibility. No longer content to view schools as objective institutions engaged in the transmission of an unproblematic cultural heritage, the new discourses illuminate how schools function as cultural sites actively engaged in the production of not only knowledge but social identities. *Critical Studies in Education and Culture* will attempt to encourage this type of analysis by emphasizing how schools might be addressed as border institutions or sites of crossing actively involved in exploring, reworking, and translating the ways in which culture is produced, negotiated, and rewritten.

Emphasizing the centrality of politics, culture, and power, *Critical Studies in Education and Culture* will deal with pedagogical issues that contribute in novel ways to our understanding of how critical knowledge, democratic values, and social practices can provide a basis for teachers, students, and other cultural workers to redefine their role as engaged and public intellectuals.

As part of a broader attempt to rewrite and refigure the relationship between education and culture, *Critical Studies in Education and Culture* is interested in work that is interdisciplinary, critical, and addresses the emergent discourses on gender, race, sexual preference, class, ethnicity, and technology. In this respect, the Series is dedicated to opening up new discursive and public spaces for critical interventions into schools and other pedagogical sites. To accomplish this, each volume will attempt to rethink the relationship between language and experience, pedagogy and human agency, and ethics and social responsibility as part of a larger project for engaging and deepening the prospects of democratic schooling in a multiracial and multicultural society. Concerns central to this Series include addressing the political economy and deconstruction of visual, aural, and printed texts, issues of difference and multiculturalism, relationships between language and power, pedagogy as a form of cultural politics, and historical memory and the construction of identity and subjectivity.

Critical Studies in Education and Culture is dedicated to publishing studies that move beyond the boundaries of traditional and existing critical discourses. It is concerned with making public schooling a central expression of democratic culture. In doing so it emphasizes works that combine cultural politics, pedagogical criticism, and social analyses with self-reflective tactics that challenge and transform those configurations of power that characterize the existing system of education and other public cultures.

Beyond Comfort Zones in Multiculturalism

Introduction: Resisting Zones of Comfort in Multiculturalism

Sandra Jackson and José Solís

When we embarked upon this work, different motivations were present. In having decided to write this book, we, like Toni Morrison and others before us, have decided to produce a book that we would like to (have) read. Our review of books and articles revealed a hiatus—one characterized by a conspicuous absence of voices and perspectives of people of color who would not let multiculturalism rest, who would not let apparent victories in school reform, hiring practices, and cosmetic curricular changes lull them into believing that they should be satisfied and settle for less than transformation in education. *Race* [Still] *Matters* (West, 1993), *The Color Line* yet persists (Franklin, 1993), *The Woman Question* (1951) still lingers beneath the fresh topsoil nurturing feminist seedlings, and *Words that Wound* (Matsuda et al., 1993) addresses resurgent and rampant racially motivated violence and hate speech in spite of First Amendment rights and protection.

Reminded that power concedes nothing, the theme of multiculturalism took on a host of traits that we were compelled to examine. From a conceptual and practical standpoint, multiculturalism seems desirable. Yet debates around the meaning of culture persist, problematizing the possibilities of multiculturalism. That so much support dominates academic, social, and political discourses on multiculturalism raises some rather serious questions about its meaning, content, and practice generally. This is not to argue against multiculturalism. It is, however, important to note what is not being mentioned in the multicultural debates. And it is here where we would like to locate this book.

What things, events, and issues have brought us in the academy to this juncture? What has propelled and compelled our attention to issues of difference, diversity, and the searching for ways to inform and enhance our mission as educators through engagement in the discourse of multiculturalism? What prompts us to wade in these troubled waters, buffeted by harsh criticism and often cynical criticism by those (such as Arthur Schlesinger, Jr., Dinish D'Souza, E. D. Hirsch, Diane Ravitch, and Allan Bloom) intent upon upholding a particular tradition, and those who perceive institutional responsiveness to difference as a ploy of accommodation and cooptation? Multiculturalism has become popularized and simultaneously demonized. In some quarters it is vilified by those resistant to change and revision in disciplinary canons and their undergirding Eurocentric assumptions about epistemology, what is most worthy of being known, and whose knowledge is legitimate, with challenges to hegemonic constructs privileging particular groups over others. In other quarters it is acclaimed as a way to address diversity, difference, representation, voice, and issues of power in teaching and learning, inclusive of curriculum, organization and structure of institutions, classroom settings, and the imperative to redress social ills in the pursuit of social justice. Particular historical and social conditions and perhaps insight and understanding about the necessity to change should indeed contribute to transform our work and the institutions in which we work, to meet challenges that go to the very core of the educational project of transformation.

While we are encouraged, in much of the literature, to celebrate diversity and difference, we are not encouraged to unpack the implications of these things for the lives and development of different peoples—especially those oppressed and colonized peoples of color whose communities in the United States stand as reminders of a legacy of subordination and conquest. This book is an attempt to disclose some of the problems of multiculturalism, and to show how a demystification of some of the implications of multiculturalism might afford us the opportunity to forge possibilities for multiculturalism grounded in the most basic exercise of cultural affirmation, self-determination. Employing multiple perspectives, the contributors of this book affirm that anything less than self-determination in multicultural development is evasive and empty of any real meaningful content and pedagogy.

Comfort zones are those arenas wherein multiculturalism has been advocated from what we argue are essentially additive, procedural, and technical perspectives. The task before us, then, is to force the parameters of those comfort zones outward, pushing for broader and more liberating constructs capable of engendering a pedagogy for transformation in a real and material sense, and not merely a recognition and acknowledgment of difference. This task is constituted by different requirements. Among these is an understanding of what the issues are. Let us point out that this book is not meant to be representative of any generalized nation, community, or group. It is an expression of different people as they examine the problems and possibilities of multiculturalism. Because multiplicities of identity intersect, the book claims no essentialisms. Yet identity is forged in particular contexts; and some of these contexts are herein alluded to. For oppressed and colonized peoples and nations, multiculturalism may have some rather different meanings; and these meanings play an important part in developing broader understandings of multiculturalism for us all, regardless of where we might locate ourselves.

For peoples whose legal agreements, treaties, and other accords and conventions with the United States have been violated, multiculturalism as a pedagogical tool often becomes suspect of reinforcing the continued reification and abstraction of their cultures and nations with little if any real meaning for educational and, as such, social transformative power. These peoples understand that the "master" yields to nothing without deriving superior results from any proposition. Here, then, multiculturalism needs to be contextualized in historical and social-cultural terms in order to arrive at a genuine terrain of possibilities, and not be merely conciliatory acts that lead to no change in the quality of the lives of oppressed and colonized peoples. A multicultural project that attends to these issues is compelled to explore geographies generally left unexamined, for the most part, by those advocating multicultural agendas.

Let us pose the following proposition to the reader: The basis of the history of the United States is predicated on primarily two major socioeconomic and political criminal acts: the genocide of indigenous populations and chattel slavery of African peoples. This is not meant to advocate a reductionist position. Rather, it is meant to raise these as issues that for many peoples remain salient points of reference. The continued oppression and repression of the exercise of self-determination for New Afrikan and African Americans; the persistence of policies aimed at the destruction of indigenous populations and land, the conquest and illegal occupation of Mexican territories resulting in the internal colonization of Mexican peoples; and the insidious continuation of classical colonialism in the case of Puerto Rico are all vivid reminders to these peoples of the racist, classist, sexist, and homophobic patriarchy that characterizes their status. If multiculturalism is to travel beyond the comfort zones, it must come to terms with the criminal acts committed by the United States against these and other peoples. Joel Kovel (1970), in his exceptional study, "White Racism," reminds us that

the integral American self has been constituted historically by its violation of Others . . . racism in all its varieties is the subjective reflex of imperialism, the fate of primary tendencies of alienation under the domination of the imperial state. Consequently, to restore peoples-rights to fully determine their own histories, it is imperative to destroy the material foundations that breed and recycle the ideology, discourse, and cultural practices of racism.

A multiculturalism that is unable or unwilling to address this issue falls short of making any real difference in educational, social, or practical contexts.

The positions taken by many of the contributors to this book draw from an understanding of international law in the context of social and cultural relations. And yet, international law, though a reference, is nevertheless limited, since the peoples against whom numerous criminal acts have been committed have never been part of the development of any international law regarding their well-being. In some significant ways, then, law as constructed by a people in the name of their public well-being constitutes an act of self-determination, a multicultural activity.

Because different peoples of color in the United States still have issues of sovereignty, land, and independence yet to be settled with the United States, legal recourse is sought at the international level. This has serious implications for multiculturalists who limit their scope to celebrating diversity, while the context remains sorely unjust and embedded in a violation of peoples' most fundamental rights as different cultures and nations. It is, in part, because of this that multiculturalism is so problematic.

The United States has violated numerous international agreements, conventions, laws, declarations, and resolutions that are of fundamental import to the peoples herein presented. Violating these charters and conventions—Nuremburg Charter, Judgment, and Principles; the 1948 Convention on the Prevention and Punishment of the Crime of Genocide; the 1973 International Convention on the Suppression and Punishment of the Crime of Apartheid; the 1948 Universal Declaration of Human Rights; the 1965 International Convention on the Elimination of All Forms of Racial Discrimination Against Native American Peoples; the resolutions on Self-Determination and Decolonization of the United Nations Charter; the 1966 International Covenant on Economic, Social, and Cultural Rights; and the Geneva Convention of 1949, violating the rights of independence fighters the treatment of protections as prisoners of war under the Third Geneva Convention of 1949 and Additional protocol of 1977—has resulted in the political incarcerations of scores of Puerto Ricans, Africans, and indigenous persons, serving virtual life sentences in U.S. prisons today. Therefore, any genuine multicultural agenda is challenged by this reality. All of the contributors to this volume, however, make clear the argument for decolonization and self-determination in a multicultural pedagogy. Any affirmation of self-determination and as such any process of decolonization has humanizing potential. This is the syntax of multiculturalism that this book advocates.

Additive, technical, and procedural changes in the content and process of developing a multicultural pedagogy are not by definition challenges to relations of power. Grounded in the rights to self-determine and a decolonizing pedagogy, any additive, technical, and/or procedural changes then become the vehicles for transforming power and, as such, education. Again, this book examines an expanded geography of multiculturalism. Unfortunately, reduced to a physical plant, education in the form of a classroom has infused multiculturalism with a characterization whose definition is constructed by traditional discursive activities conducive to the traditional classroom such as expanded syllabi, canonical changes, special events, and many holidays and celebrations. The point is that multiculturalism viewed in this light remains fundamentally problematic and accommodationist.

Pushing the comfort zones, this book includes a consideration of how multiculturalist pedagogy, in content and process, needs to be attentive to a broader set of dynamics of community from which meaning and validity are determined. The experiences and demands of different peoples are not confined to classrooms and infusions of issues and ideas therein. Homes, communities, schools, the media, and the streets are also sites where multiculturalism is developed and understood or resisted. The contributors to this book vivify the richness of histories grounded in struggle on different planes. There is not merely an affirmation of contemplative knowing, but of knowing born of commitment and action in the service of people and their multicultural development. But here culture takes on a different meaning from much of the literature on multiculturalism. Culture here is alive, dynamic, and changing, not standardized or homogenized; not a retreat to relativism, but a very fine notion of difference and diversity constantly engaged in its transformation.

Again, it is interesting to note how in the struggle to be free, to self-determine, and to develop a language of possibility in multiculturalism, oppressed and colonized peoples appear more open to difference and respect for the self-determination of diverse peoples. This book alludes to a solidarity and continuity of struggle. Because it so often lacks a serious challenge to the institutions and relations of power, much of the mainstream literature on multiculturalism continues to affirm a kind of essentialism. This is in part understood in the context of identity formation. U.S. essentialist identity is, in many ways, the result of the negation of the identities of others. Oppressors, Paulo Freire (1971) reminds us, depend upon their oppression of the "Other" for their own identity. Identity is constructed not on the basis of an affirmation of cultural heritage and development, rather identity is premised on the negation of the Other's identity. It becomes fundamental then that in order to maintain power over other peoples, they must see themselves not as different, valid, and meaningful on their own, but in the image of the master.

The ability of the United States to sustain power over the rights to self-determination of the peoples in this book also needs to be examined within the context of the politics of imposition as an historical process. Why is it that people of color in struggle are not shaken by the affirmations of other oppressed and colonized people that assert their nationhood and sovereignty? And why is it that the oppressor is so frightened by the prospect of this inevitable development? Because the colonizers would be forced to look into themselves and ask, what are we in the absence of our power over others? We would respond, "we are human, no one more than another, and all responsible for the protection of one another from ethnocide, genocide, and ecocide." Yet organizing a strict sense of who one is compared to a generalized Other facilitates organizing and categorizing difference without necessarily threatening power relations. Again, simplifying Others tends to maintain a notion of centrality in the voices of those constructing the Other. An affirmation of multiculturalism premised on self-determination, it should be clear, is not about constructing another orthodoxy. Yet in some ways it may be. Here, however, the orthodoxy is one predicated on the self-defined constructs of a difference that affirms the right of self-determination.

This book challenges any position that believes that multiculturalism can ensue in the presence of oppressive and colonial realities. A pedagogy that asserts the celebration of difference must, by implication, affirm the struggles of oppressed and colonized peoples to self-determine, lest multiculturalism be reduced to yet the latest strategy of the colonizer to "deal" with its subordinates. We are immersed in a contentious argument that has often challenged us to revisit what it means to be human, to be members of civil societies and nations. Multiculturalism in this framework is much more than attitudes, beliefs, and issues of inclusion.

In the discourse on multiculturalism that has emerged since the mid-1970s, the primary focus of the literature and research has been on the curriculum and the canon. Most of the debate has emphasized curriculum reform and teaching practices, with tension among and between various approaches: on the one hand additive, procedural, and technical, and on the other hand, that which argues for fundamental changes in educational concepts grounded in critical theory, feminist pedagogy, and arguments for democratic practices in teaching and learning. Very little has been written about higher education, and still less about challenges and implications of multiculturalism for higher education. Clearly, then, the literature regarding multiculturalism and higher education remains lacking. The editors of this project believe that educators need to problematize claims related to social change generally asserted by the literature on multiculturalism.

The generative themes of this book—From I to We: Self-Determination and the Multicultural; Racism: White Skin Privilege; Gendered Subjectivities; and Curriculum, Canon and Syllabi: Who's Teaching What and How—are posed herein to "unpack" some of the problems with the definitions and developments of multicultural projects in general, but especially in the context of the dynamics of educators insurgent in their insistence that transformation in education is imperative. These themes, we affirm, elicit a sense that more fundamentally approaches the historical, political, emotional, and social decolonization processes that are required in any emancipatory project. They force us to openly approach the subject in a serious manner that avoids skating around issues that continue to truncate the development of a multicultural agenda that addresses possibilities, beyond the mere issues of inclusion and representation. In this regard, we believe that commitment to genuine educational transformation means that we forge a dialogue of possibility, examining our own contradictions beyond the comfort zones of current multicultural discourse.

The purpose of this book is to problematize the discourse of multiculturalism. It will examine the limitations and possibilities that struggling with the above-mentioned generative themes offers to an understanding of a multicultural project and its implications for the development of educators who will, in their lived practices in teaching and learning, challenge privilege, cultural hegemony, and inequality.

In problematizing the above-mentioned themes, the book will critically examine ways in which multicultural discourse reinforces traditional pedagogies through assertions that advance multiculturalism as additive, procedural, or technical (traditionally found in logical positivist and liberal pluralist thought), while attending less to the difficult task of realizing the social vision from which multiculturalism actually gathers much of its arguments. For example, what theoretical and methodological issues present themselves to educators in the development of such an emacipatory project as the necessity of moving beyond the realm of ideas to action (to action and practices that transform teaching and learning as well as the curriculum)? What issues present themselves to educators? Here the traditional discourse of learning and teaching is challenged by emancipatory conceptions that assert a commitment to overcome racism, sexism, classism, and genocide, while affirming self-determination. In other words, what possibilities and limitations present themselves in developing a multicultural project that must be, we argue, a process of decolonizing education and, as such, society?

This book seeks to engage educators in the interrogation of multicultural discourse as necessarily a decolonizing discourse. It will do this through the affirmation of self-determination as grounded in a language that provokes educators to wrestle with ideas about how to challenge themselves and their own practices as they educate others how to teach in ways that address racism, sexism, and other forms of domination and control so that we remain mindful and vigilant in our engagement with difference(s)—curricularly and pedagogically—and resolved not to shrink from them. The book will discuss how to teach this in an inclusive and transformative way.

This text insists on pushing the boundaries of multiculturalism and crossing borders into new spaces and places regarding the complexities of culture, identity, teaching and learning, and curriculum, and ideas about the construction of knowledge. We invite educators to begin with their own assumptions, values, practices, and responses to difference. We invite our readers to join us in examining rigorously the aims and purposes of education, the underlying notions about education in a society that promotes individualism, consumerism, competition, homogenization of culture and the negation of difference, the acceptance of socially constructed things as natural, and the inclination to accept the current condition as the one best possible.

We believe that all of these things require questioning and critique. For us, the education of a people to develop independence in thought and action, and to prepare them to be actors and not passive receptors of received ideas and notions, and to dare to dream about creating a more human and just social order raises the necessity of revisiting multiculturalism, its promises and limitations, as we continue to chart where to go from here and how. Within the chapters of this book, different contributors have addressed the task of noting the limitations and possibilities of multiculturalism, drawing from the educational experiences, history, and cultures of different peoples as they forge ahead in the struggle to self-determine and decolonize. There is a reaffirmation of self and group as understood and negotiated by the different peoples presented in the book.

This text, organized into four parts, addresses the four previously mentioned generative themes. Educators of color, men and women, inclusive of Native Americans as well as a contributor from South Africa, the chapter authors rigorously examine multiculturalism in the context of multiple perspectives regarding its promises as well as its limitations in the pursuit of creating institutions, educational frameworks, practices, knowledge construction that is based on inclusion and not exclusion, curriculum in which many peoples are represented with authenticity and integrity exercising power and authority, and pedagogical practices that have at their core values and worldviews grounded in social justice.

The three chapters in Part I, "From I to We: Self-Determination and the Multicultural," address the imperative of decolonization for people of color if educational initiatives are to serve the interest of self-determination and emancipation of people who have been oppressed, exploited, discriminated against, and rendered invisible—whose experiences, histories, struggles, and voices have been silenced and erased within social, cultural, political institutions.

Ward Churchill's chapter "White Studies: The Intellectual Imperialism of U.S. Higher Education" presents a critique of Euro-American intellectual imperialism in higher education and its colonization of knowledge through privileging its own culturally defined, particular ways of thinking, seeing, understanding, and being, to the ultimate exclusion of all others. Through examination of the hegemonic legacy of white supremacy, he discusses how Eurocentric epistemologies permeate various disciplines and fields and the ways in which they have been used in the construction of Eurocentric white male dominance, by the conspicuous absence, indeed negation, of Native American perspectives. He argues for a decolonized, liberatory education, which is inclusive, anticolonial, antiracist, antisexist, and anticlassist. He does not stop at critique. Instead, he proposes strategies to transform higher education through practices that eschew the contributionist approach and call for the recruitment and retention of scholars of color who exemplify expertise in non-Western intellectual traditions and the dissolution of orthodox parameters of disciplinary boundaries.

Imari Abubakari Obadele continues the critique of Eurocentric hegemonic legacies in "Multiculturalism: War in America Continues." He problematizes multiculturalism and what he identifies as its tendencies for not going far enough in its discourses to addressing the need for fundamental change to create a racially democratic society in the United States. After reviewing the history of white supremacist ideology that has shaped this nation's government, its policies and practices, and implications for African Americans, he proposes recommendations that seek to correct "white-imposed, racist, noneducation that has been imposed upon black people over the course of over 300 years." He draws upon particular grassroots initiatives—that have grown out of struggle with local school boards and their efforts to transform curriculum, content, and processes—to illustrate possibilities for change as well as the necessity for vigilance against those who wish to subvert the movement for self-determination either by couching the issue of multiculturalism as a human relations exercise of prejudice reduction, or through maligning the initiative by attempting to reduce it to a simplistic and racially provocative venture.

Félix Masud-Piloto's "*Nuestra Realidad*: Historical Roots of Our Latino Identity" takes up the issue of imposed identities and the importance of resisting homogenization of identities. Highlighting issues relative to identity formation, Masud-Piloto examines the influence that U.S. immigration policy has had on the construction of identities of Others. Using the history of the Hispanic/Latino debate, wherein discussions on the identities of Latin Americans in the United States and a conception of their identities ensue, Masud-Piloto provides a critical account of how the use of the term "Hispanic" has served to strip Latin Americans of the contribution and relation that indigenous and African presence in Latin America has had on the construction of identity in Latin America and for any Latinos in the United States. Masud-Piloto argues that "Latina/o" more accurately accounts for the dynamics of representation and identity of all Latin Americans. He then examines the impact that the ideology behind this has had in the proliferation of immigration policies and U.S. Latin American relations.

In Part II, "Racism: White Skin Privilege," each chapter addresses the issue of race, the politics of culture, and implications for education. Cameron McCarthy and Arlette Ingram Willis' "The Politics of Culture: Multicultural Education After the Content Debate" examines multiculturalism and its "deep imbrication in rhetorical and material struggles over access, equality, and voice." They argue that any discussion of curricular reform must transcend technical and instrumental language of inclusion, content addition, and replacement that dominate the discourse. Instead, they insist that multiculturalism must address issues of representation as well as of unequal distribution of material resources and power outside of the school door.

After engaging in a critique of current multicultural approaches to education (cultural understanding, cultural competence, cultural emancipation), McCarthy and Willis offer another framework, that of a critical emancipatory multiculturalism. They argue that proponents of multiculturalism should not merely focus on curriculum content, but also advocate "broader brush strokes of educational reform": reorganization in schooling, curricular development that is multidisciplinary, agency in instructional leadership, school and community collaboration, and university-school partnerships in preservice teacher education to develop dynamic models of teaching and learning in the service of urban communities.

Marie Annette Jaimes * Guerrero's chapter "Academic Apartheid: American Indian Studies and 'Multiculturalism' " argues that while multiculturalism offers "access to new knowledge bases, it is accommodationist and assimilationist"; therefore it is inadequate to the task of creating educational institutions, curricula, and pedagogies to counteract an education that was designed to keep American Indians "second class, living in Third World conditions." In her view, only decolonization, "the dismantling of Eurocentric hegemony," offers promise of social and political transformation. She, like Churchill, draws upon the experiences of American Indians in the academy regarding curriculum and pedagogy and on the ghettoization of ethnic studies programs. After resoundly critiquing the hegemonic legacy of Eurocentrism, its particular construction of knowledge, ways of knowing, and the values underpinning its worldview, she invokes indigenism as a corrective, to combat the dominant-subordinate relations, and argues for an education that challenges genocide, ethnocide, and ecocide.

"The Doorkeepers: Education and Internal Settler Colonialism, the Mexican Experience" by Priscilla Lujan Falcón resonates with issues raised by Churchill, Obadele, and Jaimes. In her examination of settler colonialism, she reviews historical dimensions of its implications on the Mexican people. Like Churchill and Jaimes in particular, Falcón argues for decolonization for retaining cultural autonomy while gaining economic and political self-determination for Mexicans. For Falcón, multicultural education begs the question and does not address fundamental social and political issues necessary to achieve these goals: segregated schools, discriminatory state policies, underrepresentation in school teaching and staff positions, the English Only Movement and its insistence on erasure of language and social conformity, the militarization of borders, and immigration policies.

Part III, "Gendered Subjectivities," is comprised of two narrative pieces interwoven with theoretical analysis, as well as a third piece regarding a study of personal oral narratives of Puerto Rican women. The thematic chords of these works include the examination of self as a multifaceted, gendered, raced, classed identity; teaching and learning; and individual and collective resistance to domination at multiple sites in the university and the classroom, the nation, as well as within one's community and interpersonal relationships.

Sandra Jackson's "Negotiating Self-Defined Standpoints in Teaching and Learning" opens with a personal narrative that recounts her experiences as a high school teacher. In these reflections she connects them with her experiences as a university professor and the interrogation of her multiple selves as an African American, a woman, and an educator. She writes of confronting racism, sexism, classism, white supremacy, and struggles to create transformative praxis. In arguing for an insurgent pedagogy, Jackson insists on forging education and pedagogy that affirm her multiple selves, are in concert with her sense of ethics, and enable her to teach in ways that engage students to bring their multiple selves into the teaching learning context, which invites inquiry, discussion, and critical examination of issues and ideas in the pursuit of social justice.

"Entre la Marquesina y la Cocina" by José Solís, a male Puerto Rican professor, likewise begins with a personal narrative—one in which he revisits childhood reminiscences wherein he gained an early sense of topography, geography, and the mapping of space(s), sense of self, and identity. He argues against the abstraction of experience and its limitations in the struggle against colonialism. Regarding the issue of gender, whether it be in society, within educational institutions, or within teaching and learning, he contends that the discourse of equity implicitly reinforces the legitimacy of the status quo. He asserts that in the development of national liberation projects there can be no liberation without the transformation of gender, race, and class relations. In his conclusion, Solís argues that the process of decolonization is synonymous with the process of decolonizing gender and nation; anything less begs the question and is unauthentic.

In Lourdes Torres' "Deconstructing Mainstream Discourse Through Puerto Rican Women's Oral Narratives" she examines emergent themes from a case study of Puerto Rican women's representations of self and juxtaposes them to popular cultural depictions in film and social science literature. She addresses contradictions related to internalized sexism, racism, classism, as well as resistance and self-determination in the forging of identity regarding Puerto Rican women and men. The women's stories "confound monolithic and stereotypic portraits of Puerto Rican women, and their words suggest that teaching and learning about them entails the rejection of static models." This will require transformation of the curriculum as well as pedagogy.

Part IV, "Curriculum, Canon, and Syllabi: Who's Teaching What and How," examines multiculturalism and issues of school-community relations, culture and curriculum and social transformation, curricular change and pedagogical practices, uses of technology, and institutional reform in higher education. Sites involve the society, the nation, and the classroom. In "Education in Community: The Role of Multicultural Education," Terence O'Connor critiques the illusiveness of a national culture, the imposition of school identity, and problematizes faith in schooling for a great society in the wake of losing the human dimension regarding communities and groups resisting the juggernaut of a homogenization that negates differences and local color. He argues for a critique of modernism and its claims of universalism—to be replaced by revival and affirmation of local culture and the engagement of choice. In this regard, reconnecting school community relations, preparing multicultural teachers, and transforming pedagogy and making it student-centered are beginnings in the project to overcome the alienation, hostility, silence, and resistance that currently characterize the modern school.

Neville Alexander's chapter, "Core Culture and Core Curriculum in South Africa," problematizes the issue of multiculturalism within the context of another society in which racial domination has been the foundation for oppression and racial, class, and linguistic divides. He argues for a curriculum for unity and diversity. Against the backdrop of the dismantlement of white domination and privilege, he discusses challenges that must be confronted by a postapartheid South Africa, if a nonracial, democratic society is to be forged. A multiculturalism that means only attending to issues of diversity and numbers and not issues of power will result in a thin veneer of change, and will allow the persistence of a neoapartheid social order. For Alexander, the interweaving of core and tributary cultures, in a dynamic and ongoing process, is the only way that social justice in South Africa will be achieved. Identities must be forged and not imposed. He gives particular attention to language policy, early childhood educare programs, innovative curriculum development projects, and struggles against bureaucratization of change that will be central in this regard.

We move to some particulars as well as specificities in Linda Williamson Nelson's chapter, "The Peer Review Group: Writing, Negotiation, and Metadiscourse in the English Classroom," which draws on her own teaching experiences in using transformative pedagogical practices in college writing classes. She argues that the classroom with a culturally diverse population is "better suited than more . . . homogeneous classrooms, to assist students in the work of acquiring classroom discourses." Strategic student intervention through negotiation through metadiscourse (where cultures meet) in clarifying meaning of written works, in her experiences, creates in students the ability to claim the right and the ability to appropriate the discourses associated with public power while at the same time they resist conformity and retain their cultural voices. She concludes that "most students are willing apprentices in the study and practice of standard discourses, especially when their home discourses or native languages are counted for the valued and valuable currency that they are." In Nelson's classroom, students learn far more about language than that which is technical, procedural, and additive. While she argues for the appropriation of public discourse by students, she is well aware of its power as well as its limitations.

"The Cultural Ethos of the Academy: Potentials and Perils for Multicultural Education Reform" by Geneva Gay and Wanda Fox returns us to a number of issues addressed by Churchill: contending with hegemonic paradigms and forging change in curriculum, pedagogy (to which they add uses of technology), faculty recruitment and development, and the transformation of deep structures of the institution and its administration, to enact the multicultural project. The authors discuss three major topics: a conceptual framework that establishes theoretical parameters for implementing multicultural programs, salient ethics of the academy, and reform strategies that should be implemented to enact viable multicultural programs. For transformation to be enacted in the university, its culture and normative values must be radically changed to eradicate the provincialism, conformity and conservatism, social apathy, moral abdication, and political inactivity that pervade it. The authors propose reform strategies to achieve multicultural transformation in higher education, with particular attention to specific recommendations and examples regarding institutional climate and values, curriculum development, abandonment of sole reliance on lecturing and delivery of information toward the practice of student-centered pedagogy and administrative and instructional personnel. These changes are imperative if higher education is to promote the development of individuals who are critical and reflective thinkers, social activists, and ethical individuals who are committed to the elimination of all forms of oppression, domination, and exploitation in the interests of working for social justice.

Today, the challenges to education posed by multiculturalism are not confined to the voices of those demanding access, though this point remains a salient and pressing concern, evidenced by the persistence of racist, classist, and sexist policies and practices under the guise of myths regarding objectivity and difference—most recently seen in the resurgence of the racist attempts to defend intellectual superiority of the white race (Herrnstein and Murray, 1994) and the passage in November 1994 of Proposition 187 in California, denying education, health, and welfare benefits to illegal aliens. The resurrection of this argument should not surprise anyone. It is not as if such a belief had disappeared. The proponents of racist ideologies, motivated by the particular social ecology of these times, are compelled to trumpet the rallying call that "those others" are taking the country from "us" and there is a need to "take back America." Sadly enough, and again not surprisingly, the media have paid considerable attention to these latest racist proclamations. Yet, rather than encourage the public to engage in discussion of the racist framework of these studies, the media, in its sensationalist clamor, point to the studies, briefly note some of their characteristics, and leave the topic. Given the persistence of racism in this society, this hardly seems beneficial to those combatting racism and appears more likely to leave the listener with the notion that such ludicrous ideas are at least possible. The mere internalization of such a possibility fuels racism. Again, if we are convinced that such is possible, the necessary steps to circumvent access become temporal and tactical matters are facilitated by the science of racism. And here, multiculturalism poses some of its most important challenges.

Multiculturalism is forcing us to peel away the layers of policies and educational practices that reinforce the domination of peoples by naming the world for them and attaching all the Euroappropriate metaphors. However, at one of the centers of the multicultural debate resides a most profound challenge to the tradition of Eurocentricity—the dominance of European epistemologies. The knowledge factory is under the scrutiny of those demanding the democratization of knowledge and the liberation of people's experiences to become fountains of resource from which people learn of their worlds and create knowledge to transform them. This presents us all with a serious issue. On the one hand, many people are convinced of the need to "multiculturalize" a curriculum. Exactly what that means usually falls under one or more of the three categories noted above (additive, procedural, and/or technical). On the other hand, the proliferation of standardized testing at all grades today arguably exceeds any other period in history and portends a back-to-the-basics philosophy.

While this presents us with an interesting set of contradictions, note how the political economic environment is affected. The ability for the economy to absorb the pool of college graduates is painfully inadequate. More people graduating and unable to secure employment means more unemployed. One way to deal with this is to restrict access to higher education, among other ways through more competitive policies and a stronger commitment to merit. Yet if the very fabric of what constitutes the legitimacy of knowledge, and its confinement to Eurocentric conceptions, is being challenged by many multiculturalists, the meritocratic and conservative aspirations of those opponents of multiculturalism are compelled to more critically examine the motivations for sustaining the generation of myths.

When exploring the comfort zones, we are often handcuffed by our anxiety and fear. Yet such should never restrain us from struggling in the spirit of the most basic principle of any education—freedom of peoples and minds. The chapters in this book will take the reader to the borders of their comfort zones. It is here where one discovers the possibilities of multiculturalism to transform and overcome the compulsion to retreat.

REFERENCES

Franklin, John Hope. 1993. *The Color Line: Legacy for the Century*. Columbia: University of Missouri Press.
Freire, Paulo. 1971. *Pedagogy of the Oppressed*. New York: Herder and Herder.
Herrnstein, Richard and Murray, Charles. 1994. *The Bell Curve*. New York: Free Press.
Kovel, Joel. 1970. *White Racism: A Psychohistory*. New York: Pantheon Books.
Matsuda, Mari; Lawrence, Charles R. III; Delgado, Richard, and Crenshaw, Kimberlè Williams. 1993. *Words That Wound*. Boulder, CO: Westview Press.
West, Cornel. 1993. *Race Matters*. Boston: Beacon Press.
The Woman Question: Selections from the Writings of Karl Marx, Frederick Engels, V. I. Lenin, and Joseph Stalin. 1951. New York: International Publishers.

PART I

From I to We: Self-Determination and the Multicultural

2

White Studies: The Intellectual Imperialism of U.S. Higher Education

Ward Churchill

Education should be adapted to the mentality, attitudes, occupation, and traditions of various peoples, conserving as far as possible all the sound and healthy elements in the fabric of their social life.

> David Abernathy
> *The Dilemma of Popular Education*

Since schooling was brought to non-Europeans as a part of empire . . . it was integrated into the effort to bring indigenous peoples into imperial/colonial structures. . . . After all, did not the European teacher and the school built on the European capitalist model transmit European values and norms and begin to transform traditional societies into "modern" ones?

> Martin Carnoy
> *Education as Cultural Imperialism*

Over the past decade, the nature and adequacy of educational content has been a matter of increasingly vociferous debate among everyone from academics to policymakers to lay preachers in the United States. The American educational system as a whole has been amply demonstrated to be locked firmly into a paradigm of Eurocentrism, not only in terms of its focus, but also its discernable heritage, methodologies, and conceptual structure. Among people of non-European cultural derivation, the kind of "learning" inculcated through such a model is broadly seen as insulting, degrading, and functionally subordinative.

More and more, these themes have found echoes among the more enlightened and progressive sectors of the dominant Euro-American society itself.[1]

Such sentiments are born of an ever-widening cognition that, within any multicultural setting, this sort of monolithic pedagogical reliance on a single cultural tradition constitutes a rather transparent form of intellectual domination, achievable only within the context of parallel forms of domination. This is meant in precisely the sense intended by David Landes when he observed, "It seems to me that one has to look at imperialism as a multifarious response to a common opportunity that consists simply as a disparity of power."[2] In this connection, it is often pointed out that, while education in America has existed for some time, by law, as a "common opportunity," its shape has all along been defined exclusively via the "disparity of power" exercised by members of the ruling Euro-American elite.[3]

Responses to this circumstance have, to date, concentrated primarily on what might be best described as a "contributionist" approach to remedy. This is to say they seek to bring about the inclusion of non-Europeans and/or non-European achievements in canonical subject matters, while leaving the methodological and conceptual parameters of the canon itself essentially intact.[4] This chapter represents an attempt to go a bit further, sketching out to some degree the preliminary requisites in challenging methods and concepts as well. It should be noted before proceeding that while my own grounding in American Indian Studies leads me to anchor my various alternatives in that particular perspective, the principles postulated should prove readily adaptable to the experiences of other people of color.

WHITE [MALE] STUDIES

As currently established, the university system in the United States offers little more than the presentation of "White Studies" to students—general population and minority alike.[5] The curriculum is virtually totalizing in its emphasis, not simply on an imagined superiority of Western endeavors and accomplishments, but on the notion that the currents of European thinking comprise the only really natural—or at least truly useful—formation of knowledge/means of perceiving reality. In the vast bulk of curriculum content, Europe is not only the subject (conceptual mode; the very process of learning to think), but the object (subject matter) of investigation as well.

Consider a typical introductory-level philosophy course. Students will in all probability explore the works of the ancient Greek philosophers,[6] the fundamentals of Cartesian logic and Spinoza, stop off for a visit with Hobbes, Hume, and Locke, cover a chapter or two of Kant's aesthetics, dabble a bit in Hegelian dialectics, and review Nietzsche's assorted rantings. A good leftist professor may add a dash of Marx's famous "inversion" of Hegel and, on a good day, his commentaries on the frailties of Feuerbach. In an exemplary class, things will end up in the twentieth century with discussions of Schopenhauer, Heidegger and Husserl, Russell and Whitehead, perhaps an adventurous summarization of the existentialism of Sartre and Camus.

Advanced undergraduate courses typically delve into the same topics, with additive instruction in matters such as "Late Medieval Philosophy," "Monism," "Rousseau and Revolution," "The Morality of John Stuart Mill," "Einstein and the Generations of Science," "The Phenomenology of Merleau-Ponty," "Popper's Philosophy of Science," "Benjamin, Adorno and the Frankfurt School," "Meaning and Marcuse," "Structuralism/Post-Structuralism," even "The Critical Theory of Jurgen Habermas."[7] Graduate work usually consists of effecting a coherent synthesis of some combination of these elements.

Thus, from first-semester surveys through the Ph.D., philosophy majors and nonmajors fulfilling elective requirements are fed a consistent stream of data defining and presumably reproducing Western thought at its highest level of refinement, as well as inculcating insight into what is packaged as its historical evolution and line(s) of probable future development. Note that this is construed, for all practical intents and purposes, as being representative of philosophy in toto rather than of Western European thought per se.

It seems reasonable to pose the question as to what consideration is typically accorded the non-European remainder of the human species in such a format. The answer is often that course-work does in fact exist, most usually in the form of upper-division undergraduate "broadening" curriculum: surveys of "Oriental Philosophy" are not unpopular,[8] "The Philosophy of Black Africa" exists as a catalog entry at a number of institutions,[9] even "Native American Philosophical Traditions" (more casually titled "Black Elk Speaks," from time-to-time) makes its appearance here and there.[10] But nothing remotely approaching the depth and comprehensiveness with which Western thought is treated can be located at any quarter.

Clearly, students who graduate, at whatever level, from a philosophy program constructed in this fashion walk away with a concentrated knowledge of the European intellectual schema rather than any genuine appreciation of the philosophical attainments of humanity. Yet, equally clearly, a degree in "Philosophy" implies, or at least should imply, the latter.

Nor is the phenomenon in any way restricted to the study of philosophy. One may search the catalogs of every college and university in the country, and undoubtedly the search will be in vain, for the department of history that accords any recognition of the elaborate oral/pictorial prehistories of American Indians privileges the semiliterate efforts at self-justification scrawled by early European colonists in this hemisphere.[11] Even the rich codigraphic records of cultures like the Mayas, Incas, and Mexicans (Aztecs) are uniformly ignored by the historical mainstream. Such matters are more properly the purview of anthropology than of history, or so it is said by those representing "responsible" scholarship in the United States.[12]

As a result, most intro courses on American History still begin for all practical intents and purposes in 1492, with only the most perfunctory acknowledgement that people existed in the Americas in pre-Columbian times. Predictably, these typically devolve upon anthropological rather than historical preoccupations, such as the point at which people were supposed to have first migrated across the Beringian Land Bridge to populate the hemisphere,[13] or whether native horticulturalists ever managed to discover fertilizer.[14] Another major classroom topic centers on the extent to which cannibalism may have prevailed among the proliferation of nomadic Stone Age tribes presumed to have wandered about America's endless reaches, perpetually hunting and gathering their way to the margin of raw subsistence.[15] Then again, there are the countless expositions on how few indigenous people there really were in North America prior to 1500.[16] In the official discourse, genocide is an inappropriate term by which to explain why there were almost none by 1900.[17]

From there, many things begin to fall into place. Nowhere in the modern American academe will one find the math course acknowledging, along with the importance of Archimedes and Protagorus, the truly marvelous qualities of pre-Columbian mathematics: that which allowed the Mayas to invent the concept of zero, for example, and, absent computers, to work with multidigit prime numbers.[18] Nor is there mention of the Mexicano mathematics, which allowed that culture to develop a calendrical system several decimal places more accurate than that commonly used today.[19] And again, the rich mathematical understandings that went into Meso-America's development of what may well have been the world's most advanced system of astronomy are most usually ignored by mainstream mathematicians and astronomers alike.[20]

Similarly, departments of architecture and engineering do not teach that the Incas invented the suspension bridge, or that their 2,500-mile Royal Road—leveled, graded, paved, guttered, and complete with rest areas—was perhaps the world's first genuine superhighway, or that portions of it are still used by motorized transport in Peru.[21] No mention is made of the passive solar temperature control characteristics carefully designed by the Anasazi in the apartment complexes of their cities at Chaco Canyon, Mesa Verde, and elsewhere.[22] Nor are students drawn to examine the incorporation of thermal mass into Mandan and Hidatsa construction techniques,[23] the vast north Sonoran irrigation systems built by the Hohokam,[24] or the implications of the fact that, at the time of Cortez's arrival, Tenochtitlán (now Mexico City) accommodated a population of 350,000, a number making it one of the largest cities on earth, at least five times the size of London or Seville.[25]

In political science, readers are invited—no, defied—to locate the course acknowledging, as John Adams, Benjamin Franklin, and others among the U.S. "Founding Fathers" did, that the form of the American Republic and the framing of its Constitution were heavily influenced by the preexisting model of the Haudenosaunee (Six Nations Iroquois Confederacy of present-day New York and Québec).[26] Nor is mention made of the influence exerted by the workings of the Iroquois League in shaping the thinking of theorists such as Karl Marx and Friedrich Engels.[27] There is even less discussion of comparably sophisticated political systems conceived and established by other indigenous peoples—the Creek Confederation, for example, or the Cherokees or Yaquis—long before the first European invader ever set foot on American soil.[28]

Where agriculture or the botanical sciences are concerned, one will not find the conventional department that wishes to make anything special of the fact that fully two-thirds of the vegetal foodstuffs now commonly consumed by all of humanity were under cultivation in the Americas, and nowhere else, in 1492.[29] Left unmentioned is the hybridization by Incan scientists of more than 3,000 varieties of potato,[30] or the vast herbal cornucopia discovered and deployed by native pharmacologists long before that.[31] In biology, pre-med, and medicine, nothing is said of the American Indian invention of surgical tubing and the syringe, or the fact that the Incas were successfully practicing brain surgery at a time when European physicians were still seeking to cure their patients by applying leeches to draw off bad blood.[32]

To the contrary, from matters of governance, where the Greek and Roman democracies are habitually cited as being sole antecedents of the American experiment,[33] to agriculture, with its "Irish" potatoes, "Swiss" chocolate, "Italian" tomatoes, "French" vanilla, and "English" walnuts,[34] the accomplishments of American Indian cultures are quite simply expropriated and recast in the curriculum as if they had been European in origin.[35] Concomitantly, the native traditions that produced such things are themselves decultured and negated, consigned to the status of being "people without history."[36]

Such grotesque distortion is, of course, fed to indigenous students right along with Euro-Americans,[37] and by supposedly radical professors as readily as more conservative ones.[38] Moreover, as was noted above, essentially the same set of circumstances prevails with regard to the traditions and attainments of all non-Western cultures.[39] Overall, the situation virtually demands to be viewed from a perspective best articulated by Albert Memmi:

In order for the colonizer to be a complete master, it is not enough for him to be so in actual fact, but he must also believe in [the colonial system's] legitimacy. In order for that legitimacy to be complete, it is not enough for the colonized to be a slave, he must also accept his role. The bond between colonizer and colonized is thus destructive and creative. It destroys and recreates the two partners in colonization into colonizer and colonized. One is disfigured into an oppressor, a partial, unpatriotic and treacherous being, worrying only about his privileges and their defense; the other into an oppressed creature, whose development is broken and who compromises by his defeat.[40]

In effect, the intellectual sophistry that goes into arguing the radical and conservative content options available within the prevailing monocultural paradigm, a paradigm that predictably corresponds to the culture of the colonizer, amounts to little more than a diversionary mechanism through which power relations are reinforced, the status quo maintained.[41] The monolithic White Studies configuration of U.S. higher education—a content heading that, unlike American Indian, African American, Asian American, and Chicano Studies, has yet to find its way into a single college or university catalog—thus serves to underpin the hegemony of white supremacism in its other, more literal manifestations: economic, political, military, and so on.[42]

Those of non-European background are integral to such a system. While consciousness of their own heritages are obliterated through falsehood and omission, they are indoctrinated to believe that legitimacy itself is something derivative of European tradition, a tradition that can never be truly shared by non-Westerners—despite or perhaps because of—their assimilation of Eurocentrism's doctrinal value structure. By and large, the "educated" American Indian or African American thereby becomes the aspect of "broken development" who "compromises [through the] defeat" of his or her people, aspiring only to serve the interests of the order he or she has been trained to see as his or her "natural" master.[43]

As Frantz Fanon and others have observed long-since, such psychological jujitsu can never be directly admitted, much less articulated, by its principal victims. Instead, they are compelled by illusions of sanity to deny their circumstance and the process that induced it. Their condition sublimated, they function as colonialism's covert hedge against the necessity of perpetual engagement in more overt and costly sorts of repression against its colonial subjects.[44] Put another way, the purpose of White Studies in this connection is to trick the colonized into materially supporting their colonization through the mechanisms of their own thought processes.[45]

There can be no reasonable or value-neutral explanation for this situation. Those, regardless of race or ethnicity, who endeavor to apologize for or defend its prevalence in institutions of higher education on scholarly grounds do so without a shred of honesty or academic integrity.[46] Rather, whatever their intentions, they define themselves as accepting of the colonial order. In Memmi's terms, they accept the role of colonizer, which means "agreeing to be a . . . usurper. To be sure, a usurper claims his place and, if need be, will defend it with every means at his disposal. . . . He endeavors to falsify history, he rewrites laws, he would extinguish memories—anything to succeed in transforming his usurpation into legitimacy."[47] They are, to borrow and slightly modify a term, "intellectual imperialists."[48]

AN INDIGENIST ALTERNATIVE

From the preceding observations as to what White Studies is, the extraordinary pervasiveness and corresponding secrecy of its practice, and the reasons underlying its existence, certain questions necessarily arise. For instance, the query might be posed as to whether a simple expansion of curriculum content to include material on non-Western contexts might be sufficient to redress matters. It follows that we should ask whether something beyond data or content is fundamentally at issue. Finally, there are structural considerations concerning how any genuinely corrective and liberatory curriculum or pedagogy might actually be inducted into academia. The first two questions dovetail rather nicely, and will be addressed in a single response. The third will be dealt with in the next section.

In response to the first question, the answer must be an unequivocal "no." Content is, of course, highly important, but, in and of itself, can never be sufficient to offset the cumulative effects of White Studies indoctrination. Non-Western content injected into the White Studies format can be—and, historically, has been—filtered through the lens of Eurocentric conceptualization, taking on meanings entirely alien to itself along the way.[49] The result is inevitably the reinforcement rather than the diminishment of colonialist hegemony. As Vine Deloria, Jr., has noted relative to just one aspect of this process,

> Therein lies the meaning of the white's fantasy about Indians—the problem of the Indian image. Underneath all the conflicting images of the Indian one fundamental truth emerges—the white man knows that he is an alien and he knows that North America is Indian—and he will never let go of the Indian image because he thinks that by some clever manipulation he can achieve an authenticity that cannot ever be his.[50]

Plainly, more is needed than the simple introduction of raw data for handling within the parameters of Eurocentric acceptability. The conceptual mode of intellectuality itself must be called into question. Perhaps a bit of pictographic communication will prove helpful in clarifying what is meant in this respect. The following schematic represents the manner in which two areas of inquiry, science and religion (spirituality), have been approached in the European tradition.

In this model, knowledge is divided into discrete content areas arranged in a linear structure. This division is permanent and culturally enforced; witness the Spanish Inquisition and the "Scopes Monkey Trial" as but two historical illustrations.[51] In the cases of science and religion (as theology), the mutual opposition of their core assumptions has given rise to a third category, speculative philosophy, which is informed by both, and, in turn, informs them. Speculative philosophy, in this sense at least, serves to mediate and sometimes synthesize the linearly isolated components, science and religion, allowing them to communicate and "progress." Speculative philosophy is not, in itself, intended to apprehend reality, but rather to create an abstract reality in its place. Both religion and science, on the other hand, are, each according to its own internal dynamics, meant to effect a concrete understanding of and action upon the real world.[52]

Such compartmentalization of knowledge is replicated in the departmentalization of Eurocentric education itself. Sociology, theology, psychology, physiology, kinesiology, biology, cartography, anthropology, archaeology, geology, pharmacology, astronomy, agronomy, historiography, geography, cartography, demography—the whole vast proliferation of Western "ologies," "onomies" and "ographies"—are necessarily viewed as separate or at least separable areas of inquiry within the university. Indeed the Western social structure both echoes and is echoed by the same sort of linear fragmentation, dividing itself into discrete organizational spheres: church, state, business, family, education, art, and so forth.[53] The structure involved readily lends itself to—perhaps demands—the sort of hierarchical ordering of things, both intellectually and physically, which is most clearly manifested in racism, militarism and colonial domination, class and gender oppression, and the systematic ravaging of the natural world.[54]

The obvious problems involved are greatly amplified when our schematic of the Eurocentric intellectual paradigm is contrasted to one of non-Western, in this case Native American, origin.

Within such a conceptual model, there is really no tangible delineation of compartmentalized spheres of knowledge. All components or categories of intellectuality (by Eurocentric definition) tend to be mutually and perpetually informing. All tend to constantly concretize the human experience of reality (nature) while all are simultaneously and continuously informed by that reality. This is the "Hoop" or "Wheel" or "Circle of Life"—an organic rather than synthesizing or synthetic view holding that all things are equally and indispensably interrelated—which forms the core of the native worldview.[55] Here, reality is not something above the human mind or being, but an integral aspect of the living/knowing process itself. The mode through which native thought devolves is thus inherently antihierarchical, incapable of manifesting the extreme forms of domination so pervasively evident in Eurocentric tradition.[56]

The crux of the White Studies problem, then, cannot be located amid the mere omission or distortion of matters of fact, no matter how blatantly ignorant or culturally chauvinistic these omissions and distortions may be. Far more importantly, the system of Eurosupremacist domination depends for its continued maintenance and expansion, even its survival, on the reproduction of its own intellectual paradigm—its approved way of thinking, seeing, understanding, and being—to the ultimate exclusion of all others. Consequently, White Studies simply cannot admit to the existence of viable conceptual structures other than its own.[57]

To introduce the facts of precolonial American Indian civilizations to the curriculum is to open the door to confronting the utterly different ways of knowing that caused such facts to be actualized in the first place.[58] It is thoroughly appreciated in ruling circles that any widespread and genuine understanding of such alternatives to the intrinsic oppressiveness of Eurocentrism could well unleash a liberatory dynamic among the oppressed, resulting in the evaporation of Eurosupremacist hegemony and a corresponding collapse of the entire structure of domination and élite privilege that attends it.[59] The academic battle lines have therefore been drawn, not so much across the tactical terrain of fact and data as along the strategic high ground of Western versus non-Western conceptualization. It follows that if the latter is what proponents of the White Studies status quo find it most imperative to bar from academic inclusion, it is precisely the area upon which those committed to liberatory education must place our greatest emphasis.

A STRATEGY TO WIN

Given the scope and depth of the formal problem outlined in the preceding section, the question of the means through which to address it takes on a crucial importance. If the objective in grappling with White Studies is to bring about conceptual—as opposed to merely "contentual"—inclusion of non-Western traditions in academe, then appropriate and effective methods must be employed. As was noted earlier, resort to inappropriate remedies leads only to cooptation and a reinforcement of White Studies as the prevailing educational norm.

One such false direction has concerned attempts to establish, essentially from scratch, whole new educational institutions, even systems, while leaving the institutional structure of the status quo very much intact.[60] Although sometimes evidencing a strong showing at the outset, these perpetually underfunded, understaffed, unaccredited, community-based—often actually separatist—schools have almost universally ended up drifting and floundering before going out of existence altogether.[61] Alternately, more than a few have abandoned their original reason for being, accommodating themselves to the standards and other requirements of the mainstream system as an expedient to survival.[62] Either way, the outcome has been a considerable bolstering of the carefully nurtured public impression that the system works while alternatives do not.

A variation on this theme has been to establish separatist centers or programs, even whole departments, within existing colleges and universities. While this approach has alleviated to some extent (though not entirely) difficulties in securing funding, faculty, and accreditation, it has accomplished little if anything in terms of altering the delivery of White Studies instruction in the broader institutional context.[63] Instead, intentionally self-contained Ethnic Studies efforts have ended up ghettoized—that is, marginalized to the point of isolation and left talking only to themselves and the few majors they are able to attract—bitter, frustrated, and stalemated.[64] Worse, they serve to reinforce the perception, so desired by the status quo, that White Studies is valid and important while non-Western subject matters are invalid and irrelevant.

To effect the sort of transformation of institutional realities envisioned in this chapter, it is necessary not to seek to create parallel structures as such, but instead to penetrate and subvert the existing structures themselves, both pedagogically and canonically. The strategy is one that was once described quite aptly by Rudi Deutschke, the German activist/theorist, as amounting to a "long march through the institutions."[65] In this, Ethnic Studies entities, rather than constituting ends in themselves, serve as enclaves or staging areas from which forays into the mainstream arena can be launched with ever-increasing frequency and vitality, and to which non-Western academic guerrillas can withdraw when needed to rest and regroup among themselves.[66]

As with any campaign of guerrilla warfare, however metaphorical, it is important to concentrate initially on the opponents' point(s) of greatest vulnerability. Here, three prospects for action come immediately to mind, the basis for each of which already exists within most university settings in a form readily lending itself to utilization in undermining the rigid curricular compartmentalization and pedagogical constraints inhering in White Studies institutions. The key is to recognize and seize such tools, and then to apply them properly.

1. While tenure-track faculty must almost invariably be credentialed—hold

the Ph.D. in a Western discipline, have a few publications in the right journals—to be hired into the academy, the same isn't necessarily true for guest professors, lecturers and the like.[67] Every effort can and should be expended by the regular faculty—cadre, if you will—of Ethnic Studies units to bring in guest instructors lacking in Western academic pedigree (the more conspicuously, the better), but who are in some way exemplary of non-Western intellectual traditions (especially oral forms). The initial purpose is to enhance cadre articulations with practical demonstrations of intellectual alternatives by consistently exposing students to the real thing. Goals further on down the line should include incorporation of such individuals directly into the core faculty, and, eventually, challenging the current notion of academic credentialing in its entirety.[68]

2. There has been a good deal of interest over the past 20 years in what has come to be loosely termed "Interdisciplinary Studies." Insofar as there is a mainstream correspondent to the way in which American Indians and other non-Westerners conceive of and relate to the world, this is it. Ethnic Studies practitioners would do well to push hard in the Interdisciplinary Studies arena, expanding it whenever and wherever possible at the direct expense of customary Western disciplinary boundaries. The object, of course, is to steep students in the knowledge that nothing can be understood other than in its relationship to everything else; that economics, for example, can never really make sense if arbitrarily divorced from history, politics, sociology, and geography. Eventually, the goal should be to dissolve the orthodox parameters of disciplines altogether, replacing them with something more akin to areas of interest, inclination and emphasis.[69]

3. For a variety of reasons, virtually all colleges and universities award tenure to certain faculty members in more than one discipline or department. Ethnic Studies cadres should insist that this be the case with them. Restricting their tenure and rostering exclusively to Ethnic Studies is not only a certain recipe for leaving them in a "last hired, first fired" situation during times of budget exigency, it is a standard institutional maneuver to preserve the sanctity of White Studies instruction elsewhere on campus. The fact is that an Ethnic Studies professor teaching American Indian or Afro-American history is just as much an historian as a specialist in nineteenth-century British history; the Indian and the African American should therefore be rostered to and tenured in History, as well as in Ethnic Studies. This foot in the door is important, not only in terms of cadre longevity and the institutional dignity such appointments signify vis-à-vis Ethnic Studies, and it offers important advantages by way of allowing cadres to reach a greater breadth of students, participate in departmental policy formation and hiring decisions, claim additional resources, and so forth. On balance, success in this area can only enhance efforts in the two above.[70]

The objective is to begin to develop a critical mass, first in given spheres of campuses where opportunities present themselves—later throughout the academy as a whole—that is eventually capable of discrediting and supplanting the hegemony of White Studies. In this, the process can be accelerated, perhaps greatly, by identifying and allying with sectors of the professorate with whom a genuine affinity and commonality of interest may be said to exist at some level. These might include those from the environmental sciences who have achieved, or begun to achieve, a degree of serious ecological understanding.[71] It might include occasional mavericks from other fields—various applied anthropologists,[72] for instance, and certain of the better and more engaged literary and artistic deconstructionists[73] as well as the anarchists like Murray Bookchin who pop up more-or-less randomly in a number of disciplines.[74]

By and large, however, it may well be that the largest reservoir of potential allies will be found among the relatively many faculty who profess to consider themselves, philosophically at least, to be Marxian in their orientation. This is not said because Marxists tend habitually to see themselves as being in opposition to the existing order (fascists express the same view of themselves, after all, and for equally valid reasons).[75] Nor is it because where it has succeeded in overthrowing capitalism Marxism has amassed an especially sterling record where indigenous peoples are concerned.[76] In fact, it has been argued with some cogency that, in the latter connection, Marxist practice has proven even more virulently Eurocentric than has capitalism in many cases.[77]

Nonetheless, one is drawn to conclude that there may still be a basis for constructive alliance, given Marx's positing of dialectics—a truly nonlinear and relational mode of analysis and understanding—as his central methodology. That he himself consistently violated his professed method,[78] and that subsequent generations of his adherents have proven themselves increasingly unable to distinguish between dialectics and such strictly linear propositions as cause/effect progressions,[79] does not inherently invalidate the whole of his project or its premises. If some significant proportion of today's self-proclaimed Marxian intelligentsia can be convinced to actually learn and apply dialectical method, it stands to reason that they will finally think their way in to a posture not unlike that elaborated herein (that they will in the process have transcended what has come be known as "Marxism" is another story).[80]

CONCLUSION

This chapter has presented only the barest glimpse of its subject matter. It is plainly, its author hopes, not intended to be anything approximating an exhaustive or definitive exposition on its topics. To the contrary, it is meant only to act as, paraphrasing Herbert Marcuse, the Archimedean point upon which false consciousness may be breached en route to "a more comprehensive emancipation."[81] By this we mean not only a generalized change in perspective that leads to the abolition of Eurocentrism's legacy of colonialist, racist, sexist, and classist domination, but the replacement of White Studies' Eurosupremacism with an educational context in which we can all, jointly and with true parity, seek to expand our knowledge of the world in full realization that

the signposts point to a reconciliation of the two approaches to experience. Western science must reintegrate human emotions and intuitions into its interpretation of phenomena;

[non-Western] peoples must confront . . . the effects of [Western] technology. . . . [We must] come to an integrated conception of how our species came to be, what it has accomplished, and where it can expect to go in the millennia ahead. . . . [Then we will come to] understand as these traditionally opposing views seek a unity that the world of historical experience is far more mysterious and eventful than previously expected. . . . Our next immediate task is the unification of human knowledge.[82]

There is, to be sure, much work to be done, both practically and cerebrally. The struggle will be long and difficult, frustrating many times to the point of sheer exasperation. It will require stamina and perseverance, a preparedness to incur risk, often a willingness to absorb the consequences of revolt, whether overt or covert. Many will be required to give up or forego aspects of a comfort zone academic existence, both mentally and materially.[83] But the payoff may be found in freedom of the intellect, the pursuit of knowledge in a manner more proximate to truth, unfettered by the threats and constraints of narrow vested interest and imperial ideology. The reward, in effect, is participation in the process of human liberation, including our own. One can only assume that this is worth the fight.

NOTES

1. For an overview of the evolution of the current conflict, see Ira Shore, *Culture Wars: School and Society in the Conservative Restoration, 1969–1984* (Boston: Routledge & Kegan Paul, 1986); for reactionary analysis, see Roger Kimball, *Tenured Radicals: How Politics Has Corrupted Our Higher Education* (New York: Harper & Row, 1990).

2. David S. Landes, "The Nature of Economic Imperialism," *Journal of Economic History*, Vol. 21 (December 1961), as quoted in Harry Magdoff, *The Age of Imperialism* (New York: Monthly Review Press, 1969), p. 13.

3. Gerald Jayne and Robbin Williams, eds., *A Common Destiny: Blacks and American Society* (Washington, DC: National Academy Press, 1989).

4. One solid summary of the contributionist trend will be found in Troy Duster, *The Diversity Project: Final Report* (Berkeley: University of California Institute for Social Change, 1991); for complaints, see Robert Alter, "The Revolt Against Tradition," *Partisan Review*, Vol. 58, No. 2 (1991).

5. General population, or "G-Pop" as it is often put, is the standard institutional euphemism for white students.

6. A good case can be made that there is a great disjuncture between the Greek philosophers and the philosophies later arising in Western Europe; see Martin Bernal, *Black Athena: The Afro-Asiatic Roots of Ancient Greece*, Vol. 1 (Princeton, NJ: Princeton University Press, 1987).

7. Marxian academics make another appearance here, insofar as they do tend to teach courses, or parts of courses, based in the thinking of non-Europeans. It should be noted, however, that those selected for exposition—Mao, Ho Chi Minh, Vo Nguyen Giap, Kim Il Sung, et al.—are uniformly those who have most thoroughly assimilated Western doctrines in displacement of their own intellectual traditions.

8. Probably the most stunning example of this I've ever encountered came when Will

Durant casually attributed the thought of the East Indian philosopher Shankara to a "pre-plagiarism" of Kant:

> To Shankara the existence of God is no problem, for he defines God as existence, and identifies all real being with God. But the existence of a personal God, creator or redeemer, there may, he thinks, be some question; such a diety, says this pre-plagiarist of Kant, cannot be proved by reason, he can only be postulated as a practical necessity.

Will Durant, *The History of Civilization*, Vol. 1: *Our Oriental Heritage* (New York: Simon & Schuster, 1954), p. 549. It should be remarked that Durant was not a reactionary of the stripe conventionally associated with white supremacism, but rather an intellectual of the Marxian progressive variety. Yet, in this single book on the philosophical tradition of Asia, he makes no less than ten references to Kant, all of them implying that the earlier philosophers of the East acted "precisely as if [they] were Immanual Kant" (p. 538), never that Kant might have predicated his own subsequent philosophical articulations in a reading of Asian texts. The point is raised to demonstrate the all but unbelievable lengths even the more dissident Western scholars have been prepared to go in reinforcing the mythos of Eurocentrism, and thus how such reinforcement transcends ideological divisions within the Eurocentric paradigm.

9. It should be noted, however, that the recent emergence of an "Afrocentric" philosophy and pedagogy, natural counterbalances to the persistence of Eurocentric orthodoxy, have met with fierce condemnation by defenders of the status quo; see David Nicholson, "Afrocentrism and the Tribalization of America," *Washington Post National Weekly Edition*, October 8–14, 1990.

10. A big question, frequently mentioned, is whether American Indians ever acquired the epistimological sensibilities necessary for their thought to be correctly understood as having amounted to philosophical inquiry. Given that epistemology simply means "investigation of the limits of human comprehension," one can only wonder what the gatekeepers of philosophy departments make of the American Indian conception, prevalent in myriad traditions, of there being a "Great Mystery" into which the human mind is incapable of penetrating; see for example, John G. Neihardt, ed., *Black Elk Speaks* (New York: William Morrow, 1932); also see J. R. Walker, *Lakota Belief and Ritual* (Lincoln: University of Nebraska Press, 1980). For an unconsciously comparable Western articulation, see Noam Chomsky's discussion of accessible and inaccessible knowledge in the chapters entitled "A Philosophy of Language?" and "Empiricism and Rationalism," in *Language and Responsibility: An Interview by Mitsou Ronat*. New York: Pantheon Books, 1977.

11. As illustration, see Wilcomb E. Washburn, "Distinguishing History for Moral Philosophy and Public Advocacy," in Calvin Martin, ed., *The American Indian and the Problem of History* (New York: Oxford University Press, 1987), pp. 91–97.

12. For a veritable case study of this mentality, see James Axtell, *After Columbus: Essays in the Ethnohistory of Colonial North America* (New York: Oxford University Press, 1988).

13. For a solid critique of the Beringia Theory, see Jeffrey Goodman, *American Genesis: The American Indian and the Origins of Modern Man* (New York: Summit Books, 1981); also see Jonathan E. Ericson, R. E. Taylor, and Rainier Berger, eds., *The Peopling of the New World* (Los Altos, CA: Ballena Press, 1982).

14. For an exhaustive enunciation of the "fertilizer dilemma," see James C. Hurt, *American Indian Agriculture* (Lawrence: University Press of Kansas, 1991).

15. An excellent analysis of this standard description of indigenous American realities may be found in M. Annette Jaimes, "Re-Visioning Native America: An Indigenist View of

'Primitivism' and Industrialization," *Social Justice*, Vol. 19, No. 2 (Summer 1992). On cannibalism specifically, see W. Arens, *The Man-Eating Myth: Anthropology and Anthropophagy* (New York: Oxford University Press, 1979).

16. The manipulation of data undertaken by succeeding generations of Euro-American historians and anthropologists in arriving at the official twentieth-century falsehood that there were "not more than one million Indians living north of the Rio Grande in 1492, including Greenland" is laid out very clearly by Francis Jennings, *The Invasion of America: Indians, Colonialism and the Cant of Conquest* (Chapel Hill: University of North Carolina Press, 1975). For a far more honest estimate, deriving from the evidence rather than ideological preoccupations, see Henry F. Dobyns, *Their Number Become Thinned: Native American Population Dynamics in Eastern North America* (Knoxville: University of Tennessee Press, 1983); also see Russell Thornton, *American Indian Holocaust and Survival: A Population History Since 1492* (Norman: University of Oklahoma Press, 1987). Dobyns places the actual number as high as 18.5 million; Thornton, more conservative, places it at 12.5 million.

17. During a keynote presentation at the annual meeting of the American History Association in 1992, James Axtell, one of the emergent deans of the field, actually argued that genocide was an inaccurate and highly polemical descriptor for what had happened. His reasoning? That he could find only five instances in the history of colonial North America in which genocides indisputably occurred. Leaving aside the obvious—that this in itself makes genocide an appropriate term by which to describe the obliteration of American Indians—a vastly more accurate chronicle of the process of extermination will be found in David E. Stannard, *American Holocaust: Columbus and the Conquest of the New World* (New York: Oxford University Press, 1992).

18. Sylvanus G. Morely and George W. Bainerd, *The Ancient Maya* (Stanford, CA: Stanford University Press, 1963); Robert M. Carmack, *Quichean Civilization* (Berkeley: University of California Press, 1973).

19. Anthony Aveni, *Empires of Time: Calenders, Clocks and Cultures* (New York: Basic Books, 1989).

20. Mexican astronomy is discussed in D. Duran, *Book of Gods and Rites and the Ancient Calendar* (Norman: University of Oklahoma Press, 1971); also see Paul Radin, *The Sources and Authenticity of the History of Ancient Mexico* (Berkeley: University of California Publications in American Archeology and Ethnology, Vol. 17, No. 1, 1920).

21. Victor Wolfgang Von Hagen, *The Royal Road of the Inca* (London: Gordon and Cremonesi, 1976).

22. Robert H. and Florence C. Lister, *Chaco Canyon: Archaeology and Archaeologists* (Albuquerque: University of New Mexico Press, 1981); also see Buddy Mays, *Ancient Cities of the Southwest* (San Francisco: Chronicle Books, 1962).

23. Peter Nabokov and Robert Easton, *American Indian Architecture* (New York: Oxford University Press, 1988). The submerged building principles developed by the Mandan and Hidatsa, ideal for the plains environment but long disparaged by the Euro-Americans who displaced them, are not considered the cutting edge in some architectural circles. The Indians, of course, are not credited with having perfected such techniques more than a thousand years ago.

24. Emil W. Haury, *The Hohokam: Desert Farmers and Craftsmen* (Tucson: University of Arizona Press, 1976), pp. 120–151. The City of Phoenix and its suburbs still use portions of the several thousand miles of extraordinarily well-engineered Hohokam canals, constructed nearly a thousand years ago, to move their own water supplies around.

25. Cortez was effusive in his descriptions of Tenochtitlán as being, in terms of its design

and architecture, "the most beautiful city on earth." Bernal Diaz del Castillo, *The Discovery and Conquest of Mexico, 1519–1810* (London: George Routledge & Sons, 1928), p. 268. On the size of Tenochtitlán, see Rudolph van Zantwijk, *The Aztec Arrangement: The Social History of Pre-Spanish Mexico* (Norman: University of Oklahoma Press, 1985), p. 281; on the size of London in 1500, Lawrence Stone, *The Family, Sex and Marriage in England, 1500–1800* (New York: Harper & Row, 1977), p. 147; for Seville, J. H. Elliott, *Imperial Spain, 1469–1716* (New York: St. Martin's Press, 1964), p. 177.

26. Donald A. Grinde, Jr. and Bruce E. Johansen, *Exemplar of Liberty: Native America and the Evolution of Democracy* (Los Angeles: UCLA American Indian Studies Center, 1992).

27. Between December 1880 and March 1881, Marx read anthropologist Lewis Henry Morgan's 1871 book, *Ancient Society*, based in large part on his 1851 classic *The League of the Hau-de-no-sau-nee or Iroquois*. Marx took at least 98 pages of dense notes during the reading, and, after his death, his collaborator, Friedrich Engels, expanded these into a short book entitled *The Origin of the Family, Private Property and the State: In Light of the Researches of Lewis Henry Morgan*. The latter, minus its subtitle, appears in Karl Marx and Friedrich Engels, *Selected Works* (New York: International. 1968).

28. Jack Weatherford, *Indian Givers: How the Indians of the Americas Transformed the World* (New York: Crown, 1988).

29. Alfred W. Crosby, Jr., *The Columbian Exchange: Biological and Cultural Consequences of 1492* (Westport, CT: Greenwood Press, 1972); Carol A. Bryant, Anita Courtney, Barbara A. Markesbery, and Kathleen M. DeWalt, *The Cultural Feast* (St. Paul: West, 1985).

30. Redcliffe N. Salaman, *The History and Social Influence of the Potato* (Cambridge: Cambridge University Press, 1949).

31. Clark Wissler, Wilton M. Krogman, and Walter Krickerberg, *Medicine Among the American Indians* (Ramona, CA: Acoma Press, 1939); Norman Taylor, *Plant Drugs That Changed the World* (New York: Dodd, Mead, 1965).

32. Virgil Vogel, *American Indian Medicine* (Norman: University of Oklahoma Press, 1970); Peredo Guzman, *Medical Practices in Ancient America* (Mexico City: Ediciones Euroamericana, 1985). On contemporaneous European medical practices, see William H. McNeill, *Plagues and Peoples* (Garden City, NY: Anchor/Doubleday, 1976).

33. For good efforts at debunking such nonsense, see German Arciniegas, *America in Europe: A History of the New World in Reverse* (New York: Harcourt Brace Jovanovich, 1986); and William Brandon, *New Worlds for Old: Reports from the New World and Their Effect on Social Thought in Europe, 1500–1800* (Athens: Ohio University Press, 1986).

34. Carl O. Sauer, "The March of Agriculture Across the Western World," in his *Selected Essays, 1963–1975* (Berkeley: Turtle Island Foundation, 1981); also see Weatherford, *Indian Givers*.

35. This is nothing new or unique to the treatment of American Indians. Indeed the West has comported itself in similar fashion vis-à-vis all non-Westerners since at least as early as the inception of Europe; see Philippe Wolf, *The Awakening of Europe: The Growth of European Culture from the Ninth Century to the Twelfth* (London: Cox & Wyman, 1968).

36. For a much broader excursus on this phenomenon, see Eric R. Wolf, *Europe and the People Without History* (Berkeley: University of California Press, 1982).

37. For surveys of the effects, see Thomas Thompson, ed., *The Schooling of Native America* (Washington, DC: American Association of Colleges for Teacher Education, 1978); James R. Young, ed., *Multicultural Education and the American Indian* (Los Angeles: UCLA American Indian Studies Center, 1979); and Charlotte Heath and Susan Guyette, *Issues for*

the Future of American Indian Studies (Los Angeles: UCLA American Indian Studies Center, 1985).

38. Consider, for example, "Sixteen Theses" advanced by the non-Marxist intellectual Alvin Gouldner as alternatives through which to transform the educational status quo. It will be noted that the result, if Gouldner's pedagogical plan were implemented, would be tucked as neatly into the paradigm of Eurocentrism as the status quo itself. Alvin W. Gouldner, *The Future of Intellectuals and the Rise of the New Class* (New York: Seabury Press, 1979). For Marxian views falling in the same category, see Theodore Mills Norton and Bertell Ollman, eds., *Studies in Socialist Pedagogy* (New York: Monthly Review Press, 1978).

39. See, generally, Edward W. Said, *Orientalism* (New York: Oxford University Press, 1987).

40. Albert Memmi, *Colonizer and Colonized* (Boston: Beacon Press, 1965, p. 89).

41. The procedure corresponds well in some ways with the kind of technique described by Herbert Marcuse as being applicable to broader social contexts in his essay "Repressive Tolerance," in Robert Paul Wolff, Barrington Moore, Jr., and Herbert Marcuse, *A Critique of Pure Tolerance* (Boston: Beacon Press, 1969), pp. 81-123.

42. The theme is handled well in Vine Deloria, Jr., "Education and Imperialism," *Integrateducation*, Vol. 19, Nos. 1–2 (January-April 1982). For structural analysis, see Giovanni Arrighi, *The Geometry of Imperialism* (London: Verso, 1978).

43. Memmi develops these ideas further in his *Dominated Man* (Boston: Beacon Press, 1969).

44. See, especially, Frantz Fanon's *Wretched of the Earth* (New York: Grove Press, 1965) and *Black Skin/White Masks: The Experiences of a Black Man in a White World* (New York: Grove Press, 1967).

45. Probably the classic example of this, albeit in a somewhat different dimension, were the Gurkhas of the Indian subcontinent, who forged a legendary reputation fighting in behalf of their British colonizers, usually against other colonized peoples. See Patrick McCrory, *The Fierce Pawns* (Philadelphia: J.B. Lippincott, 1966).

46. See, for example, Allan Bloom, *The Closing of the American Mind* (New York: Simon & Schuster, 1988); Dinesh D'Sousa, *Illiberal Education: The Politics of Race and Sex on Campus* (New York: Free Press, 1991); Arthur Schlesinger, Jr., *The Disuniting of America* (New York: W.W. Norton, 1992).

47. Memmi, *Colonizer and Colonized*, pp. 52–53.

48. Martin Carnoy, *Education as Cultural Imperialism* (New York: David McKay, 1974); also see Laurie Anne Whitt, "Cultural Imperialism and the Marketing of Native America," forthcoming in *Historical Reflections*, 1995.

49. A fascinating analysis of how this works, distorting the perspectives of perpetrator and victim alike, may be found in Richard James Blackburn, *The Vampire of Reason: An Essay in the Philosophy of History* (London: Verso, 1990).

50. Vine Deloria, Jr., "Forward: American Fantasy," in Gretchen M. Bataille and Charles L. P. Silet, eds., *The Pretend Indians: Images of Native Americans in the Movies* (Ames: Iowa State University Press, 1980), p. xvi.

51. On the Inquisition, see Mary Elizabeth Perry and Anne J. Cruz, eds., *Cultural Encounters: The Impact of the Inquisition in Spain and the New World* (Berkeley: University of California Press, 1991). On the context of the Scopes trial, see Stephen Jay Gould, *The Mismeasure of Man* (New York: W.W. Norton, 1981).

52. For a sort of capstone rendering of this schema, see Karl Popper, *Objective Knowledge: An Evolutionary Approach* (New York: Oxford University Press, 1975).

53. Useful analysis of this dialectic will be found in David Reed, *Education for Building a People's Movement* (Boston: South End Press, 1981).

54. For an interesting analysis of many of these cause/effect relations, see Jerry Mander, *In the Absence of the Sacred: The Failure of Technology and the Survival of Indian Nations* (San Francisco: Sierra Club Books, 1991). Also see William H. McNeill, ed., *Pursuit of Power: Technology, Armed Force and Society Since A.D. 1000* (Chicago: University of Chicago Press, 1982).

55. For elaboration, see Vine Deloria, Jr., *God Is Red* (New York: Grosset & Dunlap, 1973). Also see John Mohawk, *A Basic Call to Consciousness* (Rooseveltown, NY: Akwesasne Notes, 1978).

56. A Westerner's solid apprehension of this point may be found in Stanley Diamond, *In Search of the Primitive: A Critique of Civilization* (New Brunswick, NJ: Transaction Books, 1974); also see Keith Thomas, *Man and the Natural World: A History of Modern Sensibility* (New York: Pantheon Books, 1983).

57. The matter has been explored tangentially, from a number of angles. Some of the best, for purposes of this chapter, include Tala Asad, ed., *Anthropology and the Colonial Encounter* (New York: Humanities Press, 1973); Robert Berkhofer, *The White Man's Indian: Images of the American Indian from Columbus to the Present* (New York: Alfred A. Knopf, 1978); Tzvetan Todorov, *The Conquest of America: The Question of the Other* (New York: Harper & Row, 1984); and Robert Young, *White Mythologies: Writing History and the West* (London: Routledge, 1990).

58. More broadly, the thrust this negation has always related to the interactions between European/Euro-American colonists and native cultures; see Richard Drinnon, *Facing West: The Metaphysics of Indian Hating and Empire Building* (Minneapolis: University of Minnesota Press, 1980).

59. Aside from the paradigmatic shift, culturally speaking, imbedded in this observation, it shares much with the insights into the function of higher education achieved by New Left theorists during the 1960s; see Carl Davidson, *The New Student Radicals in the Multiversity and Other Writings on Student Syndicalism* (Chicago: Charles Kerr, 1990).

60. In essence, this approach is the equivalent of Mao Tse-tung's having declared the Chinese revolution victorious at the point it liberated and secured the Caves of Hunan.

61. One salient example is the system of "survival schools" started by the American Indian Movement during the mid-1970s, only two of which still exist in any form. See Susan Braudy, "We Will Remember Survival School: The Women and Children of the American Indian Movement," *Ms. Magazine*, No. 5 (July 1976).

62. For a case study of one initially separatist effort turned accommodationist, see Maryls Duchene, "A Profile of American Indian Community Colleges"; more broadly, see Gerald Wilkenson, "Educational Problems in the Indian Community: A Comment on Learning as Colonialism"; both essays are in *Integrateducation*, Vol. 19, Nos. 1–2 (January-April 1982).

63. Ward Churchill and Norbert S. Hill, Jr., "Indian Education at the University Level: An Historical Survey," *Journal of Ethnic Studies*, Vol. 7, No. 3 (1979).

64. Further elaboration of this theme will be found in Ward Churchill, "White Studies or Isolation: An Alternative Model for American Indian Studies Programs," in James R. Young, ed., *American Indian Issues in Higher Education* (Los Angeles: UCLA American Indian Studies Center, 1981). Also see M. Annette Jaimes, "American Indian Studies: Toward an Indigenous Model," *American Indian Culture and Research Journal*, Vol. 11, No. 3 (Fall 1987).

65. So far as is known, Deutschke, head of the German SDS, first publicly issued a call for such a strategy during an address of a mass demonstration in Berlin during January 1968.

66. Mao Tse-tung, *On Protracted War* (Peking: Foreign Language Press, 1967); Che Guevara, *Guerrilla Warfare* (New York: Vintage Books, 1961).

67. For an excellent and succinct examination of the implications of this point, see Jorge Noriega, "American Indian Education in the United States: Indoctrination for Subordination to Colonialism," in M. Annette Jaimes, ed., *The State of Native America: Genocide, Colonization, and Resistance* (Boston: South End Press, 1992), p. 401, n. 115. More broadly, see Jurgen Herget, *And Sadly Teach: Teacher Education and Professionalization in American Culture* (Madison: University of Wisconsin Press, 1991).

68. The concept is elaborated much more fully and eloquently in Paulo Freire's *Pedagogy of the Oppressed* (New York: Continuum Books, 1981).

69. Again, one can turn to Freire for development of the themes; see his *Education for Critical Consciousness* (New York: Continuum Books, 1982). For the results of a practical—and very successful—application of these principles in the United States, see M. Annette Jaimes, *TRIBES 1989: Final Report and Evaluation* (Boulder: University of Colorado University Learning Center, August 1989).

70. For overall analysis, see Vine Deloria, Jr., "Indian Studies—The Orphan of Academia," *Wicazo Sa Review*, Vol. 2, No. 2 (1986); also see José Barriero, "The Dilemma of American Indian Education," *Indian Studies Quarterly*, Vol. 1, No. 1 (1984).

71. As examples, Bill Devall and George Sessions; see their *Deep Ecology: Living as if Nature Mattered* (Salt Lake City: Perigrine Smith Books, 1985). Also see André Gorz, *Ecology as Politics* (Boston: South End Press, 1981).

72. The matter is well-handled in Edward W. Said, "Representing the Colonized: Anthropology's Interlocutors," *Critical Inquiry*, No. 15 (1989).

73. See, for instance, Lucy Lippard, *Mixed Blessings: New Art in Multicultural America* (New York: Pantheon, 1990).

74. Murray Bookchin, *The Ecology of Freedom* (Palo Alto, CA: Cheshire Books, 1982); also see Steve Chase, ed., *Defending the Earth: A Dialogue Between Murray Bookchin and Dave Foreman* (Boston: South End Press, 1991).

75. Fritz Stern, *The Politics of Cultural Despair: A Study in the Rise of Germanic Ideology* (Berkeley: University of California Press, 1961); also see Wilhelm Reich, *The Mass Psychology of Fascism* (New York: Farrar, Straus & Giroux, 1970).

76. See generally, Walker Connor, *The National Question in Marxist-Leninist Theory and Strategy* (Princeton, NJ: Princeton University Press, 1984).

77. Russell Means, "The Same Old Song," in Ward Churchill, ed., *Marxism and Native Americans* (Boston: South End Press, 1983).

78. Ward Churchill and Elisabeth R. Lloyd, *Culture versus Economism: Essays on Marxism in the Multicultural Arena* (Denver: University of Colorado Center for the Study of Indigenous Law and Politics, 1990).

79. Michael Albert and Robin Hahnel, *Unorthodox Marxism* (Boston: South End Press, 1978).

80. As illustration of one who made the transition, at least in substantial part, see Rudolph Bahro, *From Red to Green* (London: Verso, 1984).

81. Marcuse, "Repressive Tolerance," p. 111.

82. Vine Deloria, Jr., *The Metaphysics of Modern Existence* (New York: Harper & Row, 1979), p. 213.

83. For insights, see Ellen Schrecker, *No Ivory Tower: McCarthyism and the Universities* (New York: Oxford University Press, 1986).

3

Multiculturalism: War in America Continues

Imari Abubakari Obadele

FOUNDATIONS OF THE EVIL OF MULTICULTURALISM

In 1985 white and black educators in the state of Louisiana organized The Louisiana Association of Education That Is Multicultural, or LAEM. This by no means marked the beginning of the new "multicultural" phase of the casualty-laden war being fought in America over education. The war to which i refer is a black-white war.[1] It is a war for control of the nature of New Afrikan education. In fact, it is a war for control of the very soul of the New Afrikan people. (The term "New Afrikan" is used here much as the term "New Englander" was originally used: an English person in a new place. New Afrikan means an Afrikan born in the United States—what we generally refer to in the United States as a "black" person.)[2]

Still, the creation of LAEM is a salient landmark because it focuses us on ten years of a new strategy in this century-old war. It focuses us on a decade of the formal marshalling of resources by the Americans (i.e., the whites), the United Statesers, under an opiatic rubric called "multiculturalism," in the continuing thrust of the whites to maintain their intellectual and physical subordination of the New Afrikans.

In this chapter i will spell out the history and nature of the academic war of the whites against the blacks in the United States. i conclude with a recounting of two pertinent recent battles. In sum, i will attempt to indicate why many New Afrikan educators, such as most of the several hundreds who participate in the work of the National Board of Education for People of Afrikan Ancestry, see multiculturalism in a much different light than people who have chosen to come to the United States from such places as Central America, Vietnam, India, and, indeed, from the Afrikan continent. Generally such persons see multiculturalism as a means of correcting historical absences and distortions in American literature and school presentations. New Afrikan teachers such as myself see multiculturalism as a new instrument in an on-going white war to continue white intellectual and physical domination of the New Afrikan people.

In preparing to grasp the genesis and nature of the Americans' war against the New Afrikans, it is helpful to note a population statistic. While the state of Nigeria has 90 million people, the largest *nation* within Nigeria, the Hausa, has only 20 million people. The nation-state of Ethiopia (i.e., a state where one nation is the overwhelming majority population) has about 50 million people. So, with more than 30 million people, the oppressed New Afrikan nation within the United States is the second largest Afrikan nation in the world.[3] This statistic poses a problem for Americans and their concept of America.

i suspect that had the New Afrikan population in the United States numbered only 250,000 or less in 1865 instead of 4.5 million, the United States might have worked out some form of self-determination and sovereignty for those within the group—say, one-half to three-quarters of the total—who wanted it. White behavior historically makes clear that it is quite another matter for them to contemplate any form of sovereignty, whether for 1865's 1–2 million New Afrikans or today's 5–20 million New Afrikans, on land which they, the whites, so selfishly possess. Yet the free exercise of the right to self-determination is obviously owed to New Afrikans whose presence here was effected by kidnapping and viciously enforced retention.

My essential argument is that, rather than facilitating the free and informed exercise of the right to self-determination by the New Afrikans—which almost certainly would result in a campaign for independent statehood on this soil by millions of New Afrikans—whites have chosen two other options. First, from the time of slavery, white government and social structure chose to attempt to terrorize us into a belief in the fundamental correctness of white domination and white possession of "America." Second, the American social structure, having failed to extinguish our thirst for education and our unceasing campaigns to achieve it, has opted to control and guide our education—indeed, to corrupt it— to the same ends as the program of terror: to make us accept the "correctness" of white domination, including white domination of the land under white-led government, and to keep from us the knowledge of our right to self-determination. Whites, also, are kept ignorant of this right, with respect not only to New Afrikans but to Indians, Puerto Ricans, Virgin Islanders, Samoans, and the peoples of Alaska.

In short, whatever the economic factors that made slavery legally and socially accepted for the vast majority of whites in the Thirteen Colonies and the successor United States, i see the political motive that i have described, and that was present from the early days of the colonial slave experience, as more important and determinant in the academic war that whites in America are waging against blacks than the economic factors.

Is multiculturalism a tool for correction? The history of the problem, the enduring thrust for white supremacist control of New Afrikan education, does not permit an affirmative answer—at least, not as multiculturalism is currently conceived and practiced.

This history is informed by the differing attitudes that Americans generally developed toward Indians, on the one hand, and New Afrikans, on the other. Indians also would be engulfed by invidious stereotypes spun and adhered to by the whites, an appropriate matter for a true multicultural corrective. But Chief Justice Roger Taney's conclusions on this matter, as he wrote in the *Dred Scott* decision (60 U.S. 397, 1857), are highly informative:

The situation of this population [the New Afrikans] was altogether unlike that of the Indian race. The latter, it is true, formed no part of the colonial communities, and never amalgamated with them in social connections or in government. But although they were uncivilized, they were yet a free and independent people, associated together in nations or tribes, and governed by their own laws. . . . It is true that the course of events has brought the Indian tribes within the limits of the United States under subjection to the white race; and it has been found necessary, for their sake as well as our own, to regard them as in a state of pupilage, and to legislate to a certain extent over them and the territory they occupy. But they may, without doubt, like the subjects of any other foreign government, be naturalized by the authority of Congress, and become citizens of a State and of the United States; and if an individual should leave his nation or tribe, and take up his abode among the white population, he would be entitled to all the rights and privileges which would belong to an emigrant from any other foreign people.[4]

Turning to the New Afrikans, Justice Taney wrote:

The question before us is, whether the class of persons described in the plea of abatement compose a portion of this people, and are constituent members of this sovereignty? We think, they are not, and that they are not included, and were not intended to be included, under the word "citizen" in the Constitution, and can therefore claim none of the rights and privileges which that instrument provides for and secures to citizens of the United States. On the contrary, they were at that time considered as a subordinate and inferior class of beings, who had been subjugated by the dominant race, and whether emancipated or not, yet remained subject to their authority, and had no rights or privileges but such as those who held the power and the government might choose to grant them.[5]

Justice Taney continued:

They [the New Afrikans] had for more than a century before [the Declaration of Independence] been regarded as beings of an inferior order, and altogether unfit to associate with the white race, either in social or political relations; and so far inferior, that they had no rights which the white man was bound to respect; and that the Negro might justly and lawfully be reduced to slavery for his benefit. . . . This opinion was at that time fixed and universal in the civilized portion of the white race. It was regarded as an axiom in morals as well as in politics, which no one thought of disputing, or supposed to be open to dispute; and men in every grade and position in society daily and habitually acted upon it in their private pursuits, as well as in matters of public concern, without doubting for a moment the correctness of this opinion.[6]

It is fair, i believe, to accept Justice Taney's report as an authoritative testimony of the nature of the negative opinion that whites generally in the United States held toward New Afrikans, even 100 years before the Declaration of Independence. There seems to be abundant evidence that this opinion among whites was the result not of careful observation but of contrived and purposeful mythmaking. It was mythmaking designed to justify the enslavement of one group of people by another group at a moment when the enslaving group held themselves, for the most part, to be Christian people.[7]

One might note that the U.S. Constitution itself, far from attempting to correct the invidious myths concerning New Afrikans, acted upon what Justice Taney described as the prevailing opinion among whites, that Afrikans were fit subjects for enslavement and deprivation of human rights *because* we were inferior to whites. Even in the wake of the Civil War, neither the U.S. government nor any of the white societies undertaking to assist the newly freed people called for or implemented any programs to destroy the two centuries of myths and vilification that had robbed New Afrikans, in the eyes of most of their white fellows, of human stature and human dignity. Such a program was a necessary prerequisite for a life of peace and mutual respect among black and white neighbors. In its absence the majority of whites seemed to feel that the violence imposed upon New Afrikans by the Ku Klux Klan and similar organizations and individuals was necessary to *white* well-being and deserved by blacks.

In the wake of congressional reconstruction, beginning in 1867, the Supreme Court quickly made clear that the violence which the hate generated by the belief in white supremacy produced was uncorrectable by federal law, so long as the perpetrators were not state officials. The case that reached the Supreme Court arose from the 1872 Colfax incident in Louisiana: a Klan-type killing of New Afrikan state deputies who had been assigned by the governor to guard a courthouse—*United States v. Cruikshank*, 92 U.S. 542 (1876).

In 1883, in *The Civil Rights Cases*, 109 U.S. 3, the Supreme Court told private owners of public accommodations (i.e., restaurants, theaters, hotels) that it was okay to refuse service to New Afrikans since the courts would not enforce "social" rights. In 1896 the Supreme Court, incredibly, told the states that they too could discriminate against New Afrikans because of race—despite the Fourteenth Amendment's explicit prohibition against such state action—*Plessy v. Ferguson*, 163 U.S. 537. These actions of the courts put the force of law and, therefore, the police, behind the enforcement of the premier American value of white supremacy. The laws and brutal police forces, backed by "hanging" judges and extensive private white violence against New Afrikans, were the rule for the 70 years of the

"Age of Segregation," lasted formally from 1896 through 1964–65 when the Black Revolution forced passage of the Civil Rights Act and the Voting Rights Act.[8]

But during the long period of law-sanctioned, police-enforced subordination of blacks to whites, the institutions of American literature, newspapers, and theater maintained a campaign of vilification. New Afrikans were portrayed as servants and clowns and criminals.[9] In the schools, until the mid-1960s, our major contributions to the world were limited in textbooks to the products of slave labor, to sports feats, and music; our epic struggle against the effects of an anti-black Constitution, against antiblack laws and practices was not described and, indeed, the textbooks limned us as people who accommodated with simple-minded goodness both to slavery and to the 100 years of law-supported oppression *after* slavery.

Note that no other oppressed group in America has received such incessant vilification. i have quoted Justice Taney's observations concerning the different foundations for the "opinions," as he put it, that Americans entertained toward Indians, on the one hand, and Afrikans, on the other. Today most elementary school children in America know the names of Cochise, Geronimo, Crazy Horse, and Sitting Bull and know that they fought honorably on behalf of their people and against American aggrandizement. Neither through movies nor through textbooks do most American students know the names of Gabriel Prosser, Denmark Vesey, Captain Garcia ("Fort Negro"), Abraham and the other Black Seminole leaders, Tunis Campbell, or the many other New Afrikan leaders who also fought honorably on behalf of their people and against white oppression.

Similarly, if one were to accept the argument that the U.S. Constitution was framed to keep rich over poor, it would remain true that none of the colonial laws or, later, the provisions of the Constitution, established the dominance of the rich over the poor as the law established the dominance of white over black. The so-called fugitive slave provision of the U.S. Constitution established that Americans, by law, would not only not celebrate freedom won by any New Afrikan but would deem such New Afrikans as objects to be brought back into slavery by any means, including the cooperation of courts and police. The laws, Justice Taney wrote, "show that a perpetual and impassable barrier was intended to be created between the white race and the one which they had reduced to slavery."[10] These laws also fueled the negative opinion held by whites against blacks.

The politically oppressed and otherwise dominated category of white women was still regarded, throughout the same long period, as superior to black males and females. Justice Taney wrote:

Undoubtably, a person may be a citizen, that is, a member of the community who form the sovereignty, although he exercises no share of the political power, and is incapacitated from holding particular offices. Women and minors, who form a part of the political family, cannot vote; and when a property qualification is required to vote or hold a particular office, those who have not the necessary qualification cannot vote or hold the office, yet they are citizens.[11]

None of this is stated to attempt to diminish the reality of the oppression of Native Americans or women. It is designed to suggest that a foundation has already been laid for a revision through multiculturalism of the treatment of Indians and women in textbooks and classrooms. Not so for the New Afrikans. We have been the specific victims of 300 years of relentless vilification. Multiculturalism as conceived and operative today demands no comprehensive attack on this seamless historic problem. i suggest that the reason is obvious: such an attack would directly challenge the Americans' premier social value, white supremacy, and open the door for a political change of major proportions: the informed and democratic exercise of the right to self-determination by 30 million New Afrikans.

As the Black Revolution was successfully challenging racist laws during the first-half of the 1960s, textbooks began to speak of "Ghana, Mali, and Songhay," usually describing these powerful West Afrikan states (existing during the European "Middle Ages") not as states but, merely, as "societies." Textbooks continued—as they do today—to suggest that ancient Egypt was white and to ignore Kush, Zimbabwe, Nok, and Ta-Seti.[12]

The extraordinary New Afrikan producer, Bill Cosby, in the late 1980s and early 1990s created a marvelous exception to vilification with his mass media television series, *A Different World* and *The Bill Cosby Show*. Spike Lee, another gifted New Afrikan producer, through the movies, gave white and black students and elders, in the early 1990s, the name of Malcolm X and a glimpse of his struggle against white oppression and hatred. But the popular media continued to perpetuate the servant-clown-criminal syndrome, making the servants occasionally police chiefs but chiefs who—like their more obvious fellows stereotypes—served a white agenda and displayed no consciousness of the historic black struggle for freedom, dignity, and opportunity. Typifying such television programs were *Starsky and Hutch*, *Hill Street Blues*, and *Designing Women*.

None of this should be viewed simply as a matter of exclusion or innocent selection of New Afrikans as delightful clowns and wonderful musicians and athletes. Rather, i urge, serious multiculturalists must keep the *political* motive in mind. No conqueror wants the expense of endless war or of forever maintaining the subjugation of an unruly people by large-scale police brutality. Throughout history and everywhere, the process of pacification chosen when genocide is inappropriate or does not work sufficiently—the process of ending the unruliness of an entire population—has involved killing and jailing the revolutionaries among the conquered people and then, on the basis of this demonstrated terror, promoting a group of leaders and teachers who are willing to urge and practice subordination to the conquerors, willing to teach the art of accommodation.[13]

In the United States the killing of revolutionaries was not, of course, confined to the era of slavery. The American Federal Bureau of Investigation (FBI) orchestrated a campaign against the Black Panther Party, the Nation of Islam, the Southern Christian Leadership Conference, and the Provisional Government of the Republic of New Afrika, which, between 1967 and the Senate's Church Committee hearings in 1974, resulted in the police killing and wounding of numerous persons and the wrongful jailing of many others.[14] This information is generally not included in the curriculum of high schools in the United States. Yet it lies in the collective awareness of New Afrikan people and, i suggest, is an appropriate area of concern for teachers earnestly seeking a true multicultural goal of friendship among neighbors of different backgrounds.

Less onerous penalties than death and prison are imposed by the American social structure upon those who resist a role in the process of making the oppressed accommodate to their oppression. Teachers who oppose the white racism of American school systems and demand and work for a systematic effort to redress 300 years of vilification of Afrikan and New Afrikan people usually became victims of mighty efforts by the white academic and media establishments to censure and fire them with prejudice. During the early 1990s the prominent examples of this treatment are Professor Leonard Jeffries of the City College of New York and Professor Tony Martin of Wellesley College. i would argue that many New Afrikan teachers, and their white allies, fear and sometimes suffer similar fates.

In sum, i am suggesting that the 300 years of vilification of New Afrikans in America is still shaping negative white opinion concerning us. i am arguing that this reality is unlike the reality of other oppressed people in America and, indeed, can not be equated to the experience of newcomers in America who have not suffered such a long, on-going calamity and whose worth can readily be bolstered by inclusion of their histories and cultures in more multicultural textbooks and classroom settings.

i am arguing that unless the reality of the 300 years of vilification, along with an appreciation of the political objectives involved with respect to the New Afrikan's right to exercise self-determination on a free and informed basis, are forthrightly considered and addressed with specific correctives, multiculturalism will remain another tool aimed at the pacification of a resisting people.

Two anecdotes from the struggle for positive education of New Afrikans and whites will illuminate, i trust, an important experience with multiculturalism as it is conceived and practiced today.

THE CONTINUING WAR: 1991 ONWARD

James Anderson's 1988 book, *The Education of Blacks in the South, 1860–1935*, is important for a number of reasons.[15] Chief among these, perhaps, is his investigation of Freedmen's Bureau records. (The Freedmen's Bureau was created by an Act of Congress on March 3, 1865.) Here and in other sources Anderson discovered the plain evidence that when Freedmen's Bureau operatives began dealing with education, they found that "throughout the entire South" New Afrikans had already established self-teaching practices and "native schools."[16] Many of these schools, according to Anderson, were in places not previously visited by the missionary societies or the Freedmen's Bureau.

Anderson stresses that while the freed New Afrikans' educational enterprises benefitted greatly from the support of northern whites, the New Afrikans "were determined to achieve educational self-sufficiency."[17] During Reconstruction, Southern legislatures, driven by their New Afrikan members, were strong, resulting in a strategy of underfunded and shortened school terms supportive of work cycles related to plantation farming. The white reformers' more subtle approach called for mass education, including the education of New Afrikans. In reality the reformers, led by Northern General Samuel Chapman Armstrong and his protégé, an extraordinarily gifted but wretched accommodating New Afrikan named Booker T. Washington, had joined the planters in renewing the white war against New Afrikan educational objectives. Those objectives, Anderson found, were New Afrikan control and unfettered education aimed at political, economic, and intellectual goals. Planters and reformers realized this resumed war was no longer to be fought against a powerless, enslaved population but against a resourceful, if relatively impoverished, free population with significant political potential.

For both the white planter and the white reformer the objective of their opposition was the same: pacification of the New Afrikan in the interest of white supremacy. The objective at a lower level was to maintain New Afrikans as an ignorant, pliable, unskilled laboring caste.

The planters firmly believed, most of them, that any mass education of New Afrikans would lead not to racial peace but to the opposite. This was so despite the unctuous assurances of Booker T. Washington, whom the U.S. rich industrialists had made nationally famous and had anointed in the eyes of northern whites and many New Afrikans everywhere as the premier leader and spokesperson for all New Afrikans.[18] (Thanks to Armstrong, Washington had become a founding leader of Tuskegee Institute in Alabama in 1881. He fashioned its curriculum on the Armstrong-Hampton model.)

But black leaders beyond Washington's orbit, including Ida Wells Barnett, Anna Julia Cooper, William Monroe Trotter, and W.E.B. Du Bois, long opposed the Hampton-Tuskegee model. They knew that the intention and practice of this model were to teach only enough literacy as one might get in a good fourth grade curriculum and no education for the higher ranks of industrial labor. These leaders sought "classical" education for New Afrikans.

Still, John D. Rockefeller's money, with that of his cohorts (e.g., the John E. Slater Fund and the Peabody Fund), had a distinct impact in shaping New Afrikan education in the South toward the Hampton-Tuskegee model. Writing in 1933, looking back at 50 years of the New Afrikan educational enterprise, one of New Afrika's most indefatigable and mentally incisive scholars, Carter G. Woodson, concluded: "Inasmuch as the industrial education idea rapidly gained ground, too, many Negroes for political purposes began to espouse it: and schools and colleges hoping thereby to obtain money worked out accordingly makeshift provisions for such instruction, although they could not satisfactorily offer it."[19]

Woodson's evaluation of the controversy between "classical" and "industrial" education was harsh. He wrote: "Unfortunately, however, the affair developed into a sort of battle of words, for in spite of all they said and did the majority of

Negroes, those who did make some effort to obtain an education, did not actually receive either the industrial or the classical education."[20]

When, as a young father, 30 years after Dr. Woodson's harsh evaluation, i and my wife Octavia withdrew our son Freddy from his Detroit junior high school because of a racist history book and curriculum guide, i did not know that we were entering a struggle that was already 100 years old. We won that 1962–64 campaign because of the black civil rights group, GOAL, whose program it was, and because of relentless coverage by the editor of the *Michigan Chronicle*, a black weekly newspaper, Al Manning.

In 1964 the Detroit school board (with only one New Afrikan member, Dr. Robinson) advised New York publishers that if they did not produce a set of books that abandoned such canards as the suggestion that we loved the master so much that we rejected freedom when offered by Union soldiers, Detroit would no longer purchase their books. The Detroit school board supported this advice/threat with the preparation and distribution of a supplement considerably more kind to New Afrikans and better representing the issues of slavery and the Civil War. The national history textbook publishers acquiesced—at least with respect to the more offensive material.

In his *The Mis-Education of the Negro*, Woodson had also written: "An observer from outside of the situation naturally inquires why the Negroes, many of whom serve their race as teachers, have not changed this program [of deficient, Euro-centric education]. These teachers, however, are powerless. Negroes have no control over their education and have little voice in their affairs pertaining thereto."[21] Woodson also added: "Taught from books of the same bias, trained by Caucasians of the same prejudices or by Negroes of enslaved minds, one generation of Negro teachers after another have [sic] served for no higher purpose than to do what they are told to do. In other words, a Negro teacher instructing Negro children is in many respects a white teacher thus engaged, for the program in each case is about the same."[22]

In 1989 Kwaku Walker, Abena Walker, and i completed a 250-page study of racial values in the textbooks and curriculum guides used in social studies in the Washington, D.C., public schools. The study also included a critique of the failure of the D.C. system, where the student population is 95 percent New Afrikan, to require teachers to understand and respect what is popularly known as "Black English." We produced and presented to the Board of Education, as part of the study, a set of nine recommendations, correctives, for curriculum reorganization. (We also included two scales for measuring racial values in textbooks for American and world history.)[23]

Here we encountered head-on the continuing reality of Woodson's 55-year-old criticism of some New Afrikan teachers' submission to white nationalist teaching. The difference in 1990 was that the New Afrikans in Washington, D.C., could no longer be said not to be in charge. The school board was majority black and the superintendent was also New Afrikan.

Our nine recommendations were built upon, inter alia, our conclusion that the

300 years of vilification had to be addressed. Recognizing that the low opinion of us generated among whites and others in America was in part built upon the perception that Afrikans possessed no creditable history, we called on the school board to require all teachers to review regularly *The Nile Valley Tapes*.[24] These tapes evolved from the historic Nile Valley Conference of scholars held at Morehouse University in Atlanta in 1984. There, not only was the celebrated black Eighteenth Dynasty examined, but also the (black) Afrikan roots of early Egyptian achievements were explored.

Recognizing that the very framework of history and social science instruction in the schools was constructed to teach a falsely glorious story of the rise of the American nation, we called for the introduction of a framework that dealt with the agendas of all three major actors (Indians, Europeans, and Afrikans), that dealt with the transformation of the racist U.S. polity into a professedly multiracial democracy, and that dealt in detail with the military struggle, as well as the nonmilitary struggle, of New Afrikans to achieve three major self-selected goals: (1) changing the United States and becoming full citizens, (2) returning to Afrika, and (3) establishing an independent state in North America on territory claimed by the United States. We called for the recognition of the right of self-determination belonging to Indians, New Afrikans, Puerto Ricans, and other peoples conquered by the Americans.

As Woodson might have predicted, these recommendations, presented formally to the Board of Education and the superintendent and reviewed by us with staff, were not only essentially ignored, but neither staff nor board offered scholarly or nonscholarly criticism or comment. Today as this chapter is being written in 1994, D.C.'s "Eighth Grade American History Curriculum Guide," replete with white supremacist characterizations and organization, remains in official use. (Among the inappropriate references is one that suggests that teachers use the movie *Gone with the Wind* as a positive aid in teaching the Civil War.)

Here we encountered black leaders of education without the will to challenge the racist framework and content that have been established by the white leaders of education, through textbooks and teachers' training curricula, in pursuit of their century-old academic and political goals. This occurred at a moment and in a setting where one might justly have expected that creative black leaders in D.C. would have used the growing popularity of multiculturalism to resume the battle for those original, self-determined, black goals of education described by Professor Anderson.

As activists regroup for another effort at getting the District of Columbia to adopt the Obadele-Walker recommendations, one lesson is that there must be stronger community and press support. With regard to the press, however, the reality is different from the days 30 years ago when black newspapers like the *Michigan Chronicle* still commanded a significant portion of black attention. Today television and the white daily press have diminished black newspapers' ability to inform and mobilize the mass of people. And the white press is hostile toward any challenge to white supremacist education. Washington, D.C., also afforded an example of this.

After the submission of the Obadele-Walker report, in 1993 Abena Walker succeeded in winning from the new superintendent (also a New Afrikan) and a divided board permission for a "school within a school" at the middle school level. One way of correcting the impact of 300 years of racial vilification for New Afrikan students is to use what is generally called an Afrikan-centered curriculum and system. This was the fundamental basis upon which Ms. Walker's *school within a school* was approved and established. Her battle continues. The initial success of the Walker project was based on the mobilization of parents and some educators. The role of the press was negative.

The *Washington Post*, playing the role of pretend liberal but championing the status quo, carried stories of the divisions existing within the school board. Mostly these stories were built upon public criticism, emanating from a new member of the school board, a vivacious New Afrikan woman long in the struggle to improve education, Valencia Muhammad. She argued, for instance, that the Walker project was too small in scope, that the Walker curriculum and system (although used in small school settings for several years) were not submitted to staff prior to the school's opening, and that Abena Walker's master's degree had been awarded by a nontraditional university of which Ms. Walker is a founder.

In the Baton Rouge, Louisiana, case the struggle to end the impact of 300 years of vilification and improve the education of New Afrikan children is more sharply focused on a campaign of the East Baton Rouge Parish school board and the state department of education to maintain the status quo, while adding a touch of multiculturalism. The state department is white-led and controlled; the Parish school board has predominantly white composition. (The city of Baton Rouge, largest in the parish, is about 30 percent New Afrikan.) The parish's daily newspaper, *The Advocate*, has played a role similar to that of the *Washington Post*, undertaking a transparently objective stance while championing white supremacist teaching.

In January 1993 i reviewed the Louisiana state guide for American history at all grade levels, on behalf of the Provisional Government, Republic of New Afrika.[25] i sent my evaluation to the state superintendent and his primary aide, Dr. William Miller. My conclusion was that the guide was "a racist, failed document, demanding immediate, substantial change."

In his reply Dr. Miller assured me that the guide had been written by a large and prestigious group of New Afrikan and white educators and, dated 1989, was designed to fulfill, inter alia, a 1987 legislative mandate to teach in high school "black history and the historical contributions of all nationalities." My critique to the state board had stated, on this point:

I am confident that the goal of the initiating legislators was not simply to have you add the name of a few outstanding Black people to the old, tired story of European discovery of America and subsequent White history. Rather, i conclude, it was to re-examine and expunge racism from the curriculum. In this task Louisiana's *American History Guide* fails miserably.

Dr. Miller's reply also said that he and Mr. John A. Jones, Jr., a member of the most recent revision committee, agreed that "some of the information and interpretations that i presented should possibly be included in subsequent revision of the American history program."[26] But within a year the department provided no further comment, no advice as to when a new revision would be under way.

Some colleagues and i then decided to challenge the East Baton Rouge Parish school system. We were Kofi Lomotey, chair of the Department of Administrative and Foundational Services of the College of Education, Louisiana State University; Raymond Lockett, chair of the Department of History at Southern University, Baton Rouge; Clyde McDaniel, chair of the Department of Social Work, Southern University, Baton Rouge; Press Robinson, a Southern University Vice President and a longtime member of the East Baton Rouge Parish school board; Jacqueline Mims, a member of the East Baton Rouge school board; and myself—all are New Afrikan.

This group made a set of presentations before the board's multicultural committee. Ms. Mims and Dr. Robinson were on that committee. An overflow audience, largely from the New Afrikan community, attended, and when the session—which had climbed in emotional intensity as the audience and some of the board members were moved by the presentations—concluded, the committee voted to recommend that the board "restructure a multicultural education advisory committee and charge it with ridding courses of what many think is a white European outlook."[27] The advisory committee would begin with the history courses. The committee also voted to commit itself to sensitivity training for all school staff.

The victory was short-lived. In the next two weeks before the meeting of the full board, Donna Deshotels, the white chairperson of the committee, was inveighed upon to table the positive recommendations of her own committee! She did this at the board meeting, outraging the once-more packed audience. The board quickly recessed.[28]

Meanwhile *The Advocate* ran commentary criticizing my statement that Thomas Jefferson was the equivalent of Hitler and should be studied in the same context. A Mike Dunne *Advocate* article charged that those arguing for change showed "the multicultural debate at its worst" and that our "real motive" was to force white students "to take a black history course."[29] This attempt of the white daily newspaper to reduce our objectives to simplistic and racially provocative terms was followed by a more sophisticated undertaking.

The newspaper promoted and sponsored a multicultural conference, attended by approximately 75 teachers, where multiculturalism was boldly promoted as a "getting to know you" enterprise. Here, also, the newspaper distributed its booklet entitled "In Celebration of Black History." The booklet lists 48 individuals divided into six categories: Education, Fine Arts, Science and Industry, Entertainment, Leaders and Politicians, and Sports. All this is under the title "Black History in

Review." The list does contain the name of Malcolm X, and there is later material on Frederick Douglass and Harriet Tubman, but nowhere else is there an indication that "Black History" includes those who took up arms in their own cause, such as Gabriel Prosser, Denmark Vesey, Nat Turner, Tunis Campbell, Abraham, or the New Afrikans who fought on John Brown's side, or the Black Panthers. Thus, the old vilification that New Afrikans lacked an intelligent comprehension of our own oppressive conditions and lacked the courage to take up arms to end those conditions was doggedly reinforced.

The newspaper's booklet also referred to New Afrikans as "African-Americans," maintaining the erroneous proposition that the Fourteenth Amendment could "make" the kidnapped persons and their progeny into U.S. citizens without their informed and democratically expressed consent. Here the newspaper undertook to continue the historic, white political objective: to prevent New Afrikans from being aware of our right to self-determination, which carries with it an inherent demand for reparations and, more important to the Americans, the possibility of millions of New Afrikans opting for independent statehood on land claimed by the United States.

CONCLUSION

Washington, D.C., and Baton Rouge cases are anecdotal evidence supporting the author's dim view of multiculturalism as it is conceived and practiced in America today.

However, i have faith that many earnest teachers are committed to one of the simple but extremely powerful goals of multiculturalism, envisioned in its best sense. That goal is true friendship among neighbors of different backgrounds, so that we passengers on spaceship Earth may get on with our quests for pure water and air, good nutrition and health, universal education, and—from my Afrikan point of view—spiritual development.

But courage is demanded, first, of teachers. It is the courage to realize that 300 years of vilification of the New Afrikan will defeat all efforts at multicultural friendship *unless* this atrocity is fully faced and fully addressed. That, i think, is the central message of this chapter. We need not despair. Precedents do exist that can be helpful. When the United States enacted the Civil Liberties Act of 1988, to compensate Japanese living in America who were held, en masse, in U.S. concentration camps during World War II, it provided for "a public education fund to finance efforts to inform the public about the internment of such individuals so as to prevent the recurrence of any similar event."

A project of this type, addressing the 300 years of invidious mythmaking and vilification of the New Afrikan and the evasion of our right to self-determination, would be an appropriate measure by government and teachers' associations toward correcting a seminal wrong and its effects that multiculturalism, as presently conceived, cannot reach.

NOTES

1. Clearly, all whites are not on the side characterized by their color; i am talking about demonstrable, operative interests of black and white group majorities. "i" is my own preferred spelling of the first-person singular.

2. Politically i decline to use the term "Afrikan-American" because the term "American" is not only a product of European conquest and presumptions but it also implies, in its hyphenated form, an acceptance of the American political ideology, which is a white vainglorious, white supremacist ideology. To accept the term "Afrikan-American" is also to accept the conqueror's presumption that he could with the Fourteenth Amendment make us—a kidnapped and oppressed people—into U.S. citizens, "Americans," without our informed, democratically expressed consent. That, of course, is not only contrary to common sense, it is contrary to settled international law. See, for instance, United Nations General Assembly Resolutions 1514 and 1541 (both in 1960) and the self-determination provisions of U.N. General Assembly Resolution 2625 (1970), the "Declaration on Principles of International Law." New Afrikans, descendants of persons kidnapped to this land and polity and held here against our will, are still entitled to exercise the right of self-determination: the right to choose—individually and collectively—to "go back" to Afrika; to go somewhere other than Afrika or the United States; to become U.S. citizens with full rights, or to establish an independent state on land now claimed by the United States (since U.S. law, and the predecessor colonial law, held us here for ten generations before the Civil War). As our political movements demonstrate today, some of us would select each of these options.

3. Brazil would have a larger Afrikan nation if they counted black people as we do in the United States. Here i am applying the international law definition of "the state"—people, land, government, and international recognition—set out in the Montevideo Treaty, ratified by the United States in 1934, *The Convention on Rights and Duties of States*, 49 Stat. 3097. The definition of "nation" may be summarized as a people bound together by distinct, historically evolved values and beliefs. See Joseph Stalin's *Collected Works*, Vol. 4: *Marxism and the National Question* (Moscow: Progress Publishers, 1953–55), pp. 300–384, and Imari Obadele, "A Macro-Level Theory of Human Organization" in *America the Nation-State* (Baton Rouge, LA: House of Songhay Commission, 1993), pp. 69–85. The "nation" still exists when it loses state power—that is, government (and army) and recognized sovereignty over its national territory—so long as the people remain bound by their historically evolved values. Examples include the Sioux or Navajo in the United States, the Uzbeks or Ukrainians in the former Soviet Union, the Yoruba or Hausa in Nigeria.

4. *Dred Scott v. Sanford*, 60 U.S. 397, 1857, pp. 403–404.

5. Ibid., pp. 404–405.

6. Ibid., p. 407.

7. See, for instance, Melville J. Herskovits, *The Myth of the Negro Past* (Boston: Beacon Press, 1958), pp. 1–32.

8. Many good sources are available. See John Hope Franklin, *From Slavery to Freedom* (New York: Alfred A. Knopf, 1967); Lerone Bennett, *Before the Mayflower* (Chicago: Johnson Publishing Co., 1969), pp. 274 et seq.; Obadele, *America the Nation-State*, pp. 264–268 and 343–377; Ralph Ginzburg, *100 Years of Lynchings* (Baltimore: Black Classics Press, 1962); and Robert Haws, ed., *The Age of Segregation* (Jackson: University Press of Mississippi, 1978).

9. i will discuss my 1962 experience with a typical history textbook later. Egregious examples of films are *Birth of a Nation* and *Gone with the Wind*; the series of Charlie Chan movies fit this category. People 40 or older have knowledge of comics such as Joe Palooka and Mutt and Jeff, which took special pains to ridicule New Afrikans.

10. *Dred Scott*, p. 409.

11. Ibid., p. 422.

12. Imari Obadele, Kwaku Walker, and Abena Walker, *Black Genius* (Baton Rouge: House of Songhay Commission, 1991). Chekh Dip, *The African Origin of Civilization* (New York: Lawrence Hill, 1967), pp. xii–xvii.

13. In our time the killing and jailing of leaders did not work in Palestine, among Catholics in Northern Ireland, or in South Afrika. It can be said to have succeeded in Zaire, with the killing of Patrice Lumumba; and for a while in Ghana with the ousting of Kwame Nkrumah; previously in the United States, with the jailing and exiling of Marcus Garvey in the mid-1920s; in the 1960s and 1970s, with the killing and jailing of Black Panther Party members and workers of the Provisional Government, Republic of New Afrika, and members of the Black Liberation Army.

14. Brian Glick, *War at Home* (Boston: South End Press, 1989); Obadele, *America the Nation-State*, pp. 343–375.

15. James D. Anderson, *The Education of Blacks in the South, 1860–1935* (Chapel Hill: University of North Carolina Press, 1988).

16. Ibid., pp. 6–10.

17. Ibid., p. 15.

18. Washington's widely publicized speech, proclaiming a New Afrikan surrender to the planter/Klan demands that we no longer seek political power in the South or social equality, and agreeing to a subordinate laboring role for us, was made at the 1895 Exposition in Atlanta.

19. Carter G. Woodson, *The Mis-Education of the Negro* (New York: AMS Press, 1933, 1977), p. 12.

20. Ibid., p. 13.

21. Ibid., p. 22.

22. Ibid., p. 23.

23. Obadele, Walker, and Walker, *Black Genius*.

24. Most of the material from the Nile Valley Conference is contained in the book edited by Ivan Van Sertima, *Nile Valley Civilizations*, incorporating *Journal of African Civilizations*, Vol. 6, No. 2 (Atlanta: Morehouse College Edition, 1984).

25. The Provisional Government of the Republic of New Afrika was founded by convention in Detroit on March 31, 1968. It leads the modern-day movement to create an independent New Afrikan state based on the five states currently known as Louisiana, Mississippi, Alabama, Georgia, and South Carolina.

26. Letter from Dr. William J. Miller, Section Administrator, Bureau of Secondary Education, Louisiana Department of Education, to Dr. Imari A. Obadele, dated March 25, 1993.

27. Mike Dunne, "Multicultural ed plan gets boost," *The Advocate* (Baton Rouge, LA) August 24, 1993, pp. 1B–2B.

28. Mike Dunne, "Multicultural issue shunted to Weiss in 8–4 board vote," *The Advocate*, September 3, 1993, pp. 1A and 4A.

29. Mike Dunne, "Worst emotional setting for Multicultural debate," *The Advocate*, March 2, 1994.

4

Nuestra Realidad: Historical Roots of Our Latino Identity

Félix Masud-Piloto

The U.S. Census Bureau's decision to homogenize immigrants from Spanish-speaking Latin American nations and their descendants living permanently in the United States by creating the label "Hispanic" unleashed a heated political debate among the affected. The new categorization was perceived by some as an improvement from the Bureau's previous label, "other," but for most of the 25 million Latin Americans and people of Latin American descent living in the United States, becoming an instant "Hispanic" implied loss of nationality, culture, and identity.

On the surface, the label was offensive for two reasons: it was an imposed, unilateral decision by a foreign bureaucracy; and it was an insensitive attempt to lump into one generic mass a people whose most distinguishing characteristics are their cultural, ethnic, racial, linguistic, and political diversity. On a deeper level, however, the Bureau overlooked the fact that Hispanic fails to recognize the many identities and cultures represented by the Latin American population living permanently in the United States. If asked, many, if not most, of the affected would have preferred to be categorized as "Latino or Latina" (hereafter called Latino/a), an identity directly linked to and forged by the independent Latin American nations, free of Spanish colonialism, and proud of their racial and cultural mixture. Latino/a is much more inclusive because it recognizes the many races and cultures that make up the people of Latin America: Amerindian, African, European, Chinese, Indian, Mulatto, and Mestizo. Hispanic, on the other hand, refers exclusively to Latin America's Spanish heritage, and excludes even the other

European, but non-Hispanic members of the Latin American family: British, French, Portuguese, and Dutch. Despite their colonial legacy, they too form part of our heritage.

This chapter will not settle the debate, it only hopes to shed some light on the historical background necessary to understand why the Hispanic and Latino labels are so polemical among Latin American immigrants and people of Latin American descent living in the United States. For this, it is essential to look back at Latin American history, and the history of U.S. participation (read interference) in the politics and economies of Latin America. Likewise, it is also essential to look at U.S. immigration history and policies in order to understand the origins of the Latino/a communities in the United States. Except for Mexicans, who can trace their lineage back to what was northern Mexico until 1848, the Latino/a population in the United States is largely made up of immigrants. Some were forced to emigrate and some did so voluntarily, some came for political reasons, and others for economic reasons. Regardless their motivation, all Latin Americans living in the United States today are here as a result of U.S. policy toward their home countries. Thus, U.S. politics and policies are at the center of the identity debate.

OUR HISPANIC AND COLONIAL HERITAGE

When we talk about Latin America's Hispanic heritage, we must avoid interpreting that heritage solely on the most tangible cultural expressions and artifacts: language, religion, music, art, food, and traditions. Cultural heritage is also determined by history, politics, and society. In the case of Latin America, as in every colonized society, that heritage was violently imposed on the native population. For nearly 400 years, the Spanish, British, French, and Portuguese empires systematically destroyed, or tried to destroy, dozens of languages, religions, and cultures that had been in existence for centuries before the Europeans' arrival in the so-called New World. Equally devastating was the enormously high cost in human lives: millions died as a result of conquest, forced labor, and slavery. It is not unusual for scholars who study that historical period to characterize the conquest of the Americas as a "holocaust," the "conquest of paradise," and the "biggest land-grab in history" (Sale, 1990; Stannard, 1992; Wright, 1992).

In Latin America, the European empires created societies dominated by class and racial distinctions. The Spanish emphasized these differences in every aspect of society, even to the extreme of categorizing the descendants of the colonists according to place of birth, *peninsulares* and *criollos*. The former, by virtue of their Spanish birth were considered racially "pure," socially superior, and trustworthy. The latter, because they were born in the colonies, were considered racially "impure," socially inferior, and untrustworthy. Spain's strict racial policies created such bitter resentment and feelings of rejection among the *criollo* population, that by the eighteenth century they began to identify more with Latin America than with the empire. This is the period that Guatemalan historian Severo Martínez

Peláez (1973) identifies as the genesis of a Latin American identity and, consequently, the birth of the independence movements.

We should not overlook the fact that like the Spanish, the Aztecs, Incas, and other native peoples of the hemisphere also emphasized race, class, and rank in their societies. This is perhaps why the leaders of Latin America's wars of independence were so concerned with creating societies that represented and protected everyone. After more than four centuries of colonialism, the leaders of Latin America faced the task not only of creating governments, but of liberating and integrating a people best characterized by their racial and cultural mixture. In 1819 Simón Bolívar urged his fellow *criollos* to remember the complexities of our people:

Let's keep in mind that our people are neither European nor North American, more a composite of Africa and America than an outgrowth of Europe, for even Spain ceases to be European by its African bloodline, its institutions, its character. It is impossible to determine properly what human family we belong to. Most Indians have been annihilated; the European has mixed with Indians and Africans. Born in the same womb of foreign fathers differing by blood and origin, we also differ according to skin color. This difference has repercussions of transcendental proportions. (Fernández Retamar, 1986, p. 8)

Bolívar dreamed of an independent and unified Latin America that would be able to defend itself against foreign enemies, and to develop economically and socially as one entity. His vision of Pan-American unity, however, was never realized. By the third decade of the nineteenth century, Latin America was wracked by civil wars, economic depressions, foreign invasions, dictatorships, regionalism, and racism. Bolívar died a frustrated and bitter man, who described his efforts to govern and unite the newly independent nations as a task as difficult as "plowing the sea" (Graham, 1994, p. 158).

Despite Bolívar's failure to unify the continent, the search for identity, self-determination, and social justice continued. In Cuba, the last Spanish colony in the Western Hemisphere, José Martí felt that neither Hispanic nor Latin American accurately reflected our new identity, since neither recognized nor celebrated the region's political independence or its rich racial and cultural diversity. He preferred *Nuestra America* (Our America), a society where every citizen, regardless of race, creed, class, or gender, would be represented, respected, and protected by a dignified and sovereign nation (Foner, 1977).

Elaborating on the concept of *Nuestra America*, Martí, like Bolívar, pondered Latin America's new racial and cultural reality:

The conquest interrupted the natural and majestic evolution of American civilization, and with the coming of the Spaniards, a strange society came into being. It wasn't Spanish because the new blood rejected the old bodies; it wasn't Indian because of the superimpositions of a devastating civilization, two worlds which, in antagonism, constitute a process. A new people, "mestizo" in form was created. (Fernández Retamar, 1986, p. 13; Maldonado Denis, 1987)

Unlike Bolívar, however, Martí did not survive Cuba's war of independence, so he never had the opportunity to govern Cuba, nor to implement his vision of a truly independent nation guided by the principle of "With all, and for the good of all" (Foner, 1977).

Latin America's attempts at creating better societies have not proven to be much more fruitful in the twentieth century than the nineteenth. Latin America today continues to be plagued by many of the problems that impeded its social progress during the early postindependence period: massive foreign debts, high infant mortality rates, high unemployment and inflation rates, discrimination against ethnic minorities, authoritarianism, militarism, and poverty. Thus, more than 170 years after independence, Latin America's greatest resources continue to be its peoples and their great spirit and capacity to resist and struggle against colonialism and neocolonialism (Castañeda, 1993; Stein & Stein, 1970). After 500 years of genocidal policies, extreme repression, and discrimination, descendants of the native populations and African slaves continue struggling to preserve their languages, customs, and religions (Galeano, 1980; Chomsky, 1993).

The most eloquent and credible testimony of these cultural wars is the fact that today dozens of native languages are spoken by millions of proud and courageous peoples from the heights of the Andes to the Valley of Mexico. In Guatemala, for example, 26 Amerindian languages are spoken by 53 percent of that nation's population. And in Paraguay, Guaraní, along with Spanish, is recognized as an official language (Galeano, 1980). Equally important has been the struggle to preserve the pre-Columbian religions and forms of worship. In addition to the many ancient rituals of worship still practiced by the descendants of the native populations, the African religions of the former slaves have not only survived, but thrived.

Couched in this historical context, it is not difficult to see why the Hispanic label, because of its gross omissions of our histories and cultures, is not only inaccurate but extremely offensive. Latino/a, while not perfect, goes much further in recognizing Latin America's cultural diversity.

U.S.-LATIN AMERICAN RELATIONS

During the 1830s, as most Latin American countries struggled to preserve their fragile independence under the threat of economic collapse, civil wars, and foreign intervention, its northern neighbor embarked on an ambitious and aggressive territorial expansion. Under the guise of "Manifest Destiny"—an obnoxious, arrogant, and obviously false belief that the United States had the "God-given right" to expand its national borders and institutions from the Atlantic to the Pacific— the United States fought an unjustified war against Mexico that resulted in the latter's loss of 50 percent of its national territory, while the United States gained control of 945,000 square miles of Mexican territory. In sharp contrast to the romantic and glorified myths of the American West, Mexican and Mexican American historians still recall the war as an act of imperialist aggression, and refer to the region as "occupied territory" (Acuña, 1988; Brack, 1975; Prago, 1973).

U.S. expansionism did not end with the Mexican War. On the contrary, throughout the rest of the nineteenth century and most of the twentieth, its domination over the governments and economies of Latin American nations increased. In 1898 the United States entered Cuba's war of independence against Spain— what American historians erroneously refer to as the Spanish-American War— and proceeded to occupy and govern the island for four years. As part of the same operation, U.S. forces also invaded and occupied Puerto Rico. In 1903 the United States instigated, organized, and financed a civil war in Colombia. The conflict concluded with the creation of the Republic of Panama, and the U.S. acquisition of the rights to build and control the Panama Canal. In 1904 the Monroe Doctrine was reinforced with Theodore Roosevelt's Corollary, by which the United States gave itself the right to act as the region's police force in order to prevent "chronic wrongdoing or impotence from disrupting civilized society." From that point on, military interventions and "gunboat diplomacy" have characterized the U.S. Latin American policy. To put it simply, governments supported by the United States would stay in power, while those it opposed, with few exceptions, would fall (Burns, 1993; Drake, 1994; Dunkerley, 1988; Roig de Leuchsenring, 1975).

In addition to its territorial expansion in Latin America, the United States has been responsible for supporting and financing the most violent, repressive, and corrupt governments in the region. A list of the heads of those governments reads like a Who's Who among Latin American dictators: Rafael Leonidas Trujillo, Dominican Republic (1930–61); François Duvalier, Haiti (1954–67); Augusto Pinochet, Chile (1973–90); the Somoza dynasty, Nicaragua (1934–79); Carlos Castillo Armas, Guatemala (1954–57); and Fulgencio Batista, Cuba (1952–59). On the other hand, the United States has consistently opposed, attacked, and often defeated revolutionary and reformist governments in the region. It opposed and obstructed the Mexican (1910) and Bolivian (1954) revolutions; overthrew the Guatemalan (1954) and Chilean (1973) reformist governments; attacked and ultimately defeated the Nicaraguan revolution (1979–90); and since 1961 has tried everything from assassinations, sabotage, defamation campaigns, economic blockade, and military intervention to destroy the Cuban revolution.

The historical record shows that constant U.S. meddling in Latin America's internal affairs, and its penchant to oppose the progressive forces of social change, have impacted and marked the region's history almost as negatively as Spain. By denying Latin Americans their rights to create societies according to their needs and conditions, and by forcing them to live under imposed social models that condemn the majority to poverty and repression, the only option left for many is to emigrate.

LATINO/A IMMIGRATION AND THE POLITICS OF U.S. IMMIGRATION

One of the biggest myths of American history is the notion that this country's immigration policy is guided by humanitarian and charitable values. The truth behind the rhetoric of "Give me your tired, your poor, your huddled masses yearning to breathe free . . ." is that U.S. immigration policy is, and has always been extremely politicized and self-interested. It is virtually impossible to separate immigration policy from U.S. foreign policy initiatives and economic interests.

The history of this "nation of immigrants" verifies the argument that every immigrant group that has come to this country has been allowed to do so for one of two reasons: economic (when the U.S. labor market has been able to absorb, and needed the newcomers), and political (as a vehicle to advance or support U.S. foreign policy initiatives). The doors are opened when it is economically or politically convenient and beneficial for the United States, and closed when it is not. Contrary to popular belief and rhetoric, this country's borders are not now, nor have they ever been, out of control (Borjas, 1990).

In the case of Latin American immigrants, it is not by coincidence that the largest groups of Latinos/as living permanently in the United States—Mexicans (17 million), Puerto Ricans (3.5 million), Cubans, (1.5 million), and Central Americans (2 million)—come from countries where the United States has had or has strong political, economic, or military interests (Moore & Pinderhughes, 1993; Spillers, 1991). As mentioned earlier, Mexico lost half of its national territory to the United States in 1848. Puerto Rico has been an American colony since 1898, and generates more profits for U.S. industry than any other Latin American country. Cuba was a U.S. client state for 60 years, and has survived a U.S. economic blockade for 35 years. In Central America, to sustain its political hegemony and economic interests, the United States has supported repressive military regimes for decades.

U.S. political and economic domination over Latin America was further enhanced during the Cold War era. Guided by superpower strategies and geopolitical considerations, it claimed, and the former Soviet Union accepted, Latin America to be under its "sphere of influence." The new mission was to stop the spread of communism, real or imagined, in the region. In reality, not much had changed since the days of the Monroe Doctrine. Only governments willing to go along with U.S. policies and strategies would be tolerated and supported, while those who opposed or questioned U.S. initiatives were isolated, and usually overthrown. Among those suffering the latter fate were Jacobo Arbenz in Guatemala, Juan Bosch in the Dominican Republic, Cheddi Jagan in Guyana; Salvador Allende in Chile, and Maurice Bishop in Grenada. Fidel Castro and the Cuban revolution have so far been the only survivors of the U.S. war against social change in Latin America.

Cuba provides a good example of how much U.S. immigration policy is driven by political motivations and foreign policy strategies. From 1959 to 1994, 1.5 million Cubans were granted virtually automatic political asylum in the United States. All Cubans had to do to gain that status was declare their opposition to Fidel Castro's government. No proof was required, just a simple verbal declaration would do.

The Cuban emigres became a powerful propaganda weapon in the U.S. Cold

War arsenal. According to the U.S. press, they were "voting with their feet," "fleeing Communist repression," and "embracing American democracy." For their political "usefulness," the U.S. government rewarded disaffected Cubans with not only an open-door immigration policy—unprecedented for Latin American immigrants—but also the Cuban Refugee Program, an aid package that provided Cuban immigrants with monetary stipends, medical care, English-language classes, and professional training. The way Cubans seeking asylum in the United States have been received is in sharp contrast with the way Haitians trying to escape the violence of the Duvaliers' totalitarian regimes, and Salvadorans escaping their government's notorious death squads have been treated among many other similar examples from Latin America. In order to have their cases heard, they had to prove a "well founded fear of persecution." As a result of that policy, during the 1980s alone, the Justice Department's Immigration and Naturalization Services (INS) ordered and executed the deportation of more than 150,000 Salvadorans, Guatemalans, and Haitians. Even today, as Haitians continue to escape the repression of an illegal military government, they are interdicted at sea and sent back without an opportunity to plead their cases (Masud-Piloto, 1988).

A case that clearly demonstrates the political opportunism of U.S. immigration policy is that of Justo Ricardo Somarriba, a Nicaraguan teacher who came to the United States illegally in March 1987. That year he applied for political asylum on grounds that due to his refusal to indoctrinate his students in Sandinista propaganda, his life was in danger. However, as in many other similar cases, the INS ruled against him twice, concluding that his claim was "frivolous." Having exhausted his means to gain political asylum, the case was closed and he was scheduled for deportation. Fortunately for Somarriba, a few days before his scheduled deportation, he won $5.3 million dollars in the Florida Lottery.

Four days after Somarriba's stroke of luck, the INS decided to hear the case again. The agency concluded that if Somarriba was deported, his millions could end up in the hands of the Sandinistas, a government the United States was trying to destroy. Thus, the new millionaire was granted political asylum, and U.S. foreign policy objectives again took priority over humanitarian considerations (*New York Times*, 1989 p. A18)

LATINOS/AS IN THE UNITED STATES: BEYOND STEREOTYPES

Latinos/as in the United States are generally viewed through stereotypical lenses. To many Americans, the common image of Latinos/as is usually distorted, inaccurate, insensitive, and formed with negative and derogatory terms. It is not uncommon for people to refer to us as "spics," "greasers," "wetbacks," "gang bangers," and "illegal aliens."

Writer and performance artist Guillermo Gómez-Peña has written extensively on the subject of Latino images. In his 1988 (p. 132) essay, "Documented/Undocumented," he explained how the average American usually perceives Latinos in false and negative characteristics:

In general, we are perceived through the folkloric prism of Hollywood, fad literature and publicity; or through the ideological filters of mass media. For the average Anglo, we are nothing but "images," "symbols," "metaphors." We lack ontological existence and anthropological concreteness. We are perceived indistinctly as magic creatures with shamanistic powers, happy bohemians with pretechnological sensibilities, or as romantic revolutionaries born in a Cuban poster from the '70s. All this without mentioning the more ordinary myths, which link us with drugs, supersexuality, gratuitous violence, and terrorism, myths that serve to justify racism and disguise the fear of cultural otherness.

Gómez-Peña's description of the average American citizen's image of Latinos/as is not far from an official view accepted and held during a period when Mexican immigration was no longer profitable for the U.S. economy. In a report prepared for the U.S. Congress in 1930, Roy L. Garis described Mexicans as follows (p. 436):

Their minds run to nothing higher than animal functions—eat, sleep, and sexual debauchery. In every huddle of Mexican shacks one meets the same idleness, hordes of hungry dogs, and filthy children with faces plastered with flies, disease, lice, human filth, stench, promiscuous fornication, bastardy, lounging, apathetic peons and lazy squaws, beans and dried chili, liquor, general squalor, and envy and hatred of the gringo. These people sleep by day and prowl by night like coyotes, stealing anything they can get their hands on, no matter how useless to them it may be. Nothing left outside is safe unless padlocked or chained down. Yet there are Americans clamoring for more of these human swine to be brought from Mexico.

Negative stereotypical images of immigrants are neither new nor uncommon. Indeed, they are as old as the United States—the expected reaction of a racist society that feels threatened by a group's increase in numbers and political and economic power. Every immigrant group to the United States has faced, at one time or another, hostility, prejudice, rejection, and outright racism. Irish, Jews, Greeks, Chinese, Japanese, Italians, Poles, Germans have suffered racism and prejudice in the United States (Jones, 1960).

The political debate over how many and which kind of immigrants to admit has been and remains heated, and is often tainted with racial (if not racist) overtones. Even Benjamin Franklin wrote that German immigrants "are generally the most stupid of their own nation . . . it is almost impossible to remove any prejudice they entertain." (Borjas, 1990, p. 3)

We cannot lose sight of the fact that this is a nation founded on military aggression, territorial expansion, cultural arrogance, and illegal immigration. U.S. history and popular lore richly document the fact that the natives of what became New England did not issue visas or entry permits to the Europeans who later drove them out of those lands. The same can be said about the "growth" of U.S. national territory. Most of it was not achieved by invitation or diplomacy, but by imperial expansion.

The United States, like Europe, cannot deny the history, nor escape the consequences, of their actions in Latin America. Nor can Latinos/as escape the legacies of our history. We are the product of more than 500 years of imperialism, repression, aggression, slavery, immigration, and resistance. Our communities in the United States are a direct consequence of U.S. foreign policy toward our home countries. As some Chicano/a writers are fond of saying, We did not cross the border, the border crossed us (Gómez-Peña, 1993).

NUESTRA REALIDAD: IMPLICATIONS FOR MULTICULTURALISM (Editors' Commentary)

The multicultural implications of U.S. policies regarding Latin Americans and Latinos/as influence the very fabric of U.S. education. The imperialist initiatives of the nineteenth century informed the racist and classist assumptions with respect to peoples of Latin America, whether located in the United States or in their own countries. Segregation policies or exclusion from education were fueled by the sentiments and attitudes generated by U.S. foreign policy in Latin America and its domestic initiatives for Latinas/os in the United States. The historical overview outlined in this chapter serves to highlight the breadth of character influencing the debates on multicultural education regarding Latinas/os.

Immigration policies have, throughout U.S. history, influenced educational policies of immigrants. The attitudes and policies for different groups have generally translated into similar ones in education. For example, the educational experiences of Cuban immigrants, in some important ways, differ significantly from those of the Mexican.

Today, the racist antics of those reviving the I.Q. myth and statements by public officials regarding the alleged inferiority of people of color, as in the case of Illinois Senator Pete Phillips, coupled with the passage in California in November 1994 of Proposition 187 (which would deny education, health care, and medical benefits to undocumented persons), exacerbate racial tension. People are not engaged in debates and discussions of the impact that U.S. political economic policies have on the lives of Mexicans and the relationship of this to immigration. More importantly, there is little if any public dialogue on the real percentages of new immigrants and the growth of the Mexican population of California. The manufacture of local sentiment is intimately tied to the proliferation of accusatory foreign policies. We saw this during the Cold War. Today there is a different war of sorts. The problem is not the structure of the United States and its history of racism and classism. The problem is again one located outside, with its illegal presence within the borders. The problem is not the social preparation of the geography within which poverty ensues, it is the impoverished. The problem is not the monopolization of wealth by the very few, it is the demands of the many to a healthy quality of life. The problem is not U.S. initiatives, and its institutional accomplices vis-à-vis the World Bank and the International Monetary Fund in other countries that sustain dictatorships and contribute to the proliferation of the genocide of indigenous peoples, the growing debt, and the destruction of the environment, it is the demands of these peoples to self-determine.

This chapter has outlined how the long history of racist and classist policies of the United States have influenced Latin America and the identity construction of Latinas/os in the United States. For those who have internalized their subordination, their appeals to their heritage seem more likely to refer to Spain, a European geography. And yet, any person of Latin American heritage must come to terms with the historical reality that the indigenous and African influences have had in forging the Latin American identity and cultures. To negate this is to reinforce one's own subjugation. Finally, this chapter presents multiculturalists with the task of considering the implications of the histories and influences of U.S. policies regarding identity construction as revealed through immigration initiatives that influence how we identify ourselves and others.

REFERENCES

Acuña, Rodolfo. 1988. *Occupied America. A History of Chicanos.* New York: HarperCollins.

Borjas, George J. 1990. *Friends or Strangers: The Impact of Immigrants on the U.S. Economy.* New York: Basic Books.

Brack, Gene M. 1975. *Mexico Views Manifest Destiny, 1821–1846. An Essay on the Origins of the Mexican War.* Albuquerque: University of New Mexico Press.

Burns, E. Bradford. 1993. *Latin America: Conflict and Creation.* Englewood Cliffs, NJ: Prentice Hall.

Castañeda, Jorge G. 1993. *Utopia Unarmed: The Latin American Left After the Cold War.* New York: Alfred A. Knopf.

Chomsky, Noam. 1993. *Year 501: The Conquest Continues.* Boston: South End Press.

Drake, Paul W., ed. 1994. *Money Doctors, Foreign Debts, and Economic Reforms in Latin America.* Wilmington, DE: Scholarly Resources.

Dunkerley, James. 1988. *Power in the Isthmus. A Political History of Modern Central America.* New York: Verso.

Fernández Retamar, Roberto. 1986. "Our America and the West" *Social Text,* 15(1): 1–25.

Foner, Philip S., ed. 1977. *"Our America:" Writings on Latin America and the Struggle for Cuban Independence by José Martí.* New York: Monthly Review Press.

Galeano, Eduardo. 1980. *Las venas abiertas de América Latina.* Mexico: Siglo Veintiuno.

Garis, Roy L. 1930. "Mexican Immigration: A Report for the Information of Congress," Western Hemisphere Immigration, Committee on Immigration and Naturalization. 71st Congress, 2d session.

Gómez-Peña, Guillermo. 1988. "Documented/Undocumented." In Rick Simonson and Scott Walker, eds., *Multicultural Literacy: Opening the American Mind.* St. Paul: Graywolf Press.

———. 1993. *Warrior for Gringostroika.* St. Paul: Graywolf Press.

Graham, Richard. 1994. *Independence in Latin America: A Comparative Approach.* New York: McGraw-Hill.

Jones, Maldwyn Allen. 1960. *American Immigration.* Chicago: University of Chicago Press.

Maldonado Denis, Manuel. 1987. *Ensayos sobre José Martí.* Rio Piedras, PR: Editorial Antillana.

Martínez Peláez, Severo. 1973. *La Patria del criollo: Ensayo de interpretación de la realidad guatemalteca.* San José, CR: Editorial Universitaria Centroamericana.

Masud-Piloto, Félix. 1988. *With Open Arms: Cuban Migration to the United States.* Totowa, NJ: Rowman & Littlefield.

Moore, Joan and Pinderhughes, Raquel, eds. 1993. *In the Barrios: Latinos and the Underclass Debate.* New York: Russell Sage Foundation.

New York Times. May 4, 1989. "Alien Wins Lottery and Right to Stay in U.S."

Prago, Albert. 1973. *Strangers in Their Own Land: A History of Mexican-Americans.* New York: Four Winds.

Roig de Leuchsenring, Emilio. 1975. *Cuba no debe su independencia a los Estados Unidos.* Santiago de Cuba: Editorial Oriente.

Sale, Kirkpatrick. 1990. *The Conquest of Paradise: Christopher Columbus and the Columbian Legacy.* New York: Plume.

Spillers, Hortense J. 1991. "Introduction: Who Cuts the Borders? Some Readings on 'America.'" In Hortense J. Spillers, ed., *Comparative American Identities: Race, Sex and Nationality in the Modern Text.* New York: Routledge.

Stannard, David E. 1992. *American Holocaust: The Conquest of the New World.* New York: Oxford University Press.

Stein, Stanley J. and Stein, Barbara. 1970. *The Colonial Heritage of Latin America: Essays on Economic Dependence in Perspective.* New York: Oxford University Press.

Wright, Ronald. 1992. *Stolen Continents: The "New World" Through Indian Eyes.* Boston: Houghton Mifflin.

PART II

Racism: White Skin Privilege

5

The Politics of Culture: Multicultural Education After the Content Debate

Cameron McCarthy and Arlette Ingram Willis

As we approach the midpoint of the 1990s, conflicts in education and society are increasingly taking the form of grand panethnic battles over culture and identity. Riding the undersides of these developments are profoundly localized struggles over the occupation and territorialization of symbolic and material space as schools and society become conflagrated by highly charged sectional centers of interests and agency. Multicultural education is deeply woven into these rhetorical and material struggles over access, equality, and voice.

Multicultural education emerged in the late 1960s as a powerful challenge to the Eurocentric foundations of the American school curriculum (McCarthy, 1988, 1990, 1991; McCarthy & Apple, 1988). It is a product of a particular historical conjuncture of relations among the state, contending racial minority and majority groups, educators, and policy intellectuals when the discourse over schools became increasingly racialized. From the outset, then, multicultural education must be understood as part of the give-and-take of the politics of accord produced in the broad civil rights struggles of American communities of color that helped to redefine the democratic face of educational and social life in this country. As such it must be seen as a particular curricular truce—part of the complex of civil rights driven initiatives that include reformist urban housing policy, expansion of the right to vote, affirmative action in the university and the workplace, and compensatory and remedial education programs in K–12 classrooms.

For a brief period (early 1960s to early 1970s) in U.S. educational history, subaltern racial groups fought a limitedly successful but very intensive "war of position" (Gramsci, 1971) within the institutions of education themselves. It is this period that Sylvia Wynter (1992) calls the "glorious decade of Black Studies." Of particular significance was the connection that subaltern school critics made between knowledge and power. These critics pointed specifically to the deep involvement of traditional, canonical school knowledge in the legitimation of authority and inequality in society. In this sense canonical knowledge was official knowledge, which undergirded official stories about social stratification and minority educational marginalization.

In contrast to the dominant preoccupations of traditional educators, African Americans and other groups of people of color emphasized a variety of transformative themes, insisting that curriculum and educational policy address the vital questions of community control, the distribution of power and representation in schools, and the status of colonized people and oppressed cultural identities in curriculum organization and arrangements. Of course, the cultural identities of people of color are not fixed or monolithic but multivocal, and even contradictory. These identities are indeed "fluid" and are theorized here as the effects and consequences of the historically grounded experiences and practices of oppressed groups, as well as the processes by which these practices and experiences come to be represented, reconstructed, and reinvented—in daily life, in the school, in the workplace, in the symbolic media, in textbooks, and in the school curriculum. The identities of people of color are therefore defined in the context of inter- and intragroup conflicts, encounters, and struggles between peoples of color and dominant white groups on the ideological terrain of education and in the production and circulation of commonsense meanings in establishment and popular culture.

But within the last two decades these transformative themes in the multicultural movement have been steadily "sucked back into the system" (Swartz, 1988, 1990). Appropriated by dominant humanism, multicultural education is now entrenched in highly selective debates over content, texts, and attitudes and values. As Warren Crichlow (1991, p. 1) argues, "this ideological encirclement currently serves to mute more fundamental challenges to the symbolic mechanisms and scholarly operations by which dominant knowledge is historically legitimated and subordinated traditions are repressed." As departments of education, textbook publishers, and intellectual entrepreneurs push more normative themes of cultural understanding and sensitivity training, the actual implementation of a critical emancipatory multiculturalism in the school curriculum and in pedagogical and teacher-education practices in the university has been effectively deferred. (Critical multiculturalism is defined here as the radical redefinition of school knowledge from the heterogeneous perspectives and identities of racially disadvantaged groups—a process that goes beyond the language of "inclusivity" and emphasizes relationality and multivocality as the central intellectual forces in the production of knowledge.)

Conservative educators and commentators have responded vigorously to the multicultural challenge, and within the past few years there has been a virulent reaffirmation of Eurocentrism and Western culture in debates over the school curriculum and educational reform (Bloom, 1987; D'Souza, 1991; Kimball, 1990; Ravitch, 1990; Schlesinger, 1992). As we shall see, proponents of multicultural education also "claw back" (Fiske & Hartley, 1978) from the radical themes associated with subaltern challenges to the dominant school curriculum and school system, emphasizing instead a normative rhetoric that accepts the broad structural and cultural parameters and values of American society and the American way. By "clawing back," we refer to the way in which some multicultural educators tend to graft the theme of diversity onto the negotiated central concerns and values of this society—values of possessive individualism, occupational mobility, and status—leaving completely untouched the very structural organization of capitalism in the United States. (This criticism can also be made of the more emergent discourse of Afrocentrism, in that proponents such as Molefi Asante [1987] fail to offer any serious class analysis of American capitalism.) Within this framework the emancipation of the individual of color is fulfilled when he or she becomes a good capitalist. It is the nonthreatening social centrality of the "good bourgeois life" for the poor in communities of color that the multiculturalist ultimately seeks to promote.

In what follows we offer a critique of current multicultural approaches to education in order to discover and extend the best intuition of their adherents: namely, that any discussion of curriculum reform must address issues of representation as well as of unequal distribution of material resources and power outside the school door. We will conclude by outlining an alternative approach to multicultural education and offering instructional suggestions that draw directly on some of the more critical insights in the curriculum and cultural studies literatures (Apple, 1992; Ellsworth, 1989; Freire, 1970; Giroux, 1985, 1992; Hall, 1988, 1992; JanMohamed & Lloyd, 1987; Said, 1992, 1993; Shor, 1987). In this critical approach, we will suggest that we need to get beyond the technical and instrumental language of "inclusion" and content addition and replacement that now dominates the multicultural field. Let us say from the outset that there are subtle and important variations within the field of multiculturalism with respect to general perspectives, core ideological assumptions, and desired outcomes advanced by its proponents.

THREE DISCOURSES ON RACIAL INEQUALITY

Multiculturalists do vary in the ways in which they mobilize the themes of culture, race, and diversity. It is therefore possible to identify three different types of multicultural discourse on racial inequality as embodied in various school curriculum and preservice teacher education program guides as well as in the articulated theories of some multicultural advocates.

First, there are those proponents who articulate *discourses of cultural understanding.* Discourses of cultural understanding are inscribed in various university-supported human relations programs that place a premium on improving communications among different ethnic groups. At the level of elementary and secondary schools, proponents stress "teaching strategies affirming the right to be different and the need for members of different cultures to respect one another" (Ogbu, 1992, p. 6). The fundamental stance of this approach to ethnic differences is that of cultural relativism. Within this framework, all social groups are presumed to have a formal parity with each other. The matter of ethnic identity is understood in terms of individual choice and preference—the language of the shopping mall (Olneck, 1989).

This stance of cultural relativism is translated in curriculum guides for ethnic studies in terms of a discourse of reciprocity and consensus: We are different but *we are all the same*. The idea that racial differences are only "human" and "natural" is, for example, promoted in the teaching kit *The Wonderful World of Difference: A Human Relations Program for Grades K-8*, in which the authors "explore the diversity and richness of the human family" (Anti-Defamation League of B'nai B'rith, 1986, p. iv). In a similar manner, Iris Tiedt and Pamela Tiedt, in their *Multicultural Teaching: A Handbook of Activities, Information, and Resources* (1986) require students to make up a list of cultural traits that would be characteristic of Sue Wong. Students are then told to complete the sentence "Sue Wong is . . ." (p. 144). This tendency to focus on the acceptance and recognition of cultural differences has led in recent years to a movement for the recognition of the cultural uniqueness of white ethnic groups—Poles, Swedes, Norwegians, and so forth—in order to counterbalance demands for the study of African American, Latino, and Native American cultures (Banks, 1988; Gibson, 1984; Sleeter & Grant, 1988). Ultimately, then, the cultural understanding approach promotes the idea of pride in one's ancestry and cultural heritage and seeks to reduce prejudice and stereotypes by fostering intercultural exchange.

A *second* emphasis in the multicultural field is that of *cultural competence*. Underpinning this approach to education is a fundamental assumption that values of cultural pluralism should have a central place in the school curriculum. This concept of social institutions as sites for the confluence of a plurality of ethnic interests was formulated in the 1960s by liberal social scientists such as Nathan Glazer and Daniel Patrick Moynihan (1975). Some educators, such as James Banks (1988), contend that there is a general lack of cross-cultural competencies, especially in the area of language, among minority and majority groups in the American populace. The American Association of Colleges of Teacher Education (AACTE) makes a particularly strong case for cultural pluralism in education. AACTE (1980, iii) maintains that multicultural education is education that values cultural pluralism.

Multicultural education rejects the view that schools should seek to melt away cultural differences or the view that schools should merely tolerate cultural pluralism. Instead, multicultural education affirms that schools should be oriented toward the cultural enrichment of all children and youth through programs rooted to the preservation and extension of cultural alternatives. Multicultural education recognizes cultural diversity as a fact of life in American society, and it affirms that this cultural diversity is a valuable resource that should be preserved and extended.

Educators who promote the idea of a cultural competence approach to curriculum reform argue for various forms of bilingual and ethnic studies programs based on pluralist values that would help to "build bridges" (Sleeter & Grant, 1988) between America's different ethnic groups. As one teacher education guide notes, "Becoming bidialectical offers students a best of both worlds existence. Bidialectical students would be able to retain the functional language, which allows full participation in their own culture. At the same time, they will be gaining a language necessary to participate more fully in the culture of the mainstream" (Spencer & McClain, 1980, p. 150). These programs aim at preserving cultural diversity in the United States, particularly the language and identity of ethnic groups such as Native Americans and Hispanics. It is expected that white students will also acquire knowledge of and familiarity with the languages and cultures of other groups. Such cross-cultural interaction, it is felt, will contribute to reduced racial antagonism between white students and students of color.

But the question of cultural competence is a matter not only for students, but also for teachers. Proponents of the cultural competence approach such as Mary Kennedy (1991) and Eleanor Wilson Orr (1987) point to technical features of minority students' speech and learning styles that put them at risk in math and science classes. These authors and their collaborators therefore offer teachers a list of how tos, such as familiarity with students' cultural backgrounds and linguistic styles, as keys to more effective pedagogical practices in the ethnically diverse classroom.

Third, models of cultural emancipation go somewhat further than the previous two approaches in suggesting that a reformist multicultural curriculum can boost school success and economic futures of African American, Latina/o and other ethnic youth. Theorists such as James Rushton and Jim Cummins argue that a reform-oriented curriculum that includes knowledge about minority history and cultural achievements would reduce the dissonance and alienation from academic success that centrally characterize minority experiences in schooling. Cummins (1986, p. 24) writes: "Considerable research data suggest that, for dominated racial and ethnic groups, the extent to which students' language and culture are incorporated into the school program constitutes a significant predictor of academic success." Such a reformed school curriculum is expected to enhance minority opportunities for academic success and better futures in the labor market for students of color. This thesis of a "tightening bond" between multicultural education and the economy is summarized in the following claim by Rushton (1981, p. 169):

The curriculum in the multicultural school should encourage each pupil to succeed wherever he or she can and strive for competence in what he or she tries. Cultural taboos should be lessened by mutual experience and understandings. The curriculum in the multicultural school should allow these things to happen. If it does, it need have no fear about the future career of its pupils.

Multicultural educators who promote the idea of cultural emancipation therefore hold a great deal of faith in the redemptive qualities of the educational system and its capacities to influence positive changes in the job market and in the society.

TOWARD A CRITICAL EMANCIPATORY MULTICULTURALISM

Although these three types of multicultural discourse significantly differ in emphasis, it is generally the case that their proponents attach an enormous significance to the role of attitudes in the reproduction and transformation of racism. Human relations and ethnic studies programs based on these approaches pursue what Banks (1988) calls the "prejudiceless goal." The strong version of these multicultural paradigms directly targets white students and teachers as the flawed protagonists in their racial relations with others. It is expected that negative white attitudes toward students of color will change if these prejudiced individuals are exposed to sensitivity training in human relations and ethnic studies programs.

In our view, the three multicultural paradigms identified here do not provide adequate theories of or solutions to the problem of racial inequality in schooling. Within these frameworks, school reform and reform in race relations depend almost exclusively on the reversal of values, attitudes, and the human nature of social actors understood as "individuals." Schools, for example, are not conceptualized as sites of power or contestation in which differential resources and capacities determine the maneuverability of competing racial groups and the possibility and pace of change. In significant ways, too, the proponents of multiculturalism fail to take into account the differential structure of opportunities that helps to define race relations in the United States. A case in point is the tendency of proponents to lean toward an unwarranted optimism about the potential impact of the multicultural curriculum on the social and economic futures of students of color. Indeed, the linear connection between academic credentials and the job market asserted by some multicultural theorists is problematic.

The assumption that higher educational attainment and achievement via a more sensitive curriculum would lead to a necessary conversion into jobs for black and other youth of color is frustrated by existing racial practices in the job market itself. Of course, the multicultural linkage of academic success to good fortune in the job market comports with "the myth," as Margery Turner (1991) points out, "of self-improvement and upward mobility in American society, [which] is that if you work hard, if you are willing to work and willing to try, you will succeed and better yourself and support your family." But a recent study of discriminatory hiring practices in the American job market conducted by the Urban Institute (1991) and directed by Turner and colleagues Michael Fix and Raymond Struyk indicates that African American young men are denied equality of opportunity with their white counterparts irrespective of education credentials. Researchers found that in the nation's capital, Washington, D.C., despite the federal government's leadership role in the elaboration of policies of equality of opportunity, "unfavorable treatment [of black college graduates] in the interview process was particularly prevalent in Washington, where black applicants were treated less favorably 60 percent of the time!" (p. 4).

The ethnographic work of Mercer Sullivan (1990) further corroborates this story of the difficult transition from school to work that African American and Latino/a youth face. In his study of youth, crime, and work in the inner city, Sullivan documents the frustrations of black "Projectville" and Puerto Rican "La Barriada" youth in the job market. He maintains that there is a racialized job ceiling that limits the working futures of these minority youth. Ogbu (1978) also comments on the racialized job ceiling that may temper the aspirations of black youth. Further, Sullivan's study corroborates the claims that Stokely Carmichael and Charles Hamilton (1967) made almost three decades ago with respect to the unfair advantages that help to boost job opportunities for white youth in the labor market. In sharp contrast to their minority counterparts, white working-class kids from "Hamilton Park" were able to secure early "off-the-books" jobs in their neighborhood and high-wage union-protected jobs later. Micaela di Leonardo (1990, p. 672) points to a further significance of Sullivan's work:

Sullivan offers . . . well-documented surprises. White, Puerto Rican and black kids had similar education levels, even though the white neighborhood had family incomes roughly twice as high as those in Projectville and La Barriada. Blacks valued education most highly, and returned most often to work on G.E.D.s and gain college credits.

Sullivan's findings and the Urban Institute's study of hiring practices in the private sector temper optimism about the responsiveness of the job market to multicultural curriculum change.

Another issue for examination is the status of the multicultural text itself and what Stuart Hall (1984) calls the "semiosis of encoding and decoding." Various studies have shown that the drive toward the elimination of prejudice through exposing white teachers and students to sensitivity training has not produced the intended result of the prejudiceless goal. Indeed, as studies of student responses to a University of Wisconsin human relations program (Fish, 1981) and the British educational television series *The Whites of their Eyes* have demonstrated, white students often make "aberrant decodings" of multicultural texts (Buckingham, 1984). Joel Fish's study of the Wisconsin human relations program showed that prejudice against blacks had increased by the end of the field-experience component of the semester-long human relations program administered at that university in 1981. (For a more recent account of the unintended effects of sensitivity programs see Sleeter, 1993.)

Besides these concerns, it must be noted that multiculturalism's proponents do not systematically pursue the very premise that set the multicultural education project in motion in the first place: the interrogation of the discourse of the Eurocentric basis of the American school curriculum that links the United States to Europe and to "Western civilization." Indeed, within the past few years contemporary conservative educators such as Allan Bloom (1987), Dinesh D'Souza (1991), E. D. Hirsch, Jr. (1987), and Diane Ravitch (1990) have sought to gain the upper hand in the debate over curriculum reform by reinvigorating the myth of Westernness and the role of Europe in the elaboration of *American* institutions and culture. No one puts this more directly than George Will (1989, p. 3):

> Our country is a branch of European civilization. . . . "Eurocentricity" is right, in American curricula and consciousness, because it accords with the facts of our history, and we—and Europe—are fortunate for that. The political and moral legacy of Europe has made the most happy and admirable of nations. Saying that may be indelicate, but it has the merit of being true and the truth should be the core of the curriculum.

In response to these frontal attacks on multicultural education, proponents have tended to propose models that emphasize the addition of "new" content about minority history to the school curriculum. The multiculturalist strategy of adding diversity to the dominant school curriculum serves, paradoxically, to legitimate the dominance of Western culture in educational arrangements in the United States. Multiculturalists have simply failed to provide a systematic critique of the ideology of "Westernness" that is ascendant in curriculum and pedagogical practices in education. Instead, they articulate a language of inclusion.

RETHINKING MULTICULTURALISM

Where does this multicultural strategy of inclusion leave us with respect to the question of race and the curriculum? How should we begin to rethink current approaches to the issue of race and curriculum organization? What are the elements of a new critical approach to multicultural education? Because of limitations of space, we will only be able to draw an outline of a critical transformative approach to multiculturalism and offer suggestions for educators.

First, such a new approach must begin with a more systematic critique of the construction of school knowledge and the privileging of Eurocentrism and Westernness in the American school curriculum. A thorough historical undertaking is needed, one that allows students to understand how ingrained Eurocentrism and Westernness has become. A review of the underlying philosophical assumptions upon which American education is based is an excellent starting point. For example, reviewing the work of several European philosophers—Auguste Comte, Herbert Spencer, and Charles Darwin, among others—would aid students in understanding the strong ties among issues of racism, classism, and gender in education in this nation.

The rather philistine assertion of Eurocentrism and Westernness on the part of conservative educators is itself a wish to run away from the labor of coming to terms with the fundamental historical currents that have shaped the United States—a wish to run away from the fundamentally plural, immigrant, and Afro-New World character that defines historical and current relations among minority and majority groups in the United States (Jordan, 1985, 1988). To claim a pristine, unambiguous Westernness as the basis of curriculum organization, as Bloom, Hirsch, Ravitch, and others suggest, is to repress to the dimmest parts of the unconscious a fundamental anxiety concerning the question of African American and other minority identities and "cultural presence" in what is distinctive about American life.

The point we want to make here is similar to one that John Berger makes in *Ways of Seeing* (1972) and Toni Morrison develops and extends in her book *Playing in the Dark* (1992): there is nothing intrinsically superior or even desirable about the list of cultural items and cultural figures celebrated by traditionalists like Hirsch and Bloom. It is to be remembered that at the end of the last century the English cultural critic Matthew Arnold did not find it fit to include in the "the best that has been thought and said" (Arnold, 1888, 1971; Czitrom, 1983) any existing American writer. This powerfully reminds us that what is "Western" is not synonymous with what is "American," no matter how hard some people may try. It also reminds us that the notion of Westernness is a powerful ideological construct—thoroughly infused with ongoing struggle over meaning and values (Bernal, 1987). What is Western is therefore highly problematic, as June Jordan (1985) has argued. How is it that African Americans, who have been in the Americas for at least as long as whites, are non-Western? Who is demarcating the West? Do we, for instance, want to say that Ernest Hemingway is in and Alice Walker is out? Where is the line of the Western to be drawn within the school curriculum? Where does Westernness end and where does Americanness begin? Multiculturalists have tended to counter the Western civilization movement by insisting on diversity and cultural pluralism. But this approach leaves untouched the very premise of the interchangeability of the culture of the United States and Europe and the notion that there is an easy fit between white America, the West, and Europe. It is this easy fit that needs to be questioned.

This brings us to our second departure from the multicultural models discussed earlier. A critical approach to multiculturalism must insist not only on the cultural diversity of school knowledge but on its inherent relationality. School knowledge is socially produced, imbued with human interests, and deeply implicated in the unequal social relations outside the school door. A critical multiculturalism should therefore be more reflexive with respect to the relationship between different social groups in the United States and developments in the United States to the rest of the world. This would mean, for instance, that we begin to see the issue of racial inequality in global and relational terms—in the context of what Immanuel Wallerstein (1990) calls "world systems theory."

The links between America's development and the underdevelopment of the Third World and the links that African Americans have had in terms of their intellectual and political engagement with the peoples of the Caribbean, Africa, and Asia must be emphasized. For example, the civil rights movement in the United States has had profound multiplier effects on the expansion of democratic practices to excluded groups in Australia, the Caribbean, Africa, and England, as well as in the United States itself. In a related sense, too, a world systems approach would call attention to the fact that the development of "Western" industrialized countries is deeply bound up in the underdevelopment and exploitation of the Third World (Rodney, 1980). C.L.R. James (1963), for example, points out that in the 1770s, at the time when the French government was helping to bankroll the American Revolution, its West Indian colony in Haiti was generating two-thirds of France's overseas trade.

By emphasizing the relationality of school knowledge, one also raises the question of the ideological representation of dominant and subordinate groups in education and in the popular culture. By representation we refer not only to mimesis or the presence or absence of images of minorities and Third World people in textbooks. More broadly, we refer to the question of power that resides in the specific arrangement and deployment of subjectivity in the artifacts of the formal and informal culture. This is what Louis Althusser (1971) calls the "mise-en-scene of interpellation"—the way in which the orchestration of cultural form in textbooks and in the popular culture generates the capacity to speak for whole groups; to arraign these groups, as it were, before a deeply invested court of appeal, draining social life of its history and naturalizing dominant/subordinate relations in the process.

This is, by and large, what textbooks do as a matter of course. For example, as Edward Said (1978) has pointed out in his brilliant book *Orientalism*, contemporary Western scholars arbitrarily draw a line of demarcation between "East" and "West," "West" and "non-West," "North" and "South," the "First World" and the "Third World." An arbitrary line of demarcation is stabilized by the constant production and reproduction of attributions, differences, desires, and capacities that separate the West from the non-West. The West is rational. The Third World is not. The West is democratic. The Third World is not. The West is virtuous, moral, and on the side of good and right. The Third World is vicious, immoral, and on the side of evil. Indeed, the electronic media images generated during the Persian Gulf conflict exploited many of these dichotomies in order to help the American viewer separate the cause of the allies of the West from that of the bad guys of the East—Saddam Hussein and the Iraqis (Schechter, 1992). This was a case of the Crusades all over again.

Framed by this discourse, as noted above, it is therefore possible to find in textbooks used in U.S. schools very negative social constructions of the Third World. The production and arrangement of images in textbooks draw intertextually on a media language that saturates the popular culture outside and inside the school. More significant than simple stereotyping, then, is the characterization of the relationship of developed countries like the United States to Third World countries such as Panama and Guatemala in Central America. As *Interracial Books for Children Bulletin* (1982, p. 5) notes about textbooks currently in use in schools across the United States:

Textbooks distort the role of the U.S. in Central America, portraying it only as the perennial "helper." The U.S. has repeatedly intervened in the internal affairs of Central American nations. Rarely are these interventions mentioned. The 34 U.S. military interventions in the area from 1898–1932—and the numerous interventions [once every year and half since WWII] overt and covert, since then—are ignored.

It is very interesting how these textbook representations of the Third World corroborate and reinforce images in the popular culture, particularly in the area of film. Though the treatment of Central America and the Third World in social studies textbooks leaves much to be desired, starker examples of marginalization and the manipulation of difference are reproduced in the popular film culture in the United States. In adventure films such as *Rocky*, *Red Dawn*, the *Rambo* films, and in space operas such as *Aliens*, thousands of alien people die in seconds on the screen and whole cultures are wiped out. One cannot but note the way in which these films anticipate the kind of high-tech war that the United States and the armies of the major Western countries waged upon Iraq in the Persian Gulf.

These are examples of a larger system of representation and production of images in the media and popular culture and school texts that position minorities, women, and Third World people in relation to dominant whites. In many cases our students depend on the media, more so than on textbooks or the classroom, for their understanding of existing relations of dominance and subordination in the world. We must therefore incorporate ways to dynamically interrogate the current production of images in the popular culture; we must find some way to critically examine film, TV, the newspaper, and popular music in the classroom.

A third point of consideration is the status of the conceptualization of race as a category within the multicultural paradigm. Current multicultural formulations tend to define racial identities in very static or essentialist terms. By this I mean that proponents tend to treat racial identities as a settled matter of physical, cultural, and linguistic traits. Minority groups are therefore defined as homogeneous entities. For example, as we discussed earlier, Tiedt and Tiedt's (1986) fictional character, "Sue Wong," is presented in their handbook for preservice teachers as a generic Chinese American. She is defined by the presumed invariant characteristics of the group.

A critical approach to multicultural education requires a far more nuanced discussion of the racial identities of minority and majority groups than currently exists in the multicultural literature. This critical approach would call attention to the contradictory interests that inform minority social and political behavior and that define minority encounters with majority whites in educational settings and in society. These discontinuities in the needs and interests of minority and majority groups are expressed, for example, in the long history of tension and hostility that has existed between the black and white working classes in this country. Also of crucial importance within this framework are the issues of the "contradictory location" (Wright, 1978) of the "new" black middle class within the racial problematic, and the role of neoconservative black and white intellectuals in redefining the terrain of contemporary discourse on racial inequality toward the ideal of a "color blind" society (McCarthy, 1990). Just as important for a nonessentialist approach to race and curriculum is the fact that because of the issue of gender, minority women and girls have radically different experiences of racial inequality than those of their male counterparts. A nonessentialist approach to the discussion of racial identities allows for a more complex understanding of the educational and political behavior of different communities of color.

Consider South Africa, where, as Michael Burawoy (1981) and Mokubong Nkomo (1984) make clear, the economic divide between the black underclass from the Bantustan and their more middle-class counterparts working for the South African state (police officers, nurses, etc.) often serves to undermine black unity in the struggle against apartheid. Similar examples exist in the United States, where some middle-class minority intellectuals have spoken out against affirmative action and minority scholarship programs in higher education, suggesting that such ameliorative policies discriminate against white males. A case in point is the 1990 ruling by the U.S. Department of Education's former assistant secretary for civil rights, Michael Williams, which maintained that it was illegal for a college or university to offer a scholarship only to minority students (Jaschik, 1990). The irony of this situation is underlined by the fact that the former assistant secretary for civil rights is a black man. Tragically, without these scholarships a number of very indigent minorities would not be able to pursue higher education. Here again, the point man on a policy that effectively undermines the material interests of African Americans and other racial and ethnic groups is a neoconservative member of the emergent minority middle class.

The point that we want to make here is that you cannot read off the political behavior of minority groups from assumptions about race pure and simple. Different class interests within minority groups often cut at right angles to racial politics (Gilroy, 1988/89). In a related sense, to predicate multicultural education on the basis of static definitions of what white people are like and what minorities are like can lead to costly miscalculations that can undermine the goal of race relations reform in education itself.

DEMOCRATIC INITIATIVES: CRITICAL MULTICULTURALISM AND THE SCHOOL CONTEXT

A new approach to multicultural education must go much further than a critique of current definitions of racial identity. A critical approach to the fostering of multiculturalism must also seek to promote democratic initiatives in curriculum, pedagogical practices, and social relations in schools. In this matter, certain facts have become painfully clear. There is now considerable documentation in both the mainstream and radical literature indicating stagnation and, in some cases, reversals in the educational fortunes of black, Latino/a, and Native American youth in the emerging decade of the 1990s (Gamoran & Berends, 1986; Grant, 1984, 1985; Hacker, 1992; Sudarkasa, 1988).

These studies also draw attention to some of the most pernicious ways in which current curriculum and pedagogical practices—not simply content—militate against minority success and alienate minority students from an academic core curriculum. For instance, studies show the following: that minority girls and boys are more likely than their white peers to be placed in low or nonacademic tracks (Fordham, 1990; Grant, 1984); that teachers' encouragement and expectations of academic performance are considerably lower for black and Latino/a students than for white students (Ogbu & Matute-Bianchi, 1986); that black students have access to fewer instructional opportunities than white students (Gamoran & Berends, 1986); and that ultimately black, Latino/a, and Native American youth are more likely to drop out of school than white youth ("Here They Come," 1986). These racial factors are complicated by dynamics of gender—black girls fare better academically than black boys but are more likely to be denied the academic and social status accorded to white girls and white boys in desegregated classrooms (Grant, 1984, 1985; Ogbu, 1978); and dynamics of class—increasingly, black youth from professional middle-class backgrounds are abandoning predominantly black institutions and opting for white–dominated state colleges and Ivy League universities, thereby imperiling the autonomy and the survival of black institutions and raising disturbing questions about cultural identity (Marable, 1985).

As we have seen, some proponents of multiculturalism have stressed attitudinal models of reform. In this manner these proponents have tended to paste over the central contradictions associated with race and the curriculum, promoting instead a professional discourse of content addition. As we emphasized earlier, changing the present content of the school curriculum is not an adequate or sufficient model for meaningful reform in the area of race relations in schooling. There is indeed a need to look at the entire range of elements in the institutional culture of schools; the constraints and barriers to teacher creativity and innovation; and the educational priorities set in district offices, by building principals, and in university-based teacher education programs. In all these areas, emancipatory multiculturalism, as a form of what Henry Giroux (1992) calls "critical literacy," is now suppressed. In addition, school critics and government officials are now talking about curriculum reform without recognizing the pivotal role of the classroom teacher. Curriculum reform proposals are coming to teachers from the outside—from researchers, politicians, and the business sector. Proposals such as "critical thinking," "scientific literacy," "problem solving in mathematics," and "multicultural education" are being presented as slogans, in some cases already packaged and teacher-proof (Apple & Beyer, 1988). No matter how well-meaning many of these new proposals are, we run the real risk of contributing to the intensification of the intrusion of the professional space of the classroom teacher.

Teachers and educators in this country's urban centers face a crisis of legitimacy with respect to the project of multicultural reform. In a society where the government has clearly reneged on the promise of racial equality raised during the

Johnson and Kennedy administrations in the 1960s, teachers and educators are being bombarded with new and contradictory demands. They are being asked to generate an ethos of harmony and equality at the same time that they are having to respond to increasing governmental pressure to foster competitive individualism in schools. This emphasis on competition reflects itself in the dominant role of standardized testing in pedagogical practices and the narrow range of classroom knowledge that is actually taught in the urban setting. Teachers feel compelled to be conservative about what they teach.

Multiculturalism, in this context, is regarded as something of a supplement to a school curriculum that is oriented toward the basics. In other ways, too, federal policy in the 1970s and the 1980s of cutting back on financial support for low-income students at all levels of schooling sent out a message that was quite destructive for the education of minorities. This message privileged excellence over equality. The irony has been that with the steady evacuation of resources and initiative from the urban school, both excellence and equality suffered. Black and Latino/a youth fell victim to a system that said and still says: YOU ARE NOT A PRIORITY—YOU DO NOT MATTER.

As we enter the midpoint of the 1990s, the gap between winners and losers is widening. Instead of the bright future anticipated by traditional multiculturalists, African American and Latino/a youth face increasingly high rates of incarceration, illiteracy, and unemployment. These developments are the bitter legacy of the Reagan and Bush years. All of this is occurring at the same time as school populations are becoming more ethnically diverse. In the largest school systems in this country, the majority of students are now minorities ("Here They Come," 1986). Current demographic projections indicate that by the third decade of the next century, one-third of the American population will be nonwhite. These demographic changes raise profound questions about school knowledge—particularly the wisdom of maintaining the hegemonic dominance of the Eurocentric curriculum in our educational institutions. The Eurocentric curriculum is, in a manner of speaking, being overtaken by events. The time has come for the vigorous pursuit of alternatives to the dominant curriculum, if we are to begin to address the complex challenges posed by the racial diversity now overtaking our schools.

SUGGESTIONS FOR EDUCATORS

Creating Community

We suggest that educators should begin by adopting the emancipatory critical approach to multiculturalism outlined above. Instructionally this means using democratic dialogue and employing several collaborative learning strategies in a technique we refer to as creating community. The process is likened to Freire's (1970) suggestion of the formation of cultural circles to encourage participation and colearnership. He states that "a cultural circle is a live and creative dialogue in which everyone knows some things and does not know others, in which all seek together to know more" (Freire, 1970, cited in Shor, 1987, p.41). Creating a community requires the instructor to develop a nonauthoritarian stance, adopt a student-centered and multicultural approach, to model democratic and participatory instruction, and to be observant/research-minded (Shor, 1987). A key component of transformation is time. Extended time is needed in class for dialogue and out of class for reflection.

Dialogue should begin with students describing their daily life experiences. Participants are thus exposed to viewpoints, experiences, and interpretations that may differ from their own. Recognizing that their personal realities and assumptions about race are learned and that not everyone shares their sense of reality, is the beginning of what Freire (1970) calls conscientization for many students. Four important outcomes are realized at this point. First, unchallenged notions of official knowledge are challenged. The content of the discussions and the open context in which all colearners equally share challenges the official knowledge that have silenced others. Second, the diverse notions shared by all bring many face-to-face with their, heretofore, unvoiced acknowledgement of racial biases. Often the private conversations and beliefs about race surface during discussions, thus making public the conversations held outside of class and making public the fears many students have never voiced publicly. Third, through discussion of their future roles as teachers, students become aware of their positions of power as teachers. Finally, discussions center on how to use this new knowledge to affect and transform schooling in a democratic manner.

Initial personalized conversations should be followed by social and institutional conversations. We suggest beginning by problematizing the issue of school knowledge: questioning how canonical knowledge has been formulated, supported, validated, and perpetuated as the only acceptable way of knowing. The mutual discussions by class participants will undoubtedly offer a range of responses. These responses will reflect the political, cultural, and self-awareness aspects of each individual, thus enabling all to grow and stretch their personal and social realities. The problems posed are never solved. The goal here is not to solve them but to cultivate in students the disposition to question what they have considered reality. Apple (1992, p. 9) argues that "in these situations, the role of education takes on even more importance, since new knowledge, new ethics, and new reality seek to replace the old."

Understanding the Interconnectedness of Race, Image, and Power

The problematization of cultural images conveyed by the media can serve to open discussions about the democratic use of language and the power of images. Addressing the stickiness of "political correctness" head-on is important. Frank discussions should focus on racial terms and stereotypical images used to polarize people that are a part of the media. Meeting these issues in face-to-face contact, to foster better understandings of their impact on society, is not easily accomplished. Yet the trust and comfort established during the community-building phase through democratic dialogue supports these efforts. What is important is the quality of the discussions; while they should not dissolve into a heated sling of epithets, they need to be open enough for students to begin to reflect on personal and institutional realities.

Codification of images needs to begin with personal experiences and grow to discussions of local, national, and international concern. Using the experiences from the daily life experiences, past and present, of students we can begin to address their reality. Expanding students' growing awareness of the power of media in racialized society, by offering them a new lens through which to view the media, predisposes students to question other mismatches of their reality.

Additionally, as students consider their future roles as teachers, they need to address the representedness of minorities, women, and Third World people in relation to dominant whites as portrayed in school textbooks. Apple (1992, pp. 4-5) notes that "it is naive to think of the school curriculum as neutral knowledge. Rather, what counts as legitimate knowledge is the result of complex power relations and struggles among identifiable class, race, gender, and religious groups." He goes on to state "controversies over 'official knowledge' that usually center around what is included and excluded from textbooks really signify more profound political, economic, and cultural relations and histories. Conflicts over texts are often proxies for wider questions of power relations." Discussions at this point should give way to actual examination of school texts and analysis of how they convey messages of power.

Other discussions of power and how it is manifested during interpersonal communications between students and teachers can now occur. The discussions should include an examination of levels of expectations, orality, and written communication. We have used multicultural literature as a vehicle for these discussions, which offers an opportunity to reflect on growing self-awareness of racial understandings, sociohistorical and sociocultural backgrounds of racial groups within the United States, school knowledge, and the power of language and images used to represent minorities, women, and Third World people.

CONCLUSION

These developments should not lead to paralysis but to action for comprehensive reform in schooling. Proponents of multiculturalism should not merely focus on curriculum content but should introduce broader brush strokes of educational reform that would promote structural reorganization in schooling. Such structural reorganization should involve as a first priority the restoration of the professional space of the teacher.

Second, there needs to be a concerted effort to foster full academic integration and guarantee equality of access to instructional opportunity for minority and disadvantaged students. Schools and school district personnel must set goals for equality of educational outcomes as well.

Third, instead of falling back on the language of content inclusion, multicultural reform must mean a dynamic approach to school knowledge that emphasizes heterogeneity of perspectives, multidisciplinarity, intellectual challenge and debate, and vigorous interrogation of received knowledge and traditions. Such an approach to knowledge in the multicultural classroom would liberate teachers and students from the tyranny of the textbook. Multiculturalism should cultivate student's autonomy with respect to multiple sources of information, and not require their necessary submission to corrective bits of knowledge presented as already-settled truth and realism—the good multicultural truth versus the bad fiction of stereotypes.

Fourth, there is a complex of critical institutional issues that must be addressed as part of any program of multicultural reform. These should include, among other things, clear instructional leadership in the school that attempts to build on the dynamic potentials of diversity in the faculty and student bodies; reconsideration of testing and evaluation items to reflect the rise of new knowledge in African American Studies, Chicano Studies, Women's Studies, and so forth; and the fostering of collegiality and peer supervision among faculty from different intellectual disciplines and social backgrounds. Fifth, school and district personnel must come up with strategies of interpretation of the needs of the urban context as a product of close collaboration and dialogue with minority parents and communities. These strategies of interpretation of the urban center should lead to specific curriculum and institutional initiatives that give priority to the needs of disadvantaged youth. Schools must not continue to be armies of occupation in the inner city. Sixth, preservice teacher education programs at universities and colleges across the country must, together with school districts and school principals, set a moral tone as well as establish strategies for dynamic models of multiculturalism in education.

Ultimately efforts to redefine the curriculum in the name of multiculturalism must get beyond the narrow prescription of incremental addition and replacement. A critical approach to multicultural reform must make salient connections between knowledge and power. Such an approach would bring the entire range of traditional and contemporary arrangements in schooling into focus for examination with a view toward transformation.

REFERENCES

Althusser, L. 1971. "Ideology and Ideological State Apparatuses." *Lenin and Philosophy and Other Essays*. London: Monthly Review Press, pp. 127–86.

American Association of Colleges of Teacher Education. 1980. *Multicultural Teacher Education: Preparing Educators to Provide Educational Equity*, Vol. 1. Washington, DC: Author.

Anti-Defamation League of B'nai B'rith. 1986. *The Wonderful World of Difference: A Human Relations Program for Grades K–8*. New York: Author.

Apple, M. 1992. "The Text and Cultural Politics." *Educational Researcher*, 21(7) (October): 4–11, 19.

Apple, M. and Beyer, L., eds. 1988. *The Curriculum: Problems, Politics and Possibilities.* Albany: State University of New York Press.

Arnold, M. 1971. *Culture and Anarchy: An Essay in Political and Social Criticism*, edited by I. Gregor. Indianapolis: Bobbs-Merrill.

————. 1988. *Civilization in the United States: First and Last Impressions of America.* Boston: Cupples.

Asante, M. K. 1987. *The Afrocentric Idea.* Philadelphia: Temple University Press.

Banks, J. 1988. *Multiethnic Education: Theory and Practice.* Boston: Allyn and Bacon.

Bastian, A.; Fruchter, N.; Gittell, M.; Greer; C., and Haskins, K. 1986. *Choosing Equality.* Philadelphia: Temple University Press.

Berger, J. 1972. *Ways of Seeing.* London: Penguin, 1972.

Bernal, M. 1987. *Black Athena: The Afroasiatic Roots of Classical Civilization*, Vol. 1. London: Free Association Books.

Bloom, A. 1987. *The Closing of the American Mind.* New York: Simon and Schuster.

Buckingham, D. 1984. "The Whites of Their Eyes: A Case Study of Responses to Educational Television." In M. Straker-Welds, ed., *Education for a Multicultural Society.* London: Bell, pp. 137–143.

Burawoy, M. 1981. "The Capitalist State in South Africa: Marxist and Sociological Perspectives on Race and Class." In M. Zeitlin, ed., *Political Power and Social Theory.* Greenwich, CT: JAI Press, pp. 279–335.

Carmichael, S. and Hamilton, C. 1967. *Black Power.* New York: Vintage Books.

Crichlow, W. 1991. "Theories of Representation: Implications for Understanding Race in the Multicultural Curriculum." Unpublished manuscript. University of Rochester, School of Education.

Cummins, J. 1986. "Empowering Minority Students: A Framework for Intervention." *Harvard Educational Review*, 56(1): 18–36.

Czitrom, D. J. 1983. *Media and the American Mind: From Morse to McLuhan.* Chapel Hill: University of North Carolina Press.

di Leonardo, M. 1990. "Who's Really Getting Paid?" *The Nation*, May 14, pp. 672–676.

D'Souza, D. 1991. *Illiberal Education: The Politics of Race and Sex on Campus.* New York: Free Press.

Ellsworth, E. 1989. "Why Doesn't This Feel Empowering? Working Through the Repressive Myths of Critical Theory." *Harvard Educational Review*, 59(3): 297–324.

Fish, J. 1981. "The Psychological Impact of Field Work Experiences and Cognitive Dissonance upon Attitude Change in a Human Relations Program." Doctoral dissertation, University of Wisconsin-Madison. Dissertation Abstracts International, 42/08B3494.

Fiske, J. and Hartley, J. 1978. *Reading Television.* London: Methuen.

Flickema, T. and Kane, P. 1980. *Insights: Latin America.* Columbus, OH: Merrill.

Fordham, S. 1990. "Racelessness as a Factor in Black Students' School Success: Pragmatic Strategy or Pyrrhic Victory?" *Harvard Educational Review*, 58(4): 54–84.

Freire, P. 1970. *Pedagogy of the Oppressed.* New York: Continuum.

Gamoran, A. and Berends, M. 1986. *The Effects of Stratification in Secondary Schools: Synthesis of Survey and Ethnographic Research.* Madison: National Center on Effective Secondary Schools, University of Wisconsin-Madison.

Gibson, M. "1984. Approaches to Multicultural Education in the United States: Some Concepts and Assumptions." *Anthropology and Education Quarterly*, 15: 94–119.

Gilroy, P. 1988/89. "Cruciality and the Frog's Perspective." *Third Text*, 5 (Winter): 33–44.

Giroux, H. 1985. "Introduction." In P. Freire, *The Politics of Education: Culture, Power, and Liberation*. South Hadley, MA: Bergin and Garvey.

———. 1992. *Resisting Difference: Cultural Studies and the Discourse of Critical Pedagogy*. In L. Grossberg, C. Nelson, and P. Treichler, eds., *Cultural Studies*. New York: Routledge, pp. 199–212.

Glazer, N. and Moynihan, D. P., eds. 1975. *Ethnicity: Theory and Experience*. Cambridge, MA: Harvard University Press.

Gramsci, A. 1971. *Selections from the Prison Notebooks*, edited by Q. Hoare & G. Nowell-Smith. London: Lawrence.

Grant, L. 1984. "Black Females' 'Place' in Desegregated Classrooms." *Sociology of Education*, 57: 98–111.

———. 1985. "Uneasy Alliances: Black Males, Teachers, and Peers in Desegregated Classrooms." Unpublished manuscript, Southern Illinois University, Department of Sociology.

Hacker, A. 1992. *Two Nations: Black and White, Separate, Hostile, and Unequal*. New York: Scribner's.

Hall, S. 1984. "Encoding/Decoding." In S. Hall, D. Hobson, A. Lowe, and P. Willis, eds., *Culture, Media, Language: Working Papers in Cultural Studies, 1972–79*. London: Hutchinson, 1984, pp. 128–138.

———. 1988. "New Ethnicities." In *ICA Documents 7: Black film and British cinema*. London: Institute of Contemporary Arts, pp. 27–30.

———. 1992. "Cultural Studies and Its Theoretical Legacies." In L. Grossberg, C. Nelson, and P. Treichler, eds., *Cultural Studies*. New York: Routledge, pp. 277–294.

"Here They Come Ready or Not: An Education Week special report on the ways in which America's population in motion is changing the outlook for schools and society." 1986. *Education Week*, May 14, pp. 14–28.

Hirsch, E. D., Jr. 1987. *Cultural Literacy: What Every American Needs to Know*. Boston: Houghton Mifflin.

Interracial Books for Children Bulletin. 1982. "Central America: What U.S. Educators Need to Know." [special double issue], 13(2 & 3): 1–32.

James, C.L.R. 1963. *The Black Jacobins: Toussaint L'Ouverture and the San Domingo Revolution*. New York: Vintage.

JanMohamed, A. and Lloyd, D. 1987. "Introduction: Minority Discourse—What Is To Be Done?" *Cultural Critique*, 6: 5–17.

Jaschik, S. 1990. "Scholarships Set Up for Minority Students Are Called Illegal." *The Chronicle of Higher Education*, 37(15): A1.

Jordan, J. 1985. *On Call: Political Essays*. Boston: South End Press.

———. 1988. "Nobody Mean More to Me Than You and the Future Life of Willie Jordan." *Harvard Educational Review*, 58(2): 363–374.

Kennedy, M., ed. 1991. *Teaching Academic Subjects to Diverse Learners*. New York: Teachers College Press.

Kimball, R. 1990. *Tenured Radicals: How Politics Has Corrupted Our Higher Education*. New York: Harper & Row.

Kinzer, S. 1981. "Isthmus of Violence." *Boston Globe Magazine*, August 18, p. 4.

Marable, M. 1985. *Black American Politics*. London: Verso.

McCarthy, C. 1988. "Reconsidering Liberal and Radical Perspectives on Racial Inequality in Schooling: Making the Case for Nonsynchrony." *Harvard Educational Review*, 58(2): 265–279.

————. 1990. *Race and Curriculum*. London: Falmer Press.

————. 1991. "Multicultural Approaches to Racial Inequality in the United States." *Oxford Review of Education*, 17(3):301–316.

McCarthy, C. and Apple, M. 1988. "Race, Class and Gender in American Educational Research: Toward a Non-synchronous Parallelist Position." In L. Weis, ed., *Class, Race, and Gender in American Education*. Albany: State University of New York, pp. 9-39.

Morrison, T. 1992. *Playing in the Dark: Whiteness and the Literary Imagination*. Cambridge, MA: Harvard University Press.

Nkomo, M. 1984. *Student Culture and Activism in Black South African Universities: The Roots of the Resistance*. Westport, CT: Greenwood Press.

Ogbu, J. U. 1978. *Minority Education and Caste: The American System in Cross-cultural Perspective*. New York: Academic Press.

————. 1992 "Understanding Cultural Diversity and Learning." *Educational Researcher*, 21(8): 5–14.

Ogbu J. U. and Matute-Bianchi, M. 1986. "Understanding Sociocultural Factors in Education: Knowledge, Identity, and School Adjustment." In California State Department of Education, ed., *Beyond Language: Social and Cultural Factors in Schooling Language Minority Students*. Los Angeles: Evaluation, Dissemination and Assessment Center, California State University, pp. 73-142.

Olneck, M. 1989. "The Recurring Dream: Symbolism and Ideology in Intercultural and Multicultural Education." Paper presented at the annual meeting of the American Educational Research Association, San Francisco, March.

Orr, E. W. 1987. *Twice as Less: Black English and the Performance of Black Students in Mathematics and Science*. New York: W. W. Norton.

Ravitch, D. 1990. "Diversity and Democracy: Multicultural Education in America." *American Educator*, 14(1): 16–48.

Rodney, Walter. 1980. *How Europe Underdeveloped Africa*. Washington, DC: Howard University Press.

Rushton, J. 1981. Careers and the Multicultural Curriculum." In J. Lynch, ed., *Teaching in the Multicultural School*. London: Ward Lock, 1981, pp. 163–170.

Said, E. 1978. *Orientalism*. New York: Vintage Books.

————. 1992. "Identity, Authority, and Freedom: The Potentate and the Traveller." *Transition*, 54: 4–18.

————. 1993. *Culture and Imperialism*. New York: Knopf.

Sarup, M. 1986. *The Politics of Multiracial Education*. London: Routledge.

Schechter, D. 1992. "The Gulf War and the Death of T.V. News." *The Independent*, January/February, pp. 28–31.

Schlesinger, A. M., Jr. 1992. *The Disuniting of America*. New York: W. W. Norton.

Schmidt, P. 1989. "Educators Foresee 'Renaissance' in African Studies." *Education Week*, October 18, p. 8.

Shor, I., ed. 1987. *Freire for the Classroom: A Sourcebook for Liberatory Teaching*. Portsmouth, NH: Boynton/Cook Publishers.

Sleeter, C. 1983. "How White Teachers Construct Race." In C. McCarthy and W. Crichlow, eds., *Race, Identity and Representation in Education*. New York: Routledge, pp. 157–171.

Sleeter, C. E. and Grant, C. A. 1988. *Making Choices for Multicultural Education: Five Approaches to Race, Class and Gender*. Columbus, OH: Merrill.

Spencer, N. L. and McClain, S. R. 1980. "Essential Understandings, Rationale, and Objectives for Teaching Standard English." In American Association of Colleges for Teacher Education, eds., *Multicultural Teacher Education: Preparing Educators to Provide Educational Equity*, Vol. 1. Washington, DC: American Association of Colleges for Teacher Education, pp. 127–153.

Spivak, G. C. 1990. *The Post-colonial Critic: Interviews, Strategies, Dialogues*, edited by S. Harasym. New York: Routledge.

Sudarkasa, N. 1988. "Black Enrollment in Higher Education: The Unfulfilled Promise of Equality." In National Urban League, ed., *The State of Black America 1988*. New York: National Urban League, 1988.

Sullivan, M. 1990. *Getting Paid: Youth Crime and Work in the Inner City*. Ithaca, NY: Cornell University Press.

Swartz, E. 1988. *Multicultural Curriculum Development*. Rochester, NY: Rochester City School District.

———. 1990. "Cultural Diversity and the School Curriculum: Context and Practice." Paper presented at the annual meeting of the American Educational Research Association, Boston, April.

Tiedt, I. and Tiedt, P. 1986. *Multicultural Teaching: A Handbook of Activities, Information, and Resources*. Boston: Allyn and Bacon.

Turner, Margery. 1991. University of Southern California Radio, "Market Place," May 14.

The Urban Institute. 1991. *Hiring and Discrimination against Young Black Men*. Policy and Research Report, 21 (2): 4, 5. Washington, DC: Author.

Wallerstein, I. 1990. "Culture as the Ideological Battleground of the Modern World System." In M. Featherstone, ed., *Global Culture: Nationalism, Globalization and Modernity*. Beverly Hills, CA: Sage, pp. 31-56.

Will, G. 1989. "Eurocentricity and the School Curriculum." *Morning Advocate* (Baton Rouge), December, p. 3.

Wright, E. O. 1978. *Class Crisis and the State*. London: New Left.

Wynter, S. 1992. "The Challenge to our Episteme: The Case of the California Textbook Controversy." Paper presented at the annual meeting of the American Educational Research Association, San Francisco.

6

Academic Apartheid: American Indian Studies and "Multiculturalism"

Marie Annette Jaimes * Guerrero

AMERICAN INDIAN STUDIES: MULTICULTURALISM OR INDIGENISM

Today the term "multiculturalism," which has come to mean many different things, both positive and negative, to different groups of people, has become appropriated and therefore exploited for many causes and ideologies that have little to do with education, knowledge, or wisdom. At its worst, multiculturalism as an educational epistemology (a theory of knowledge) has been criticized as a socialization process that ultimately leads to social leveling in the schools. In the academic debate, it is challenging the conventional discourse with cross-cultural and cross-gender exchanges or dialogues for alternative discourse. At the same time, it is a threatening word for those who are holding to the status quo, at the expense of any genuine cultural integrity for mainstream as well as ethnic/minority populations. This chapter argues that multiculturalism lends itself to accommodation and assimilation, while the movement for decolonization works toward social reform for native self-determination and self-sufficiency.

American Indians, especially those who live off the reservations, and often called "ethnic" or urban Indians, are considered an ethnic/minority population. Such a designation does not connote their Indian status if they still have affiliation with their tribal community, as many do. American Indians are instead perceived among a growing population of native peoples and their families living off the reservations as a substandard ethnic culture within the United States. This is due to coercive federal policies of allotment and termination, as well as relocation programs enforced since the 1940s. This also involves the dire economic conditions found on most reservations, with high unemployment and unavailable or poor housing.[1] At the same time, urban Indian populations that find themselves in metropolitan enclaves of U.S. society, the result of colonizing campaigns such as relocation and termination periods, are denied access to state and federal social services when they do not meet the ever-more-restrictive criteria of an ethnic minority population. This creates urgent problems when attempting to meet basic needs such as housing and commerce as well as social services in education and health.

This chapter has as its audience educators and education administrators at all levels, as it examines multiculturalism and American Indian studies. In addressing issues of maintaining institutional status quo and the inclusivity of the educational/academic curriculum, James Banks in his *Teaching Strategies for Ethnic Studies* has written on the incremental stages of multiculturalism as "Levels of Integration of Ethnic Content." He presents multiculturalism as a hierarchy: Level 1, Contributions Approach, which focuses on cultural or ontological (traditions, customs usage) contributions; Level 2, Ethnic Additive Approach, where content, concepts, themes, and perspectives are added to curriculum without changing structures; Level 3, the Transformative Approach, where the structure of the curriculum is changed from the perspective of diverse ethnic and cultural groups; Level 4, the Social Act Approach, when students make decisions on important issues and take actions to help solve them.

Banks' overall schema is grounded in a Eurocentric American educational theory and seems predicated on Abraham Maslow's developmental stages of maturity. Banks' treatment in my view is therefore a surface attempt to correct the prevailing Eurocentric social hegemony in general education. Level 4 interests me the most since it calls for social reform. However, Banks does not explain the structural base or worldview that undergirds the extant social political system. This leads one to conjecture that his model is operating within a paradigm of accommodation and adaptation rather than any social reform. Hence, his Levels 3 and 4, which advocate cultural diversity, lack coherence when presented as constituent parts that develop from Levels 1 and 2, making his effort incremental and cosmetic at best.[2]

A number of other multiculturalists also share this orientation: Sonia Nieto, Donna Gollnick and Philip Chinn, and Ricardo Garcia. Hence, the context in which multiculturalism as a socioeducational movement has emerged, in response to the conventional curriculum and its attendant Eurocentric/ethnocentric structures and epistemological biases, has to be comprehended in light of an understanding of the politics of identity, history, and struggle.

For native peoples who want to preserve and restore their cultural traditions and belief systems, any educational reform would have to challenge the existing dominant-subordinate construction. Social hegemony, as moral philosophy, perpetuates the myths of Euro-American superiority at the expense of native cultures/

cosmologies and the indigenous worldview (that all living entities are interrelated and integrated within the whole of the universe). Here, native thinkers are universal beings that welcome new thoughts, ideas, and inventions, but within the indigenous values and knowledge bases. Ward Churchill writes on this subject from a Native American metis perspective, in his treatise "White Studies: The Intellectual Imperialism of Contemporary U.S. Education." In his examination of the difference in the conceptual modes of knowledge base and inquiry, he compares what he terms the "European Conceptual Model" (predominantly linear, wherein reality is predicated on science, speculative philosophy, and religion) in contrast to the "Native American Conceptual Model" (characterized as "wholistic" and circular in the interconnectedness and integration of science, philosophy, and spirituality in determining reality).[3]

Churchill's contrasting analysis could be made broader by examining the limited scope of linear-derived Newtonian scientism and Darwinian economics, which are being challenged by quantum theories in physics, in what has been called "the new sciences." In the European paradigm that prevails in U.S. academe, such linearity at the expense of (w)holism is exacting conformity in its fundamentalist structures and predetermined assumptions as well as conclusions. This is at the price of more universal intellectual legitimacy, and at the expense of what I refer to as "indigenous dialectics." Jerry Mander's "table of inherent differences," between what he designates "native peoples" and "technological peoples," is particularly noteworthy as an illustration despite its generalities. Nevertheless, I do not agree with him that these differences are necessarily irreconcilable within the broader schema of what I have termed "indigenous dialectics" for the reconciliation of opposites as opposing forces within the universal whole.[4] It is in this context, then, that I take Churchill's conceptual comparisons further in positing that the European Conceptual Model, in contrast to what Churchill calls the Native American Conceptual Model, is instead a traditional indigenous worldview that manifests a universalism in valuing all living things.

As a case in point, regarding this intellectual discourse, the notion of philosophy, both in its epistemology (which has come to mean "science") and the masculine Logos (from Martin Heidegger's Logocentrism which feminists term as phallocentrism or phallogocentrism) at the expense of the feminine Eros and its metaphysics (meaning "beyond physics," as well as Aristotle's systems of ideas"), is an extremely Eurocentric construct that permeates all other academic disciplines as exact bodies of knowledge and, therefore, reality or conventional wisdom as truth.[5] Significant in this discourse are the time/space/place constructions as human-derived and in contrast to the natural rhythms (i.e., seasonal cycles) in indigenous knowledge and traditional practice, which several native and nonnative scholars have examined.[6] Any doubts about this human intervention and male-centeredness, at the expense of indigenous peoples and their relations and reciprocity with nature, are quickly dispelled when one looks at any higher educational institution's courses of studies in philosophy, which have spawned rationalism and humanism, among other philosophies. Churchill, on the other

hand, describes Indian intellectualism (others have called it "intellectual sovereignty") as being predicated on structures of a circulinear mode and belonging to
the tradition of "the relational indigenous worldview." The ideology of "Western
civilization," on the other hand, is "the arrangement around a central thematic
. . . the integrated assertions (as a system of ideas) . . . that constitutes a sociopolitical program."[7]

Churchill's critique of Eurocentrism is that it is characterized by linear modes
of thinking that rationalize an ideology of Indo-European and Euro-American
superiority over indigenous reality and approaches to life. This scientific paradigm
perpetuates claims of universal epistemology.

The word "ethnocentrism" was coined to advocate an interdisciplinary critique
of what was termed "invariant" structure in modern society, which is human value
orientation that is the opposite of absolutism found as a dominant strain in Struc-
turalism.[8] The international scholar Edward Said has also written extensively on
the subject of knowledge as power to determine reality, in order to maintain
ethnocentrism and imperialist aims in colonization as process.[9] J. H. Stanfield
states:

The fact that ethnocentrism has a knowledge base and thus has culture-bound parameters
challenges ideas about the universality of social knowledge. Not all people "know" the
same way. What greatly determines whether the cognitive style of one population is to
dominate another's is its ability to monopolize essential resources and institutions. That
ability does not come from "better means of reasoning." . . . Thus, sentimentalist expression, ethics, and morality have no place in social scientific inquiry, particularly since they
cannot be measured or used to develop predictive explanation models. In this tradition,
the *scientific* as factual is divorced from the *humanistic* and *artistic* as impressionistic (emphasis added).[10]

Stanfield's work actually explores how social knowledge is stratified through
the ethnocentrism of European-descent ruling populations; it then proceeds to
analyze the American social sciences as products of European-descent cognitive
styles. This is what the author refers to as "hegemonic racial domination."

Culture is defined as the affective perceptions, normative standard modes of subsistence,
modes of communication, technology, religious beliefs, and political ideas which materi-
alize the interactional forms which constitute life worlds of a population and its members.
How we create, define, and validate social knowledge is determined largely through our
cultural context. . . . Historically ethnocentrism has both initiated and legitimized the unequal distribution of resources and privileges among human populations [and with] Anglo-
Saxonism the major ideological force behind the European colonization of nonwhite
populations. In a more sophisticated form, it has transformed traditional colonialism into
Third World neocolonialism. Ethnocentrism becomes especially destructive when one human population monopolizes crucial resources.[11]

Today, Eurocentrism is manifested in geneticist propaganda that makes the
"scientific" conclusion that all native peoples of the Americas are immigrants from

Asia, and are offspring of the Chinese as a single "race" of people. This is difficult to argue against or counter by most American Indian groups, who have little or no access to genetic engineering theories. Nonetheless, these Eurocentric ideas do not meld with indigenous creation stories and oral histories, as recorded by the peoples native to this hemisphere. There is as well a rising tide of Indian scholarship, supported by non-Indian research, that is countering the geneticist assertions by primarily stating that in regards to the conventional "Bering Strait" theory—which purports that all American Indians presumedly came across the Bering Strait from Russia—the footprints were actually going the other way, from the Americas to Asia and Siberia.[12]

What this ethnocentrism has wrought in academic institutional settings is a form of "academic apartheid" that marginalizes Ethnic Studies (as well as Women's Studies) as fringe programs of less merit and credibility. This defines its subordinate status within the institution (in hiring, course development, departmental determinations, etc.) as well as its survival when confronted by program cuts. In contrasting indigenous knowledge with Eurocentrism, one justifies its subordination in juxtaposition to rigorous science and its objectivity in subcultural (meaning less than) terms like ethnoscience, ethnomusicology, ethnic studies and art, and so on, comparing these to the presumed advanced, progressive stature of Western civilization. Robert Bocock raises critical questions about sociology and philosophy as orthodox disciplines, regarding dogmatic, mechanistic, determinist, and positivist attributes that maintain an ideology favorable to their dominant interests, while at the expense of subordinated groups and their traditional knowledge base.[13]

Leading Native American scholars are countering this framework and challenging its exclusionist assumptions. Among those already mentioned should be added Clara Sue Kidwell, at Berkeley, who has written on "Science and Ethnoscience," which challenges the dichotomies contrasting the indigenous worldview with Western sciences.[14] There are illustrative polarities that get in the way of a holistic reality, and which can be extrapolated from the following schema: quantitative vs. qualitative, specialization vs. integration, temporal vs. spatial, objective vs. subjective, mechanistic vs. purposive, position vs. momentum, individualism vs. collective, absolutism vs. metaphysics, civil law vs. natural law, materialist vs. idealist, nationalism vs. tribalism, atomistic vs. holistic, and so on. Vine Deloria is quoted in his book *The Metaphysics of Modern Existence*:

Western science must reintegrate human emotions and intuitions into its interpretation of phenomena. . . . In the re-creation of metaphysics as a continuing search for meaning which incorporates all aspects of science and historical experience, we can hasten the time when we will come to an integrated conception of how our species came to be, what it has accomplished, and where it can expect to go in the millennia ahead. (Hence our next immediate task is the unification of human knowledge.)[15]

This approach is what some native scholars are calling indigenism as a liberation movement and a worldview that is an integrated orientation to life with nature. This worldview is at times referred to as the "Fourth World" or the "Host World," which emphasizes indigenous guardianship of the Earth centered in a reciprocal relationship with the natural world and its features as well as nonhuman species, in the plant and animal spheres.[16] I have written elsewhere that traditionally native peoples, as natural peoples, forged their indigenous identity from the environment, and particularly the bioregion of their respective homelands that determined their concepts of nationhood.[17]

In articulating these concepts on native cosmologies and the indigenous worldview, it is important to comprehend high tech and postmodernist conditions in terms of the fractured mirror of our existence, which lends itself to distortions and a skewness that are wrought from polarities, dichotomies, and even polemics that can be found in the wholeness encompassing all life forms within the natural world. In contrast, native cultures and cosmologies can be seen as variations on the same spiritual themes and symbols, and truths that all human cultures share, in the Creator's universal plan within a natural order.

Carl Jung, the famed German psychoanalyst/philosopher, theorized about a "collective unconscious" that all human cultural groups shared. He was inspired by what he had learned among the Pueblo peoples in New Mexico, among others, in his encounters with "natural" peoples.[18] Ironically, his broad vision of archetypes for a universal humanity attracted the Nazis, which led to some speculation that he was a Nazi sympathizer. Such phenomena may need to be understood with critical dialectics perceived in collective human behavior, a point that is beyond the scope of this chapter. I, however, use this Marxian term as it pertains to indigenous thought processes that have been espoused by native (Lakota) writers.[19] I referred earlier to this as "indigenous dialectics," and this is particularly relevant to native groups on reservations as well as in more urban settings, attempting to attain self-sufficiency in a postindustrial capitalist society while at the same time wanting to preserve their traditional indigenous lifeways.[20]

As illustrations in these dialectical differentiations (as an extrapolated term) of native peoples' lifeways and traditions within the indigenous worldview as contrasted to the modern, technological view, the following descriptors are contrasted in conceptual/textual art:

imagined or displayed; bewildered or classified; generalized or reinvented; celebrated or lost; protected or consumed; climatized or confined; collected or forgotten; questioned or evaluated; mythologized or politicized; admired or analyzed; salvaged or disposed; accumulated or claimed; composed or decoded; polished or ignored; traded or stored; named or disciplined; transformed or neutralized; simulated or photographed; restored or neglected; studied or subtitled; owned or moved; narrated or rationalized; valued or typified; selected or fetishized; juxtaposed or registered; treasured or countered; negotiated or obfuscated.[21]

These issues are the heart of this chapter and its examination of the role of the multicultural movement in the context of European conquest and U.S. colonization. A key point, then, is that while multiculturalism offers access to new knowledge bases, only decolonization, as the dismantling of Eurocentric hegemony, offers the promise of social and political transformation. Multiculturalism, in addition, favors treating American Indians as ethnic/minorities rather than as descendants of indigenous peoples and members of tribal nations, whether the latter have federal recognition or not. This can be seen as a second instance in which the Eurocentric paradigm, with multiculturalism touted by liberals as a microcosm of it, is in conflict with an indigenous movement for decolonization that requires more radical social change and reform. This concept is predicated on the original meaning of the word "radical," which is "to go to the root of a problem."[22] From this conceptualization, therefore, a transformative multiculturalism is beginning to be voiced in educational discourse and dialogue, one in contrast to the multiculturalism so often espoused by liberals predicated on accommodationist theoretics that result in assimilationist strategies and agendas.

COLONIZATION AND ACADEMIC APARTHEID

American Education and American Indians

It is the state of affairs and an unfortunate fact that we are living in times when there are ethnic scholars, as well as nonethnic academicians and educators, who are advocating a multicultural vision for American education at all levels without challenging the paradigmatic status quo that creates such problems as educational disparity and social hegemony. These well-known and respected personages, who are usually well-versed in U.S. racism and sexism rampant in the societal institutions, are still advocating accommodationist resolutions to a predominantly nonethnic and even antiminority mind-set that perpetuates these social ills for Euro-American privilege and the presumed superiority of Western civilization.

In the American Indians' colonizing experience, in particular, there is a substantial case for decolonization before any genuine multiculturalism can take place, as a first step in countering the dominant-subordinate construction imposed on native peoples and established by U.S. colonizers through federal Indian policy. This would then acknowledge the problem that can ease the tension that has been wrought in the mandated policies of assimilation and marginalization that native peoples have been subjected to in the process of their colonization by the Euro-American invasion. Decolonization would allow for reparations to be made in terms of compensation that would enable the establishment of restoration and preservation of programs in education. A good illustration of such an initiative was witnessed when federal monies were being used to restore as well as preserve Native American languages in bilingual education. Yet this program was criticized and federal support was withdrawn. Resistance to bilingual education culminated in the blatantly racist and ethnocidal "English-Only" movement.[23] Decolonization programs would counter the social hegemony that perpetuates the myth of the intellectual superiority of Western civilization at the expense of indigenous peoples, our cultures and contributions to modern society, and our sophisticated traditional knowledge bases.

Such an educational plan would have to be community centered and concerned with survival skills for employment and careers, as well as providing opportunities for academic and intellectual endeavors—all from an indigenous worldview of balance with and within the natural order—what some native scholars (cited later) are calling Indigenism. This worldview also involves an indigenous identity that was derived from a people's relationship with nature, as a bioregional environment within a more encompassing ecosystem. Anything less will only exacerbate the genocide, ethnocide, and ecocide that is being committed against indigenous peoples in North America and throughout the globe.

Yet, before any solutions can be sought, the dimension of the problems has to be recognized and acknowledged within an historical contextualization that is linked with analysis of contemporary issues. Among those issues: the majority of non-Indian "experts" on Indian subjects, at the exclusion of indigenous perspectives; the institutional structures that support an ideological bias (also referred to as Euro-American-centrism) in reinforcing conventional academics that preserves the status quo, such as the "myth of objectivity" for credentialing; institutional barriers to native participation; and the reality that some American Indian studies proponents are preoccupied with the personalization of the subordinate experience. This leaves us open to double-standard criticism that our scholarship is based on personal bias, and is also correlated with not being able to meet qualifications due to a substandard status (i.e., ethnoscience, ethnomethodology, etc.).

Any solutions to the problems wrought by U.S. colonization in American Indian Studies would have to address the cultural, economic, and environmental spheres with sociopolitical agendas from native peoples, which challenge the conventional wisdom of academic dogma and orthodoxy that has institutionalized a kind of academic apartheid. These challenges require indigenous interpretations of knowledge bases that are predicated on indigenous experiences to both animate and inanimate phenomena. Such a solution would also require access to funding and accreditation for alternative schools and programs, taking into consideration the rights of indigenous peoples on an international level and within international forums as in the United Nations, as well as responsibilities and obligations at the national level.

A Traditional Native Legacy and Colonial Historicism

In 1792 Benjamin Franklin recorded the reply of Cornplanter, a Seneca leader, to Thomas Jefferson in response to Jefferson's overture to provide free education for selected Iroquois youth:

You who are wise, must know that different Nations have different Conceptions of things, and you will therefore not take it amiss, if our ideas of this kind of Education happens not to be the same as yours. We have had some experience of it. Several of our young people were formerly brought up at the Colleges of the Northern provinces; they were instructed in all your Sciences; but, when they came back to us, they were bad Runners, ignorant of every means of living in the Woods, unable to bear either Cold or Hunger, . . . spoke our Language imperfectly, were therefore neither fit for Hunters, Warriors, nor Counsellors; they were totally good for nothing. We are however not the less obliged by your kind Offer, tho' we decline in accepting it; and to show our grateful Sense of it, if the Gentlemen of Virginia will send us a Dozen of their Sons, we will take great Care of their Education, instruct them in all we know, and make Men of them.[24]

Contemporary Native American scholars, one of the most prominent being Vine Deloria, Jr., have built on this critique that the Euro-American educational ways are not appropriate for the traditional ideas of a more realistic Indian education that is community oriented, predicated on cultural traditions, and emphasizes survival skills. Deloria even went so far as to call the Euro-American indoctrination of Indian youth in the U.S. school system to be a form of cultural imperialism with the intent of eradicating native culture and belief systems.[25] The historical record of federal Indian policy in this and other arenas has substantiated this to be the case, as evidenced in the infamous mission and boarding schools as well as the present-day situation of Indian students in U.S. public schools.[26]

The history of colonialism in North America also parallels the history of U.S.-Indian relations in the educational sphere and other related arenas, such as health and other social services, and correlates with the expropriation of Indian lands and resources. Native scholars have described particular policy orientations, some being more liberal (meaning generous with federal funds) than others, but all having assimilationist aims and goals at the expense of indigenous cultures and belief systems. Jorge Noriega, in his essay on "American Indian Education in the U.S.: Indoctrination for Subordination to Colonialism," describes federal funding cycles and argues that for the following periods a policy framework based on colonization emerged: A treaty period that stipulated educational appropriations from 1700 to the 1800s; followed by the reformulation of Protestant mission schools originating with Catholic Spaniards since the 1500s; in the nineteenth century, military boarding schools were farming and factory outlets utilizing Indian labor, both males and females, as vehicles of American colonialism; in the twentieth century, there was a federal mandate to mainstream Native Americans into public school systems and Indian education programs (requiring the infamous 506 Forms, discussed later); this was followed by contract schools on reservations, tribal community colleges in the 1970s (the first one was established in 1969 as the Navajo Community College, located in Tsaile, Arizona); to be followed by controversial block grants that escalated competition among tribal schools and their communities; and finally college tracking into technobureaucratic roles among "educated" native individuals, resulting in a cultural brokering strata for pseudo-leadership in the Indian ranks as well as a high graduate dropout rate.[27]

Felix Cohen's seminal legal canon, *The Handbook of Federal Indian Law* (1941), laid the legal ground for tribal sovereignty. He has been followed by Deloria's arguments, among them his edited *American Indian Policy in the 20th Century* (1985) and in texts coauthored with C. M. Lytle, *American Indians, American Justice* (1983) and *The Nations Within: The Past and Future of American Indian Sovereignty* (1984). Inspired by these scholars and their earlier works, Noriega writes: "In 1819, Congress established the 'Civilization Fund,' an annual appropriation of $10,000—in addition to those monies already allocated for the purpose—for 'education of the frontier tribes' " (p. 377). This was followed, in 1820, by acceptance of a proposal by then Secretary of War John C. Calhoun, that future treaties with indigenous nations be required to directly incorporate provision of additional cash annuities for instruction so that Indians might "be initiated in the habits of industry, and a portion taught the mechanical arts." For implementation of the intended program, the government relied primarily on missionaries supplied by the American Board of Commissioners for Foreign Missions, established collectively by the Congregational, Presbyterian, and Dutch Reform churches in 1810. It was in this context that the real contours of what might be described as the "U.S. model" of colonialist education began to emerge.[28]

Cohen wrote that the original relationship between the Treaty Indians and the early American colonialists was meant to be bilateral as the Indians interpreted their understanding of it. But major court decisions, most notably the Marshall Doctrine (1830s) defined this arrangement as a unilateral one that enabled the United States to subordinate Indian nations, what Marshall labeled as "domestic dependent nations." In this scenario, the U.S. government constructed a unilateral relationship with native peoples as tribal groups that established a wardship, or what is often called a "trusteeship," manifesting paternalism that is actually masking colonialism. I have termed this notion of trusteeship as a dominant-subordinate construction in U.S.-Indian relations. This enabled the U.S. Congress and certain government entities in the Department of the Interior to act "in behalf of the Indian groups' best interests" through the Office of War, with the native tribal groups as conquered peoples after Indian-settler wars, and later implemented by the Department of the Interior via the Bureau of Indian Affairs (BIA).[29]

Included in certain treaty agreements between Indian nations and the U.S. government, as in the case of the Continental Congress at the time, were educational appropriations to build schools and services for Indian youth (the results of which have been noted earlier). Yet this bureaucratic system operated at the Indian peoples' expense, by way of land and resources seized from them, often in the name of the common good for the United States and its mainstream citizenry. The United States asserted eminent domain on Indian lands by military might, operating under the guise of trust lands to protect the Indians from themselves (as uncivilized), while political campaigns cleared the path for white settlement. Therefore, this separation of designated reservation-based communities from so-called surplus lands was conveniently deliberate for the expropriation of Indian lands and the continuing diversion of water for national projects.[30] This has actually led to the exploitation of natural resources found on Indian lands

and overall environmental degradation of the natural habitat, with lethal consequences leading to health problems among the native peoples as well as surrounding areas and populations. The most visible cases of this devastation of land and
exploitation of natural resources on reservation lands are the "national sacrifice
areas" located in the Four Corners of the Southwest: Black Mesa among the Hopi;
Big Mountain among the Navajo/Dineh; and Laguna Pueblo, Acoma Sky City, in
New Mexico.[31]

Between the late 1880s and the early 1900s, leading Euro-American intellectuals called themselves "Friends of the Indians." Several of these educational leaders were also members of presidential cabinets that, under Theodore Roosevelt's
administration, gathered in what was called the Mohonk Proceedings, in upstate
New York, in order to discuss the future of American Indians in terms of their
American educational opportunities.[32] These cabinet members perceived that they
acted with good intentions to counter the harsher years of what was called the
Indian wars and the military defeats that led to their containment on reservations.
Hence, these "Friends" were influential in formulating federal Indian policy in a
concerted campaign to assimilate Indian students by eradicating the "Indianness"
in them vis-à-vis American education (evidenced in the earlier mission/boarding
schools). This was in preparation for the second-class citizenship they would
experience upon their return to the reservations, including their role in the cheap
labor force and domestic servitude for the wealthier citizenry. This subordination
of native peoples as national and cultural entities led to their impoverishment on
reservations and to their consequential dependency on U.S. federal entities. To
insure this hegemonic process for educational and intellectual colonization, the
boarding school years of the 1930s solicited the military kidnapping of Indian
children from their communities to take them to far-away places where Indian
youth were punished for being "Indian," speaking their native language, and
practicing their cultural traditions.

In the governing of these military-like institutions with their rigid and punitive
rules (i.e., one could not speak one's native language), there were infamous
schoolmasters, both men and women. These puritan zealots used Indian youth
as laborers in factories and farms in order to pay for their upkeep. A case in point
is a school that was really a textile factory utilizing native young women in Chico,
California. One of these particularly pathological headmasters was Eleazar Whee-
lock, a founder of Dartmouth College, who used Indian male youth as psychiatric
guinea pigs in his social indoctrination to make them into second-class Indian
Christians and missionaries. The grounds of some of these boarding schools are
dotted with the cemeteries and tombstones of Indian youth who died from the
harshness of life in government boarding schools. These military-regimented institutions exacted punitive corporal punishment in accordance with rigid rules of
coercion and suppression when the Indians resisted incarceration or even persisted in speaking their own native language. Such insubordination would at times
lead to an early death, correlated with a high incidence of suicide among the
youth.[33]

These years also saw the high point in scientific racism, manifested in U.S. laws against miscegenation to protect the purity of the white citizenry against all native groups who were perceived as a single race. The irony here is that at the same time there was, and had been since the early days of European contact, a high rate of exogamy, by way of intermarriage as well as nonmarital miscegenation, between natives and non-native peoples. However, this did not deter British imperialists and puritan fathers among American colonialists from passing laws against this mixing of the races in the more civilized regions of the colonies. Such caste-based laws, which evolved from a racist pseudoscience called Crania Americana, predicated on the measurement and comparison of native skulls with European and other racially designated groups, has since been debunked. Based on Morton's taxonomy of human physical development, samplings of Indian skulls among native groups were used as a justification, according to size and shape, for the presumption of a biological ideology to substantiate the inferiority of the American Indians as a race. This practice also involved their comparison to other groups of color, all of which were viewed in contrast to white male European standards of superiority. The American Indians and the Africans as distinct racial stocks were each considered inferior according to the white scientists.[34]

Regarding the dimensions of this colonizing situation, there remain distortions in academics and scholarship. For example, there is the manipulation of demographics to establish low counts of pre-Columbian and pre-European conquest indigenous populations (i.e., Kroeber, Mooney, et al.).[35] Regarding these historical periods, there are also the early anthropologists and paleontologists (among others) who perpetuated the stereotypes of primitive peoples and cultures. In their Eurocentric view, the indigenous lacked the standards of European civilization in agriculture, engineering, pharmacology, metallurgy, and religious/spiritual beliefs.[36] This convenient rationale for conquest was also used as predatory justification to commit genocide against indigenous peoples in the Americas.

In more contemporary times, ethnic-targeted populations are off-reservation Indians, while reservation-based Indians are designated as tribal communities; the latter are also now further categorized as historic or nonhistoric tribes by the BIA (as noted elsewhere in this chapter). These subordinating classifications are perpetrated regardless of any indigenous rights based on international law, which binds the United States to recognize and respect its obligations and responsibilities to its native populations. This colonizing situation has divided native peoples as another ethnic/minority population into various subgroups. Generally speaking, these divide-and-conquer tactics converted and reinforced the dependency on federal programs of reservation Indians.

This is in contrast to off-reservation, mostly urban, Indians who are denied services in some areas (as noted earlier), as in the case of metropolitan Chicago with the second largest Indian population. The reasons for this are due to some members of other groups of color pressuring state and federal authorities not to recognize the native population as another ethnic minority. This situation produces a classic "catch-22" where the urban Indian groups are further marginalized, and end up falling through the social service cracks, especially regarding urgent needs for education and health services. Ironically, then, there is the overt undermining of American Indians by the census takers and federal Indian policy, so that federal agencies can abrogate their federal obligations in Indian services. This is especially urgent in these economic deficit times, when the U.S. federal system diverts social service funds to fight wars and escalate punitive law and order campaigns against communities of people of color. Also ironic is the preponderance of historical revisionists who invoke social Darwinism today to uphold the distortion regarding the rights of conquest by Euro-Americans who dispossessed the indigenous peoples, while, according to international laws, ignoring or disavowing the traditional rights of indigenous peoples and their respective nations.

In yet another systemic and therefore covert act of racism, there is the absence or downplaying of the democratic contributions of native nations in the historicism of U.S. nationalism, as in the case of the Iroquois Confederacy in the East, which influenced the American system of government. Native scholarship has only recently made inroads into correcting this misrepresentation of native legal practices and political contributions to governance (see the works of Donald A. Grinde, a native historian, and Bruce E. Johansen).[37] Such alternative works from a native perspective are important in order to challenge the white social hegemony of American history that holds sway over American education. However, these authors are remiss in not pointing out in their illustrative analyses, that Iroquois nationhood was traditionally predicated (and may well still be) on matrifocal spheres of decision making and leadership among clan mothers. Such authority among the elder women could be viewed as a derivative of the domestic sphere in indigenous communalism, which is in contrast to the public political persona of modern-day nationalism and male-dominated leaders. The latter contributes to a lack of political ethics with its class inequities and executive authorities who are above the laws they implement, while at the same time oppressing the masses they were elected to represent.

Generally speaking, then, political authority was vested in elder native women from a domestic base in pre-Christian indigenous societies. This was juxtaposed to the patrifocal spheres of decision making and influence that were kept in check as a public base of operations involving communal rituals and ceremonies. Most native nations in pre-Columbian times were found to be matrilineal rather than patrilineal. Some anthropologists have even speculated that all original indigenous societies started out matrilineal, but circumstances (i.e., a paucity of women for childbearing), led them to patrilineality, which is not the same as the patriarchy derived from Western European city-states. Both matrifocal and patrifocal spheres were complementary to each other for a balance of power exemplifying a close approximation to egalitarian models of democracy, which is rare in human social history.

Ward Churchill asserts that this systematic and systemic ideological bias is due to both "sins of omission and commission," about "the length of indigenous occupancy in America," inversion of juridical theory in the "Discovery Doctrine," the "decimation by disease" thesis to explain the high attrition among native populations, the "both sides were guilty" rationalization, the "outright denial of inconvenient patterns of events" still put forth by so-called revisionists to date, and the revision of sociopolitical realities that reject the "standard contrast and comparison methodologies in assessing motives, policies, and impact of Euro-American conquest and colonization on Native America."[38]

This mythologizing of native peoples as "a single 'race' of people" actually begins with the Bering Strait Theory, which purports that all indigenous peoples are relative newcomers to the American hemisphere, presumedly Asian immigrants. Such thinking is now being supported by the geneticists who claim to be deconstructing DNA in comparative racial/racist groups.[39] In an American Indian Movement (AIM) statement, Churchill and Russell Means expound on this academic bias, which results from the inclusion of Eurocentric scholarship as "facts" about Native American in mass commentary and news reporting.[40] This propagandizing can also be seen in popular mainstream fiction and Hollywood cinema, and always at the expense of the Indian while perpetuating the superiority and supremacy of the (predominantly male) white race.[41]

U.S. Indian policy then has been and continues to be assimilationist at the expense of the preservation and survival of indigenous knowledge of native cultures and nations. This is the present-day situation despite the case of multiculturalism being couched in liberal yet still oppressive terms, which nonetheless promote assimilation. Decolonization challenges the prevailing Euro-American centrism and argues for a more genuine self-determination predicated on a positive affirmation of self and people. The history of the politics of Indian identity reveals a host of practices and policies aimed at undermining a decolonization initiative. This will be the topic of the next section.

Cultural Diversity and the Politics of Indian Identity

During the late 1920s, there was a systematic campaign to mandate American education for all Indian students in public school systems. Federal funds went directly to different school districts for the express purpose of establishing Indian education programs under the 1928 Snyder and Johnson-O'Malley Acts. At first, Indian youth and their parents resented and resisted this new education mandate, resulting in a high truancy rate among reservation Indian students in the public schools. There was also a misuse of these funds in their expropriation to buy books for libraries and equipment for gyms that did not directly benefit the Indian students as intended. That was before the years of more watchful accountability from school and district administrations, including pressure by Indian parent committees established to participate in these programs.

The twentieth century also saw the federal policy pendulum swing from very conservative to more liberal Indian education funding, which eventually led to an acknowledgment among the white experts that there was a large and growing population of Indians in urban centers. This was due in part to federal Indian policy: allotment in the 1800s, relocation from the 1940s to the present, and termination in the 1950s, all of which forced Indians to leave the reservations due to economic conditions and high unemployment. The more liberal years were also the result of the activities and leadership of the American Indian Movement in the 1970s. Liberalization was particularly important in the wake of the Wounded Knee Occupation by AIM in 1973, on the Pine Ridge Reservation in South Dakota. This act drew much-needed attention to the growing misery of Indian peoples and resistance to it in the United States.[42]

In comprehending the concerns and problems besetting the Indian populations in the United States today, one must examine the colonizing circumstances that persist in a postindustrial technological society. In this social context, educational opportunities for native students are often dependent on whether or not an individual person can prove that she or he is American Indian, more often based on federally determined criteria, such as meeting a blood quantum degree as well as other less controversial requirements (i.e., residing on a reservation is correlated with most likely being a tribally enrolled member). The issue of federal Indian identification is a highly political one for American Indians today, since all those who claim Indian identity have to have a tribal enrollment number for BIA certification in order to be considered a federally recognized Indian or tribe. Tribal membership for educational services as federal benefits were first left up to the tribes themselves. But later new legislation was introduced, resulting in the infamous 506 forms, which would be used to certify proof of tribal membership with federal recognition by government entities. Requiring a lot of bureaucratic staff and federal paperwork for the Indian parents and tribes, this process, regulated by the BIA, was implemented in the 1970s.[43] The Arts and Crafts Act for BIA Certification (P.L. 101-644-104, Stat. 4662), a mandated congressional law signed under the Bush administration, stipulates certification among Indian artists in the Indian art market. It was amended from an earlier 1930s act, concerned with exploitation of the U.S.-based Indian market by foreign replicas of native arts and crafts. The act now states that it is a criminal act for any individual to self-proclaim him- or herself an "Indian" artist if they can't show BIA certification. Consequently, uncertified individuals can now be fined and jailed for impersonating an "Indian," and galleries that sell their art as "Indian" art can be fined into bankruptcy.

Such certification can be arbitrary and partisan in both federal and tribal political policy-making spheres, since it is based on a race formula and a eugenics coding. This is in contrast to the cultural criteria that traditionally determined one's membership in a tribal group. This new policy has contributed to insularism at the expense of the younger mixed-blood generations among native groups, many of whom have pending enrollments. One ramification of the policy has created serious problems for these individuals and groups, denying them access to educational, health, and other social service entitlements from state and federal agencies. In a related campaign, during the 1950s the federal government declared whole tribal groups, as well as individuals, no longer federally recognized, and even extinct in some cases. More recently, in 1992, the Bush administration announced that the federal government can terminate tribes for any reason with no real cause.[44]

The sociographic results of U.S. Indian policies and practices are a good measuring stick of the dependency Indian peoples are forced to experience through reliance on federal service funds and agencies in order to meet basic human needs in education, health, and housing. At the same time, the BIA as the entity that implements and regulates these federal and state services is again being threatened by closure, this time headed up by Senator Daniel Inouye, a Japanese American from Hawaii, who chairs the Senate Select Committee for Indian Affairs in Congress. Even though Indians have had many complaints about the BIA, they have generally held the position that a federal bureau is better than not having one to represent Indian peoples' interests before the United States. It should also be noted that there is a process whereby an Indian community can petition Congress for federal recognition or reinstatement of past recognition. But this process is both very long and expensive, with no guarantees that the goal will be attained. In addition, federal recognition by the government undermines Indian/tribal self-sufficiency among native groups.

Such colonizing controls by the federal authorities have had dire affects on many Indian students across the board, especially for those who do not qualify for educational programming and fellowships. These BIA certification tactics also have repercussions in the hiring of Indian faculty, administrators, and staff, resulting in their token representation. This kind of tokenization for employment in education is meant to meet civil rights standards of cultural diversity for ethnic/minority representation. However, native peoples have only recently been designated another ethnic/minority that is subcultural to the mainstream nonethnic populations. In addition, in the selection of such ethnic individuals to meet affirmative action criteria in educational settings, it is assumed that the person in this position will operate within the existing paradigm of institutional as well as intellectual academe rather than challenge the Eurocentric hegemony. Hence, academic politics can and do play a big part in determining which ethnics get hired. The keepers of the gates are more inclined these days to offer jobs to those least likely to rock the boat.

There is also the issue, by extension, of what I call the cloning of Indian identity police who now go around institutional settings, usually behind closed doors rather than face-to-face, to denounce the hiring of others, in slanderous and libelous ways, for not being real Indians if they can't produce their certification card or tribal enrollment number. There are, in reality, many reasons why native peoples do not have BIA certification. These cases are generally not by choice, but due to political reasons (that the U.S. government should not be interfering with an internal affair and even sovereign affairs of tribal membership). In the final analysis, federal Indian blanket policies of this mode are extremely oppressive, since they are also violations of an individual's fundamental rights in terms of one's sociocultural identity.

Today, we live in extremely oppressive times that see even neoconservative tribal leaders adopting the BIA divide-and-conquer tactics, which deny rights to native individuals due to divisive partisan politics in the Indian world. These tactics often operate under the misguided attitude that the fewer Indians there are, the more federal support there will be for the remainder of them. I propose, instead, that the various tribal groups reestablish their traditional kinship systems in order to determine their tribal membership based on traditional cultural criteria, and to counter the prevailing federal control and regulation in this arena. This is especially needed in light of the fact that the terms "American Indian" and "Native American" are actually politically constructed categories, from both legal and legislative spheres, which began with the Columbian invasion. Yet, in more contemporary times a "pan-Indian" or rather intertribal Indian experience has been wrought due to the conquest and blanket colonization of the indigenous peoples of the Americas, but with an outcome that is still ongoing.[45]

Today, one finds professional Indian organizations that are now claiming what they prematurely call ethnic fraud among suspected individuals who may not have the proper pedigree papers to call themselves American Indian or Native American.[46] This is in turn encouraging the Indian identity police to instigate hit lists and witchhunts on university campuses, targeting certain individuals whom they charge with impersonating or masquerading as Indians. These ethnic buzzards are sometimes even backed by sacred cows, who are more likely motivated by self-interest and other personal agendas.

There are also the cultural brokers in these Indian ranks, who get paid by federal subsidies to influence policy and implement rules at the expense of other less-stationed Indians. The latest targets of these reactionary groups have been radicals in the universities who they claim are monopolizing Indian intellectualism as pseudo-Indians, while at the same time they use their works, which threaten dominant class status.[47] The issues that should be addressed in attempting to understand this problematic situation for a dialectical resolution must begin with asking why native peoples, as individuals or groups, are the most controlled and regulated population in the United States. The glib answer by federal authorities and bureaucrats is that they require government monitoring and accounting regarding federal and state entitlements in education, health, and other social services. This matter is about conquest and colonization of a settler nation that has become racistly astute at practicing economic genocide by negating and denying one group to the advantage of another or others.

IN CONCLUSION: MULTICULTURALISM OR
DECOLONIZATION FOR INDIGENOUS PEOPLES?

Given the foregoing examination of sociopolitical dynamics of Euro-American cultural hegemony, I argue that multiculturalism lends itself to accommodation and assimilation, while a movement for decolonization works toward social reform for native self-determination and self-sufficiency. For traditional indigenous peoples, the latter also has to be predicated on social ethics and cultural integrity as well. In my earlier work on "American Indian Studies: An Overview and Prospectus," built on Churchill's and Deloria's works, my treatise challenges the subcultural status of American Indian Studies to be considered a fringe ethnic studies program, and therefore marginally relevant to the hegemonic Westernized curriculum in higher education institutions. This analysis therefore calls for the need to counter Western ideology and its conception of history by demystifying, dismantling, and deconstructing its hegemonic construction of racial and intellectual superiority over other non-Western peoples and cultures.[48] Mary Kay Downing and William Willard have accurately described my work in their survey review on American Indian Studies (AIS), wherein they state: "Jaimes, looking back at [R.] Thornton's article, suggests that [SIS] should in the 1990s move away from an attempt to seek an exclusively academic disciplinary status of and about the indigenous people of North America and move toward involvement in a global context of the experience of all indigenous people."[49]

The actual pedagogical practices for domination and colonization in American education, as analyzed above, are systemic in their institutional racist and sexist forms. A more covert, but no less abusive, illustration can be seen in the treatment of Native American literature predicated on oral histories of native peoples for mythic knowledge that is philosophical and religious in its intent. In academic contexts it is denigrated and treated as colorful folklore for commercial goals in contrast to elitist writers of Euro-American canons, both past and present. This subordination of indigenous thought and orality can be criticized as a form of literary colonization within the Eurocentric paradigm of written works.

This body of literature contributes an emergence of an American Indian Studies curriculum, upon which a fully accredited discipline with legitimate institutional standing should develop. Before this can be accomplished, however, institutional standards that support structural barriers to preserve the status quo of academic apartheid need to be challenged. These barriers encourage ethno-specific curriculum and programming debates, all of which need to be addressed head-on. This development also needs to critically address the kinds of models to implement within institutions, such as multiethnic program centers or autonomous units as separate departments that are not subordinated to a conventional or traditional discipline. This also involves issues over hiring, promotion, and tenure, and the composition of degree-granting programs. American Indian Studies more often than not receive the short stick in any multiethnic program or center. Furthermore, there is an inclination to hire from among the male ranks, at the exclusion of indigenous women.

Regarding gender parity or its lack, it has been substantiated that ethnic women in academe are the last to be hired in an Ethnic Studies or Women's Studies program, and that native women find themselves at the very bottom of this situation, where neither Ethnic Studies nor Women's Studies have had much interest in the native women's experiences or perspectives. There is also the need to establish more proactive professional associations among native scholars, both within more mainstream associations (i.e, the American Indian Professoriate) or independent of such (i.e., the American Indian Scholars Association). In addition, strategies need to be developed to reassess the publish or perish practices that consume academics, in general. Further, discussions need to continue regarding decisions whether or not to operate within mainstream presses and media, seek out alternative enterprises, or establish independent native-determined journals and book publications to facilitate dissemination and distribution of indigenous research and scholarship, as well as materials for the general public.

On the subject of identity, Satya Mohanty, a visiting English scholar from India, now at Cornell University, recently stated in a presentation, "Identity is a way of making sense of our experiences . . . to define and reshape our values and commitments, . . . and what can be perceived as a search for a genuine post-colonial identity that is linked with our historical legacy."[50] Such a conception would include our relationship with our environment as indigenous peoples.[51] Another important area is discovered in the global dimensions for an American Indian Studies. Here studies could incorporate the experiences of all indigenous peoples, and what can preferably be called Inter-American Indigenous Studies and Indigenous Global Studies. This reconceptualization of the discipline in its own right can counter the parochialism and ethnocentrism that abounds in the sociopolitical spheres, and that perpetrates political factionalism and divisiveness within ethnic and reservation-based communities as well as American society at large.

A reconceptualization of Native American Studies within the above framework is based on a broader international as well as interdisciplinary foundation, advocating a more enlightened comprehension of the affairs of humankind, power, and politics. It can also be seen as a positive alternative to a multicultural movement that is actually business as usual, albeit with a Band-Aid approach, but one that never really challenges the denigration of ethnic/minority populations who still have to contend with Euro-American standards and Eurocentric values for educational and career success. Acknowledging and legitimizing an indigenous worldview that encompasses the study of all human beings and nonhuman species in our natural existence with Mother Earth, and one that seeks truths from the contributions of indigenous knowledge and ancient wisdom that have been passed down the ages, will restore this worldview. This Indigenism recognizes collective commonalties and their interrelatedness at the same time it acknowledges and respects differences. This is what is meant in the Lakota blessing, *metakuyeayasi*, translated as "all my relations." To achieve this goal, American Indian Studies must decolonize its indigenous worldviews. Education and teaching of indigenous people that are not rooted in indigenous worldviews will only serve to sustain our colonial reality and maintain the status quo.

NOTES

1. Citing the 1980 and 1990 U.S. Census Reports; also, *Indian Country* (Washington, DC: League of Women Voters Education Fund, 1976). In addition, refer to Lenore A.

Stiffarm with Phil Lane, Jr., chapter 1, "The Demography of Native North America: A Question of American Indian Survival," in M. A. Jaimes, ed., *The State of Native America; Genocide, Colonization and Resistance* (Boston: South End Press, 1992), pp. 23–53.

2. James Banks, *Teaching Strategies for Ethnic Studies*, 4th ed. (Boston: Allyn & Bacon, 1987). See also Sonia Nieto, *Affirming Diversity.* (New York: Layman, 1992); Donna Gollnick and Philip Chinn, *Education for a Multicultural Society* (New York: Merrill, 1994); Ricardo Garcia, *Teaching in a Pluralistic Society,* 2nd ed. (New York: HarperCollins, 1991); and Leonard David with Patricia Davidman, *Teaching with a Multicultural Perspective: A Practical Guide* (New York: Layman, 1994).

3. Ward Churchill, "White Studies: The Intellectual Imperialism of Contemporary U. S. Education," *Integrateductaion,* special issue on American Indian Education, Vol. 19, Nos. 109–10 (January–April 1981), pp. 51–57.

4. Jerry Mander, *In Defense of the Sacred: The Failure of Technology and the Survival of the Indian Nations* (San Francisco: Sierra Club Books, 1991), pp. 214–219. In this context, then, what needs to be recognized by way of indigenous dialectics is that prodevelopment schemes have to be conducted with long-term human consciousness and environmental ethics from a "Native Land Ethic" (Ward Churchill's term in *Struggle for the Land* [(Monroe, ME: Common Courage Press, 1993]), and in the context of the broader indigenous worldview.

5. Definitions from W. L. Reese's *Dictionary of Philosophy and Religion: Eastern and Western Thought* (Atlantic Highlands, NJ: Humanities Press, 1980); Robert Warrior, Native American theologian, is credited with the term "intellectual sovereignty," in his "Intellectual Sovereignty and the Struggle for an American Indian Future," *Wicazo Sa Review,* Vol. 8, No. 1 (Spring 1992), pp. 1–20.

6. On time/space/place constructions, see Vine Deloria, Jr., "Thinking in Time and Space," Chapter 4 in *God Is Red: A Native View of Religion*, 2nd ed. (Golden CO: North American Press, 1992). Also see M. A. Jaimes, "Native American Identity and Survival as 'Indigenism': Environmental Ethics for Economic Development," in Steven Gregory and Roger Sanjet, eds., *Race* (New Brunswick, NJ: Rutgers University Press, 1994), pp. 41–61. In addition, there are books by non-Indian authors: Anthony Aveni, *Empires of Time: Calendars, Clocks, and Cultures* (New York: Basic Books, 1953); more recently is Michael O'Malley, *Keeping Watch: A History of American Time* (New York: Viking Press, 1990).

7. Churchill, "White Studies."

8. See Samir Amin's *Provocative Eurocentrism*, translated by Russell Moore (New York: Monthly Review Press, 1989).

9. Edward W. Said, "The Politics of Knowledge," in Paul Berman, ed., *Debating P.C.: The Controversy Over Political Correctness on College Campuses* (New York: Dell, 1992), pp. 172–189. He has since been myopically accused of "essentialism" by his competitive peers.

10. J. H. Stanfield, "The Ethnocentric Basis of Social Science Knowledge Production," *Review of Research in Education*, Vol. 12 (1985), pp. 387–415.

11. Ibid., pp. 388, 394–396, 409–410, also noting Reginald Horsman, "American Racial Anglo-Saxonism," in his *Race and Manifest Destiny* (Cambridge, MA: Harvard University Press, 1981).

12. An AIM statement, "About That Bering Strait Land Bridge . . . (Turn the Footprints Around)," by Russell Means and Ward Churchill was written in response to an article by Tim Friend, "Genetic Detectives Trace the Origin of the First Americans," *USA Today*, September 21, 1993, p. D5.

13. Robert Bocock, *Hegemony*, Key Ideas Series, Peter Hamilton, ed. (New York: Routledge, 1986).

14. Clara Sue Kidwell, on "Science and Ethnoscience," in *The Weewish Tree* (San Francisco: Indian Historian Press, n.d.), pp. 43-54.

15. Vine Deloria, Jr., *The Metaphysics of Modern Existence* (New York: Harper & Row, 1979).

16. Ward Churchill, "I Am Indigenist," pp. 403–451, in his *Struggle for the Land*; he cites Bonfil Batalla on the concept of the Fourth World. Also see Winona LaDuke's preface to Churchill's *Struggle for the Land*, pp. 3–6, on "host" nations. Both are cited in M. A. Jaimes, "Re-Visioning Native America: An Indigenist View of Primitivism and Industrialism," *Social Justice: Columbus on Trial*, special issue, Vol. 19, No. 2 (1992).

17. Jaimes, "Native American Identity and Survival as 'Indigenism.' "

18. See Carl G. Jung, *Man and His Symbols* (New York: Doubleday, 1964) on his theory of the "collective subconscious."

19. Frank Black Elk, on "Lakota dialectics" in his illustration of Lakota critical thought articulated in his "Observations on Marxism and Lakota Tradition," pp. 137–157, in W. Churchill, ed., *Marxism and Native Americans*, 2nd ed. (Boston: South End Press, 1990). (translated into German [Bremen: AGIPA, 1993]).

20. Regarding constructs in general, there is Mander's "table of inherent differences," in his *In Defense of the Sacred*. It should be noted that the federal-Indian agreements have time and again been violated when the federal educational agendas are at odds with the tribal community's expectations of preserving their native cultures, traditions, and belief systems. It is not that Indians are resistant to change or not interested in modernization, because their survival depends on just that. Yet, traditionally oriented native peoples often have different and conflicting priorities, values, and therefore agendas to what has been imposed upon them from the federal authorities, with the ultimate goal of assimilation at the expense of restoration and preservation of what is uniquely indigenous, both culturally and spiritually.

21. From Lothar Baumgarten's 1993 exhibition entitled "America Invention," at the Guggenheim Museum, New York City, show entitled "Unsettled Objects," with preface by Scott Momaday, a notable native writer. Thanks to a former student of mine, Lee Marshall, for calling this to my attention. As an artist, she has exceptional insight into the ability for abstraction within the human mind.

22. The *Oxford English Dictionary*, 24th edition, defines the word "radical" as of Greek origin (Oxford: Oxford University Press, 1971–85), p. 2403.

23. W. Churchill and M. A. Jaimes, "Behind the Rhetoric: 'English Only,' " *New Studies on the Left*, Vol. 13, Nos. 1 & 2 (Winter-Spring 1988), pp. 42–51.

24. Jorge Noriega, Chapter 13, "American Indian Education in the U.S.: Indoctrination for Subordination to Colonization," in Jaimes, *The State of Native America* (from the Papers of Benjamin Franklin), p. 376, note 30.

25. Vine Deloria, Jr., "Education and Imperialism," *Integrateducation*, special issue on American Indian Education, Vol. 19, Nos. 109–10 (January–April 1981), pp. 58–63.

26. M. A. Jaimes, "American Indian Identification/Eligibility Policy in Federal Indian Education," doctoral dissertation, Arizona State University; Chapter 3, "Overview of Historical Background."

27. Noriega, "American Indian Education," pp. 371–389.

28. All these works are cited in ibid., p. 377.

29. Ward Churchill, "Perversions of Justice: Examining the Doctrine of U.S. Rights to

Occupancy in North America," pp. 33–83 in *Struggle for the Land*, citing the *Loneworld v. Hitchcock* case that first officially used the term "tribe" for tribal nations. In addition, see Churchill's "Naming Our Destiny: Towards a Language of Indian Liberation," *Global Justice*, Vol. 3, Nos. 2 & 3 (Summer and Fall 1992),pp. 22–33. In this essay, Churchill deconstructs the original meanings and present-day terminology between "tribe" and "nation" in regard to indigenous peoples to North America. The legal history of the U.S.-Indian construction is actually spotted with fraud and other duplicitous acts by the U.S. authorities. In this federal trust or guardianship arrangement, the federal authorities were supposed to act in the best interests of the Indian nations, which are now called "tribes" since the 1903 *Lonewolf* Decision.

30. Marianna Guerrero, Chapter 6, "American Indian Water Rights: The Blood of Life in Native North America," in Jaimes, *The State of Native America*, pp. 189–216.

31. Ward Churchill, with Winona LaDuke, Chapter 8, "Native North America: The Political Economy of Radioactive Colonialism," in Jaimes, *The State of Native America*, pp. 241–266.

32. Alexandra Harmon, summary of essay entitled, "When An Indian Is Not An Indian: 'Friends of the Indian' and the Problem of Indian Identity," *Journal of Ethnic Studies*, Vol. 18, No. (1991), pp. 95–123, on the Proceedings of the Seventh Annual Meeting of the Lake Mohonk Conference of Friends of the Indian (1988, 1989).

33. Noriega, "American Indian Education."

34. Stephen J. Gould, on "Morton's Skulls" (1839 study) and "Crania Americana" in his *The Mismeasure of Man* (New York: W.W Norton, 1981), pp. 20–60.

35. A. L. Kroeber: "Cultural and Natural Areas of Native North America," University of California Publications in American Archeology and Ethnology, Vol. 38, Sec.11 (1939), and *Handbook of the Indians of California* (New York: Dover, 1976 [originally published in 1925]). See James Mooney (on Cherokee removal), *Historical Sketch of the Cherokee* (Chicago: Aldine, 1975 [originally published in 1900]). Also see Francis Jennings, *The Invasion of America: Indians, Colonialism, and the Cant of Conquest* (Chapel Hill: University of North Carolina Press, 1979). Jennings's work was premised on disputing Kroeber and Mooney as "undercounters." See Henry Dobyns, *Their Numbers Become Thin: Native American Population Dynamics in Eastern North America* (Knoxville: University of Tennessee Press, 1983). Dobyns's later work substantiated the higher counts.

36. Jaimes, "Re-Visioning Native America," pp. 5–34, referring to indigenous knowledge bases in agriculture and economics, architecture and archeo-astronomy, sciences and engineering, and so on.

37. Donald A. Grinde, Jr. and Bruce E. Johansen, *Exemplar of Liberty: Native America and the Evolution of Democracy* (Los Angeles: University of California, American Indian Studies Center, 1991). This text follows Grinde's earlier solo book, *The Iroquois and the Evolution of Democracy* (San Francisco: Indian Historian Press, 1977). Johansen's earlier text on the subject is *Forgotten Founders: How the American Indian Helped Shape Democracy* (Boston: Harvard Common Press, 1982). Grinde's latest work on the subject is "Iroquois Political Theory and the Roots of American Democracy," in Oren Lyons and John Mohawk, eds., *Exiled in the Land of the Free: Democracy, Indian Nations, and the U.S. Constitution* (Santa Fe: Clear Light, 1992).

38. Dialogue with Ward Churchill (director of American Indian Studies [AIS]) on his 1993–94 AIS program agenda for the Center for Studies of Ethnicity and Race in America, University of Colorado (September 1993 in Boulder, CO). In addition, refer to Russell Thornton's demographic text, *American Holocaust and Survival: A Population History Since*

1492 (Norman: University of Oklahoma Press, 1987), and David E. Stannard's more recent book, *American Holocaust: Columbus and the Conquest of the New World* (New York: Oxford University Press, 1992).

39. Friend, "Genetic Detectives Trace the Origin of the First Americans."

40. Churchill and Means, AIM statement, "About that Bering Strait Land Bridge," in response to *USA Today* news hype (Friend article).

41. M. A. Jaimes, "False Images: Native Women in Hollywood Cinema," *Turtle Quarterly*, Fall 1993.

42. Jaimes, *"American Indian Identification/Eligibility Policy,"* Chapters 3 and 5 ("An American Indian International Perspective").

43. Ibid., Chapter 1, "Prospectus of Study," citing the "506 Forms," pp. 9–10.

44. "BIA Can Declare Tribes Extinct," American Indian Anti-Defamation Council (AIADC) newsletter, July 1992, Denver, p. 13; also citing the *Denver Post*, July 3, 1992 (quoted verbatim):

SEATTLE: The Bush administration has quietly asserted it has the power to declare any Indian tribe in the nation extinct, even if the tribe has been recognized by a congressionally ratified treaty. The new policy is stated deep in the text of a [BIA] decision last month denying recognition to the Miami tribe of Indiana. The BIA, an agency of the Interior Depart., says it has no plans to use the power to disqualify already-recognized tribes, though it claims the right to do so if they fall short of agency requirements on continuing existence.

45. Robert K. Thomas, his treatise "On Pan-Indianism," in Deward Walker, ed., *The Emergent Native Americas: A Reader in Culture Contact* (Boston: Little, Brown, 1972), pp. 741–746.

46. Elisabeth Lynn-Cook, "Meeting of Indian Professors Takes Up Issues of 'Ethnic Fraud,' Sovereignty and Research Needs," *Wicazo Sa Review*, Vol. 9, No. 1 (Spring 1993), pp. 57–59. This is what I have assessed as a premature statement on ethnic fraud put out by the American Indian Professoriate, of which I am a member. However, I do not hold to this position due to its escalation of already divisive tactics being used to deny nonfederally recognized Indians, groups as well as individuals, their Indian identity by others, both federally recognized Indians and non-Indians alike, to divide and conquer native peoples.

47. A relevant editorial with an academic scope is by Donald Lazere, "Conservative Critics Have a Distorted View of What Constitutes Ideological Bias in Academe," *The Chronicle of Higher Education*, November 9, 1988, p. A52.

48. M. A. Jaimes, "American Indian Studies: Towards an Indigenous Model," *American Indian Culture and Research Journal*, Vol. 11, No. 3 (Fall 1987); also citing Churchill ("White Studies") and Deloria ("Education and Imperialism") essays in *Integrateducation*.

49. Mary Kay Downing and William Willard, "American Indian Studies and Inter-Cultural Education," *Wicazo Sa Review,* Fall 1991, p. 2; including a review of Jaimes' "American Indian Studies: An Overview and Prospectus," *Wicazo Sa Review*, Fall 1985.

50. Quote from Satya Mohanty's presentation, "The Epistemic Claims of Cultural Identity: On *Beloved* and the Postcolonial Condition," sponsored by the Society for the Humanities with the English Department at Cornell University, April 15, 1992. *Beloved* is a powerfully poignant novel by Toni Morrison.

51. Jaimes, "Native American Identity and Survival as 'Indigenism.' "

7

The Doorkeepers: Education and Internal Settler Colonialism, the Mexican Experience

Priscilla Lujan Falcón

Within the world vision of the U.S. settler colonialist state, the Mexican people have had a long experience as an internal colony. The purpose of this chapter is to examine settler colonialism's impact on the sociopolitical and educational conditions of the Mexican people after the War of 1848 and the implication of these relevant to the multicultural debate today.

The historic relations between the Euroimmigrant population and the Mexican people have generally been defined by dominant Eurocentric paradigms and theories. Social science theories couched in models of assimilation were born of the Euroimmigrant experience. Spanning the spectrum from the melting-pot version to models of cultural pluralism, explanations of difference have been developed from within the context of the Euroimmigrant worldview. The rationale for this is found in the assumption that, within the United States, everyone is an immigrant who voluntarily entered the United States. Concepts such as assimilation, consensus, melting pot, and integration are central themes of these theories. The early melting-pot models of assimilation were narrow, restrictive, and, for the most part, based on conformity to the dominant Euroimmigrant society. The cultural pluralist models tended to be broader and allow for the display of diversity based on the criteria determined by the dominant society, in essence the "doorkeepers."

The doorkeepers emerged from within the dominant society, and their power is a reflection of the broader societal relationships of oppression and dependence. On the other hand, cultural pluralist models are the foundation of educational trends toward multiculturalism. The concern here is that multiculturalism and cultural diversity issues continue to be defined by the dominant society, of Euroimmigrant doorkeepers. Despite the call being made for multicultural education, the power relations within educational institutions have not changed. The doorkeepers remain the same, determining the content of education in its forms and processes, including multiculturalism.

A second set of assumptions within social science theory centers on individual mobility within the society. Accordingly then, an immigrant naturally starts at the bottom and, through work and assimilation, finds a fulfilling life. If one does not want to assimilate and does not succeed in climbing the socioeconomic ladder, then cultural deficiency theories, in their many forms, are applied as quick explanations for such failure. Cultural deficiency theories originated with the Euroimmigrant dominant society as their explanation of why people of color in general and specifically the Mexican population were at the bottom of the socioeconomic ladder.[1] These theories suggest that family structure, values, language, and traditions are somehow less than those of the Euroimmigrants, while imposed values and lifestyles have been positioned as models to be emulated.

The history written by the colonizer is not the same history experienced by the colonized. Sociopolitical relations between the Mexican and the Euroimmigrant tend to be characterized, by the Euroimmigrant dominant society, as a conflict of cultures. What does this mean? The most common interpretation has been "that meeting of Spanish-speaking and English-speaking peoples in the southwest has brought two historical cultures into contact and insofar as they are different, into conflict."[2] According to Herschel Manuel, there are four generalizations to be made in assessing conflict of cultures: (1) the underlying culture of a people is the product of long past; (2) the culture of a people changes at varying rates as a result of forces within the group and of contacts with other cultures; (3) cultures that develop in isolation from each other and in different environments tend to diverge; and (4) when two people are brought together geographically, cultural differences tend to keep them apart and cultural likenesses bring them together.

The weakness with this type of analysis is that it precludes any consideration of internal settler colonialism, which here refers to the conditions imposed upon Mexican people by the United States after the U.S.-Mexico war of 1848. Typically, between 1900 and 1994, it has been common to appeal to the use of analysis such as "deficiency theories" and "cultures in conflict" as explanations of the colonial relationships between the Euroimmigrant and the Mexican. The questions not addressed by these paradigms raise issues regarding the nature of colonialism and the conquest. Why was colonialism imposed on the conquered Mexican population? What are the structures and mechanisms of colonialism? How was it that colonialism created asymmetrical power relationships with the Euroimmigrant population as dominant and the Mexican as subordinate? How has the colonial experience impacted the education of Mexicans?

The pivotal point of this work is drawn from the issue of internal settler colonialism experienced by the Mexican people since the military conquest by the

United States in 1848. The dominant society of Euroimmigrants created social, political, educational, and cultural institutions within which the conquered populations were to function. From 1848 through 1994, those power relations have changed very little. The Euroimmigrant society dominates and determines educational policy for the internally colonized Mexican people, including the most recent trend of determining the fabric of multiculturalism and diversity. For example, Mexican history, culture, society, philosophy, sociology, psychology, literature, and worldview are not being institutionalized into the public schools. Instead, selected aspects of the above are being attached to the current core of discourse regarding curriculum. Multiculturalism is equivalent then to attachments. Multiculturalism here constitutes the selective application of educational materials attached to the current curriculum without a process of institutionalization and transformation at all levels of education. The dominant society, owing to its power within, tends to make the selections and attachments of educational materials to the curriculum. Multiculturalism and diversity are in the hands of the Euroimmigrant society, which continues to act as doorkeepers for what will or will not be allowed in educational institutions.

INTERNAL SETTLER COLONIALISM

The birth of internal settler colonialism can be traced directly to the military conquest and forceful incorporation of Mexico's northern territories and its inhabitants into the United States. Mexicans, however, are not colonized in the classic sense. Internal colonialism differs from classic colonialism in that it entails not the subordination of a distant land, but the conquest and colonialization of a contiguous territory.[3] Internal settler colonialism suggests the physical movement of Euroimmigrants into a non-European land base, state, region or territory, displacing or eliminating the native inhabitants.[4] Once the territory was conquered and the local elites were deposed from power, the indigenous institutions were completely destroyed.

Internal settler colonialism of the Mexican people by the United States began at the point of occupation of half of Mexico's national territory. Neither the issues nor the process surrounding internal settler colonialism have been addressed by the dominant society. The colonial discourse suggests that while Mexicans were once militarily conquered, today they are a volunteer immigrant group.[5] The naming of Mexicans as an immigrant group fails to address the questions and conditions of colonialism. A person of Mexican ancestry living in the United States, whether a recent arrival or a native of the occupied Southwest, is nevertheless subject to the same conditions of internal settler colonialism.[6]

The refusal to acknowledge the Mexican people as a colonized population allows the United States and its Euroimmigrant-dominant society to avoid addressing questions of internal settler colonialism, and as such sovereignty and self-determination. It affords the United States the luxury of not having to address the legitimacy of voluntary and involuntary citizenship, the presence of military bases along the border created after the war of 1848, or even to question the legitimacy of the special police agencies such as the Immigration and Naturalization Service (INS) and the Border Patrol. The Euroimmigrants entered the United States as individuals or families on a voluntary basis. The Mexican people's entry into the United States was by conquest and not by choice. The Mexican nation's people, land base, and natural resources were usurped by the United States in accordance with state policy of colonization.

The argument that Mexicans are immigrants ignores the fact that the 2,000-mile border was established and imposed by the conquering nation. It is a politically and militarily imposed border established at gunpoint and resulted in the signing of the Treaty of Guadalupe Hidalgo. The United States strategically placed military installations at or near the border, such as Fort Bliss in Texas, Hauchuca in Arizona, Fort Williams Air Force Base in Phoenix, Davis Monthan Air Force Base in Tucson, and Camp Pendleton near the border of Baja and Alta California. Despite the military maneuvers at the border and the countless attempts to construct barbed-wire fences, steel curtains, trenches,[7] and other sorts of border blockades to discourage and exclude Mexicans from the occupied homelands, the Mexican people have continued to cross the border.

SEPARATION AND DIVISION

The separation and division of the Mexican people is a false one and by no means permanent. The constant migration of Mexican people has functioned to reinforce *Mexicanidad*, meaning culture, language, and traditions within the community. This process poses a direct challenge and resistance to internal settler colonialism and its deculturalizing agenda aimed at destroying Mexican identity. One can travel from Mexico City to Chicago, Los Angeles, or even New York City and never have to speak a word of English, nor leave the continent. Los Angeles has more people of Mexican origin than any other city in the world with the exception of Mexico City. The Euroimmigrant experience was completely distinct. Psychologically and sociologically, ties to the homeland were severed with the abrupt crossing of the Atlantic Ocean. For centuries the Mexican people and their ancestors before them have traversed back and forth from the Valley of Mexico to the occupied lands.

With the structures of internal settler colonialism came the introduction of new policing agencies for the Mexican population: The Immigration and Naturalization Service and the Border Patrol ("La Migra") were officially created by an act of Congress in 1924. They are part of U.S. colonial state policy—special police agencies established to control the colonized Mexican population. As a colonial police agency the Border Patrol/La Migra exists side by side with the local police forces that patrol communities. The INS/Border Patrol monitor checkpoints approximately 100 miles north of the Mexico-U.S. border. Given the power of the INS to detain, jail, or deport, the checkpoints symbolize the intimidation and harassment for Mexicans with or without documents. It is interesting that the

United States in its foreign policy advocated the destruction of the Berlin Wall while it increased spending to the INS/Border Patrol to strengthen the "U.S. wall."

Since its formation, violence along the border has been a common condition. More recently, the American Friends Service Committee/U.S. Mexico Border Program reported documented shootings, killings, and beatings of migrant workers by roving gangs of white youth in northern San Diego County. The rising number of human rights violations of the Mexican population along the border is increasing. Since 1991, Army, Marines, and National Guard troops are already patrolling the U.S.-Mexico border from San Diego/Tijuana to Laredo/Nuevo Laredo. Regular Army troops were stationed along the Rio Grande near Laredo, Texas, while Marines are stationed in other parts of Texas, New Mexico, and Arizona to provide support to the Border Patrol. The United States has turned parts of the border into a quasimilitarized zone.[8] The National Guard has played a similar role in the San Diego area. Border Patrol agents have the authority to carry personally owned semiautomatic pistols. The American Friends Service Committee/U.S. Mexico Border Program has documented cases of Mexicans who were killed and many others who were wounded by Border Patrol agents.[9] Several of the shooting incidents involved the collaboration of the San Diego police in a coordinated effort, called the Border Crime Prevention Unit. In 1990 the Border Crime Prevention Unit, which had been suspended and criticized for abuses, disbanded, and was replaced with the Border Crime Intervention Unit, a similar swat team composed of Border Patrol and local police. U.S. policy then suggests that the border has become a "war" zone.[10] Within this context, then, the politics of the economy reinforces the oppressive conditions faced by Mexicans.

The economy is a very integral part of the structures of internal colonialism. U.S. policy in periods of economic depression had been to resort to deportations of large numbers of Mexican-origin population. Yet Mexican labor has historically played a fundamental role in the development of many major industries in the United States: agribusiness, garments, electronics, heavy industry, automobiles, steel, and restaurant, hotel, and other service industries. The settler colonial state has continually practiced both deportation and importation of labor as a way to provide a solution for economic problems, whether to guarantee large pools of surplus labor or to deter workers from seeking better wages or working conditions. Deportation programs were implemented during the 1920s, 1930s, 1950s, 1970s, 1980s and currently in the 1990s. During World War I Mexican labor was brought into the United States to combat labor shortages. During the recession in 1920–22, Mexicans were deported en masse. Anti-Mexican sentiment was on the increase as exemplified by the actions of labor unions, racist mobs, vigilantes, and the Ku Klux Klan. As the stock market went into decline, Mexican workers were perceived as the cause of unemployment and depression, encouraging nativist sentiments and anti-Mexican attitudes and actions by the American Federation of Labor, the American Legion, and the American Eugenics Society to call for the closing of the Mexico-U.S. border and immediate mass deportations.

From 1929 through 1938,[11] 500,000 to 600,000 Mexicans and their children were deported.

With World War II came yet another demand for Mexican labor and the negotiation of the infamous *Bracero* program between the United States and Mexico. On September 29, 1942, the first 1,500 workers arrived in Stockton, California. By 1945 there were 58,000 *Braceros* in agribusiness and 62,000 working in the railroads. The wages, housing, treatment, and living conditions of these workers were deplorable. In January 1954 the United States endorsed the "open border" as an official policy. This allowed an increasingly large pool of workers to come into the United States and at the same time decreased the wages being paid to Mexican labor.

In spite of the open border policy, U.S. authorities were deporting Mexicans in mass numbers. The AFL-CIO officially campaigned against the Mexican workers. In 1954, state law enforcement agencies—including INS officials, Border Patrol, the FBI, the Army, the Navy, other federal agents, local sheriffs, and police—all conducted militarized dragnets called "Operation Wetback," which resulted in the incarceration or deportation of approximately 2 million Mexicans.[12] Since 1954 similar operations have been conducted periodically, maintaining a perpetual state of tension.

Operation Wetback was a model for the 1982 "Operation Jobs," which was a nationwide deportation sweep undertaken by the INS. Created in 1981 by the Reagan administration, the Task Force on Immigration and Refugee Policy submitted numerous proposals concerning U.S. immigration policy. The Task Force proposed that the president be given broad powers to deal with illegal aliens, including: sealing the border and harbors to prevent unwanted aliens from getting into the country; restricting travel by Americans both domestically and to a country named in an emergency declaration; and locating apprehended aliens in detention camps, from which they could be released only at the discretion of the attorney general.[13] For fiscal year 1982, the administration allocated the task force's recommended sum of $35 million for the development of permanent detention centers.[14] It is very feasible to conclude that these detention centers could someday be used for Mexicans with or without papers, much like the experience of the Japanese during World War II. To the present, the same ideological thrust has motivated U.S. considerations of Mexicans.

During the late 1980s and into the decade of the 1990s, an anti-Mexican campaign was spearheaded by proponents of the English Only Movements led by U.S. English and English First. U.S. English coordinated grassroots campaigns in a state-by-state attempt to make English the official constitutional language of each state. Currently, 17 states have passed such amendments to their constitutions. Meanwhile, English First has introduced bills through Congress declaring English as the official language.

As the economic crisis worsened in the 1990s, an anti-Mexican campaign emerged from the governors of the following states: Lawton Chiles in Florida, Pete Wilson in California, Ann Richards in Texas, and Fife Symington in Arizona.

These governors are requesting payment for providing undocumented workers federally mandated services.[15] "Immigrants pay nearly $30 billion more in taxes every year than they receive in benefits and services, and most use welfare less than native-born Americans."[16] According to a study conducted by the Urban Institute, Mexican migrants are not a drain on the U.S. economy and in many cases create jobs by starting new businesses and filling jobs that U.S. citizens would not think of attempting.[17] Today, the strategy of these states is familiar to many; the Mexican community is being scapegoated for the economic problems and crises facing the U.S. economy.

INTERNAL SETTLER COLONIALISM AND EDUCATION

As part of settler colonialism, the United States has endeavored to keep the Mexican population subordinated and uneducated. Education remains a vehicle, a key, without which life becomes restricted and the world remains closed. The methods of education in any country reflect its social and economic systems and respond to the needs arising from this. In a racist context, segregation and inequalities are rationalized in order to categorize and locate different groups in ways that respond to social and economic production and reproduction, here reinforcing the case of internal colonialism for Mexicans.

Education with its enormous racial disparities is not simply the result of a lack of resources, as some would suggest, but is more importantly a result of a colonial education. The aim of anticolonial education is to reappropriate identity, history, culture, and nationhood—all of which lead toward the full development of the person in their rehumanization from the state of dehumanization under colonialism. The separation of educational facilities for Mexicans from Euroimmigrants has been achieved not simply within schools, but by separate administrative structures, segregated methods of finance, differences in syllabi, and by different expectations of achievement imposed to resonate with different expectations for employment. During the beginning of the twentieth century, education was geared for the effective preparation of Mexicans for future occupations as unskilled labor.

For over 100 years from 1848 through the 1960s, the Mexican population was denied equal entrance into the U.S. public school system. During the early colonial period, the states attempted to consolidate control over the newly acquired territory by imposing social institutions, language, and a U.S. legal system. Colonized by Euroimmigrants, the Mexican homeland became characterized by imposed institutions of the dominant society. The population in the colonized territory was segregated based on Mexican-European color lines. School boards established a de jure segregationist policy that would last through the 1960s. Public school segregation in this colonial setting was part and parcel of national education politics and practice. School segregation was clearly a reflection of the larger society. Segregation existed in all residential communities, along with dual labor and wage systems, political inequality, socioeconomic disparities, and racial oppression. The practice of segregation was a condition of colonialism established within the public education system. It was a reproduction of dominant-subordinate, imperial-colonial relationships. Segregated education, at its best, meant that the Mexican community might have minimal access to a Eurocentric education, while the pattern of colonialism and subordination was maintained.

Historically, the U.S. policy concerning education of the Mexican people has functioned at two levels: promoting segregation and the myth of assimilation. Mexicans were completely excluded from equal participation in educational institutions between 1848 and the early 1900s. Throughout the twentieth century there has existed an unwritten policy of assimilation, segregation, and conformity, which the Civil Rights Commission under the Civil Rights Act of 1964 has documented. Mexican people have had to wage struggles and strikes, legal battles, boycotts, confrontations, and demonstrations to obtain a Eurocentric education within the settler colonial state.

From the beginning of California's statehood, Mexicans became subordinate in what had been their land. So complete was Yankee domination during the last half of the nineteenth century that when the presence of Mexicans was again noticed it was a foreign immigrant group.[18] Euroimmigrants settled, imposed their worldview to legitimize the conquest, and as part of their new world vision attempted to transform the Mexican people into foreigners. The asymmetrical power relations were very clear. Under settler colonialism the Mexican people as indigenous to the land were displaced and had absolutely no rights, including the right to education. Psychologically, the immediate dilemma for the Mexican people was their survival in a hostile imposed state.

In California, the state made little effort to educate Mexican children. In fact, some of the first legislation to address this issue arose in 1921 with the creation of migratory schools. Prior to this there were schools established in urban areas that served Mexican children. These schools were segregated, poorly equipped and financed, and it is noted that not much has changed to this day. According to Irving Hendrick, consistent with the goals of Americanization of the foreign born, it was clear that Mexican children had their attention directed toward a curriculum completely foreign to their experience. The cultural value contrast between the public schools and the Mexican parents was substantial.[19] Some 20 years later in 1944, 47 percent of the total Mexican school-age population received no education; of those in school, 72 percent were in the first three grades; and the percent of high school graduates was almost nil.[20] In Texas, the exclusion of Mexican children was as sweeping as in other former Mexican states.

In 1930 Mexican parents in the Del Rio, Texas, school system suggested that school officials were arbitrarily and illegally depriving Mexican children of facilities used by other races. Most Mexicans were then classified on their birth certificates as being of the white race. Today this remains a problem. In the case of the *Independent School District v. Salvatierra*, Mexicans demanded an end to segregation by the Del Rio school system. The trial court granted an injunction against the segregated school. The Texas Court of Civic Appeals upheld the lower court ruling but voided the injunction. The court held that due to pedagogical judgment, in this case, "language deficiency," segregation was justified.[21]

In 1947 three University of Texas student organizations legally challenged local school administrators in Beeville, Sinton, Bastrop, Elgin, and Cotulla where Mexican students were segregated in grades one through eight. Superintendents of Beeville and Sinton defended their practices based on "language deficiency issues."[22] In California, the Ninth Circuit Court ruled in *Westminster School District v. Mendez* (1947) that the segregation of Mexican children by California schools was found to be unconstitutional, while justification to continue segregation was found again in "language issues."[23] In Texas, the *Minerva Delgado et al. v. Bastrop I.S.D.* segregation case attempted to put a stop to these practices. On June 15, 1948, a judgment was issued stating that the practice of segregating pupils of Mexican or Latin descent in separate schools or classes was prohibited.[24]

Though these court rulings in California and Texas began to chip away at the rigid segregation system, loopholes remained. The 100-year system of segregation practices, customs, and usage was not to be easily undone. The battles against the settler colonial state's racist educational policy persisted. The U.S. Commission on Civil Rights in its Mexican American Education Studies, a project that began in the late 1960s, revealed the following: Mexican school-aged children attend schools segregated from their Anglo counterparts, therefore the Civil Rights Act of 1964 (Title IV, Section 405) should be applied to Mexican school segregation;[25] there was an underrepresentation of Mexicans in the education professions and on school boards;[26] the language and culture of the Mexican children was not only ignored but suppressed by the schools;[27] the schools to which Mexican children were assigned were underfinanced in comparison to schools attended by Anglo children;[28] teachers treated Mexican children less favorably and failed to involve them as active participants in the classroom;[29] the dropout percentages reached above 50 percent in the period, 1960–92, between entrance and graduation, and those who remained achieved at lower levels then their Anglo counterparts.[30]

Mexican people have had to struggle against settler colonialist educational policy for 150 years for the right to walk into foreign public schools and universities. Once inside the educational institution, the issue becomes one of content. The content of education in the United States is based on a Eurocentric worldview. The right to mother-tongue instruction—that children should be taught the medium of their own native language—is neither tolerated nor supported by U.S. society. In fact, the norm was corporal punishment for speaking Spanish on school grounds. As a result, and alongside segregated schools, many generations of Mexican parents have refused to teach their children Spanish, assuming that to learn English translated into success. This strategy by many Mexican parents failed. Sure, their children did in fact learn English, but success within the Eurocentric system was not the overwhelming result. What Mexican parents failed to understand was that whether speaking Spanish or English within an English-dominant state, children were nonetheless faced with colonial structures and conditions.

English is the de facto official language of the United States and education occurs in that medium. The negation of instruction in Spanish is part of the colonial pattern of an assimilation myth and conformity to the values and culture of the dominant white society. As a Mexican people living within the confines of an occupied homeland, the right to language remains a basic human right—one violated by the assumption that conquest and colonialism of people and their lands gave the United States license to define.

The foundation of settler colonial education is rooted in the ideology of manifest destiny—the divine right of the Euroimmigrant to carve out a state from the nations of the Native Americans and the Mexicans. History textbooks have been written to project the justification and legitimation of this divine plan. The treatment of the Mexican people in U.S. history is in most cases completely absent or, when present, tends to be a grossly incomplete narration. Eurocentric settler colonial education has inculcated feelings of inferiority within the Mexican population through the historic policies of language deficiencies and segregation. This has had a profound impact on the retention of Mexicans in school.

It should be noted that in the 1990s the dropout rate within the Mexican community fluctuated between 50 and 65 percent. For the 1960s through the 1980s, the figures were comparable. The excessively high numbers of Mexicans who are not receiving an education and who are dropping out of the public schools suggest that they are rejecting the colonial education imposed by the dominant society. Gloria Murry suggests that large numbers of Mexican students drop out of school because of lack of relevant education and meaningful cultural diversity. She suggests that educational reform should take a critical look at how a multicultural curriculum might improve the education of all children.[31] One of the weaknesses with this suggestion is that the issue of dropouts runs deeper than a question of reform. Dropping out of school suggests a resistance to colonialism and a condemnation of the Eurocentric worldview with a serious penalty paid for dearly by Mexican youth. Dropping out of the educational system is an act of resistance that usually results in the youths retreating back into the barrio, seeking the safety of community and identity yet unprepared to transform the situation within which the community exists. The past and current dropout rates are not a symptom of cultural deficiency or lack of a study skill or some other technical problem, but rather a form of resistance to colonialism. The colonial content of education is the foundation of instruction, because the educational system was created by the settler colonial state, therefore even if the instructor happens to be a person of color very little changes.

Euroimmigrant educational intitutions in relationship to the conquered Mexican population have functioned as an instrument of domination and assimilation. The socialization process in public education is aimed at assimilating the Mexican population. The public education institutions control ideas, values, and shape self-images. Psychologically Mexicans have historically been made to feel inferior. They do not see a positive reflection of themselves in history or in their contributions to society.

The curriculum of public schools in the United States, derived within a Euroimmigrant worldview, perpetuates the heroes, nationalism, and values of Euro-Americans. For example, the celebration of the pilgrims at Thanksgiving, the Fourth of July, Washington as the father of this country all reflect Euroimmigrant patriotism and values. Yet, in many cases, these same events have a negative historical meaning for Mexicans and Native Americans. There has been no attempt at institutionalization of Mexican holidays or heroes—such as September 16th, Mexican Independence, Cinco de Mayo, Hidalgo, Morelos, Zapata, and so on.

What is being debated in multiculturalism with relation to the Mexican experience are attachments that are bits and pieces of cultural or historical events that remain nonthreatening to the settler colonial worldview. Fiestas, folk dances, myths, cultural foods and dress, individual assimilationist successes—these are acceptable kinds of attachments of the Mexican experience. On the other hand, to question and study the historic socioeconomic and political relations between Mexicans and the Euroimmigrants from the worldview of the Mexican people is resisted and viewed as a threat to the social fabric of the United States, and it is heightened by the political and educational policies of the past two decades.

It is interesting to note that the multicultural debate and English Only Movement have flourished during the same period. The English Only Movement of the late 1980s and early 1990s is the most current form of cultural genocide being perpetuated against the Mexican people. John Tanton has asked quite unabashedly, "will the present majority peaceably hand over its political power to a group that is simply more fertile? As whites see their power and control over their lives declining will they simply go quietly into the night? Or will there be an explosion?"[32] Tanton's comments in August 1988 led to the resignation of Walter Cronkite from the Board of Advisors of U.S. English. Tanton would not retract the statement, although he resigned when it became clear that the agenda of the founders and financiers of U.S. English were centered on an unholy trinity—population control, immigration restrictions, and language restrictions.

The current English Only Movements are a continuation of the long Euroimmigrant tradition of ethnocentrism, cultural intolerance, and cultural genocide. Born within the upper ranks of the Reagan administration, the language amendment movement brought together state agencies such as the Organization of American States, the Council for Inter-American Security, U.S. congresspersons, and two domestic groups: U.S. English and English First.[33] The language amendment movement is the product of a well-financed campaign that has antecedents in the antiimmigrant lobby and in the population control crusade. The leading group, U.S. English, Inc., boasts of a membership of 350,000 nationwide and commands an annual budget of over $7 million.[34]

In 1985 the Council for Inter-American Security conducted a special study concerning the domestic policy of bilingual education. A special report issued by Rusty Butler of the Council entitled "On Creation of a Hispanic America: A Nation Within a Nation?" made the case for defending passage of a proposed twenty-seventh amendment to the Constitution declaring English the official language.[35]

Senator Steve Symms (R-Idaho) suggested that bilingual education and bilingual ballots have created an apartheid system. Therefore, to correct the condition he has sponsored legislation in the Senate calling for English as the U.S. official language.[36] In his report, Butler suggests that bilingual education has perpetuated the maintenance of heritage, language, and allegiance to Mexican roots, diminishing a sense of Americanism. Butler attacks bilingual education, claiming, among other things, that it has security implications that could guide terrorism and it is no longer an educational but a political issue.[37]

The passage of the English Only amendment in California was a victory for the advocates of the English Only Movement. Between 1986 and 1989, similar proposals were considered by voters and legislators in 39 states, bringing the total of "official English amendment states" to 17.

U.S. English was organized in 1983, an offshoot of the Federation for American Immigration Reform (FAIR), a Washington D.C.-based lobby advocating tighter immigration restrictions. Its founders were former Senator S. I. Hayakawa, the first sponsor of the English language amendment, and John Tanton. Tanton served as president of Zero Population Growth before founding FAIR. U.S. English was born highlighting the cultural impact of immigration and calling for stricter immigration controls.[38] By 1988 U.S. English outgrew FAIR, with whom they continue to work closely, channeling grants to Americans for Border Control and Californians for Population Control. U.S. English states as its goal to organize and help finance state-by-state campaigns to make English the official language in a minimum of 37 states, laying the requisite groundwork for passage of a federal amendment to the Constitution.[39]

English First is also spearheading a national English Only Movement. It claims a membership of 200,000 and an annual budget exceeding $2 million. English First was created for the express purpose of adding a language amendment to the Constitution. It is the only such organization registered to lobby Congress for direct action.[40]

The English Only Movement and its supporters are expressly antibilingual education. The English Only Movement and its supporters are procolonial state policies of assimilation and conformity to Eurocentric worldviews. These forces are calling for the cultural genocide of the Mexican people and have been able to mobilize a serious grassroots base of support.

CONCLUSION

The Mexican people are an internal colony of the United States and as such must enter into a process of transformation and decolonization. U.S. settler colonialism is not simply the application of a theory, but the historical experience of the Mexican people in the United States.

Internal colonialism functions because of the asymmetrical power relations. As a part of internal settler colonialism the Mexican people have been rendered subordinate and dependent; myths of cultural assimilation within this context pivot on cultural genocide.

To achieve self-determination, the thrust for Mexicans must be decolonization. The mechanism of internal colonialism must be recognized, addressed, and up-rooted. This transformation process must be addressed in order to affect meaningful change. Multiculturalism and cultural diversity that places itself within a settler colonial context is doomed to failure.

NOTES

1. The term "Mexican" will be used throughout this chapter to mean all persons of Mexican origin, both those born in the United States and those born in Mexico. For a treatment of assimilationist models, see Celia Heller, *Mexican American Youth: Forgotten Youth at the Crossroads* (New York: Random House, 1966); Alvin Rudolph, "The Incarcer-ated Mexican American Delinquent," *Journal of Criminal Law, Criminology and Political Science*, June 1962, pp. 224–238; Marry Straus and Gerald Hotaling, "A Cultural Consistency Theory of Family Violence in the Mexican American and Jewish Ethnic Groups," in *The Social Causes of Husband and Wife Violence* (Minneapolis: University of Minnesota Press, 1980), pp. 68–85; Octavio I. Romano, "Editorial," *El Grito: Journal of Contemporary Mexican American Thought*, Fall 1968, pp. 2–4; Octavio I. Romano, "The Anthropology and Soci-ology of the Mexican Americans: The Distortion of Mexican American History," *El Grito: Journal of Contemporary Mexican American Thought*, Fall 1968, pp. 23–26.

2. Herschel T. Manuel, *Spanish Speaking Children of the Southwest: Their Education and the Public Welfare* (Austin: University of Texas Press, 1965).

3. Alfredo Mirande, *The Chicano Experience: An Alternative Perspective* (Notre Dame, IN: University of Notre Dame Press, 1985).

4. Frantz Fanon, *The Wretched of the Earth* (New York: Grove Press, 1963); Robert Blauner, *Racial Oppression in America* (New York: Harper & Row, 1972).

5. Mirande, *The Chicano Experience*, pp. 1–13.

6. Ibid.; and James Cockeroft, *Outlaws in the Promised Land: Mexican Immigrant Workers and America's Future* (New York: Grove Press, 1986).

7. John Anner, "The Ones To Watch Out For," *The Trendsletter*, Vol. 5, No. 1 (Winter 1991/92), p. 5. According to Anner, in 1992 surplus military aircraft landing material was being welded into a solid wall separating Tijuana from San Diego in southern California.

8. Human Rights in Mexico, A Policy of Impunity, An Americas Watch Study, June 1990, New York.

9. Yolanda Rodriquez, and John Glionna, "Border Agent Fires into Van," *Los Angeles Times*, May 26, 1990.

10. Roberto Martinez and Maria Jimenez, "Human Rights On The U.S./Mexico Border Hearings," Subcommittee on Human Rights and International Organizations, Committee on Foreign Affairs, U.S. House of Representatives, Washington, DC, April 18, 1990.

11. Rodolfo Acuna, *Occupied America* (New York: Harper & Row, 1988), p. 202.

12. Cockeroft, *Outlaws in the Promised Land*, p. 77.

13. Ibid., p. 245.

14. Ibid., p. 246.

15. Daniel Wood, "Legal Fight Over Illegal Aliens," *The Christian Science Monitor*, May 12, 1994, pp. 1, 4.

16. Peter Copeland, "Immigration Myths," *Albuquerque Tribune*, May 26, 1994.

17. Peter Copeland, "Economic Impact," *Rocky Mountain News*, May 25, 1994, p. A 26.

18. Irving G. Hendrick, "Early Schooling for Children of Migrants Is Disputed in Study of Immigrants," *Aztlan*, Vol. 8 (Spring 1977), p. 11.

19. Ibid., pp. 15, 16.

20. Carl Allsup, "Education Is Our Freedom: The American G.I. Forum & The Mexican American School Segregation In Texas, 1948–1957," *Aztlan*, Vol. 8 (Spring 1977), p. 27.

21. Ibid., pp. 30, 31.

22. Ibid., p. 32.

23. Ibid.

24. Ibid., p. 34.

25. Inter-agency Committee on Mexican American Affairs, Testimony Presented at the Cabinet Committee Hearings on Mexican American Affairs, El Paso, Texas, October 26-28, 1967.

26. U.S. Commission on Civil Rights, Ethnic Isolation of Mexican Americans in the Public Schools of the Southwest, Report I, 1971.

27. U.S. Commission on Civil Rights, The Excluded Student: Educational Practices Affecting Mexican Americans in the Southwest, Report III, 1972.

28. U.S. Commission on Civil Rights, Mexican American Education in Texas: A Function of Wealth, Report V, 1974.

29. U.S. Commission on Civil Rights, Teachers & Students: Differences in Teacher Interaction with Mexican American & Anglo Students, Report IV, 1973.

30. U.S. Commission on Civil Rights, The Unfinished Education: Outcomes for Minorities in the Five Southwestern States, Report II, 1971. In addition, selective exclusion is based on settler colonial standard measures such as ACT, SAT, GPA, and other standardized examinations devised from within a Eurocentric, Euroimmigrant worldview and then applied to the colonized populations.

31. Gloria Murry, "Cultural Diversity as a Quintessential Component of Education Reform." *New Direction for Educational Reform*, Vol. 1, No. 1 (1992), pp. 55–60.

32. Priscilla Falcón and Patricia Campbell, "The Politics of Language and the Mexican American: The English Only Movement and Bilingual Education," ed. George Shepherd, Jr. and David Penna, in *Racism and the Underclass: State Policy and Discrimination Against Minorities* (Westport, CT: Greenwood Press, 1991); Peter Strescino, "U.S. English Chief Resigns Her Position," *The Pueblo Chieftain*, October, 18, 1988, p. A1; Laird Harrison, "U.S. English's Link to Anti-Immigration Groups," *Asian Week*, August 15, 1986, pp. 1, 7, 16, 17.

33. Falcón and Campbell, "The Politics of Language," pp. 145, 146; Lawrence Mosqueda, "English Only Has Deep Roots in the Ultra Right," *The Guardian* (New York), November 30, 1988, p. 6.

34. Falcón and Campbell, "The Politics of Language," p. 148; Robert Lindsey, "Debate Growing on Use of English," *New York Times*, July 21, 1986, p. 1.

35. Rusty Butler, "On Creation of a Hispanic America: A Nation Within a Nation?" Report prepared for the Council for Inter-American Security (Washington DC: Council for Inter-American Security, 1985).

36. Shepherd and Penna, *Racism and the Underclass*, p. 145.

37. Ibid., p. 146.

38. James Crawford, *Bilingual Education: History, Politics, Theory and Practice* (Trenton, NJ: Crane, 1989).

39. Sue Lindsay, "U.S. Group Joins English Effort," *Rocky Mountain News*, September 24, 1988, p. 10; U.S. English, Update, Vol. 8, No. 4 (July-August 1990).

40. Crawford, *Bilingual Education*, p. 66.

PART III

Gendered Subjectivities

8

Negotiating Self-Defined Standpoints in Teaching and Learning

Sandra Jackson

FRAMING: A PERSONAL NARRATIVE

As I look back on my teaching experiences when I was a high school English teacher, I remember vividly a number of occasions in which I encountered resistance from white students and teachers that personified challenges to me—my person, what I embodied, my knowledge and expertise, indeed my competence and values as an educator. During that time, I was teaching in a large public high school system in a school that had been undergoing dramatic changes in the demographic hue and class makeup of the student body. The particular school was characterized by many as what once had been a "flagship school," touted for its excellence and its ability to prepare many students who went on to graduate from the nation's most prestigious and selective colleges and universities. Once upon a time, this school had been predominantly white, middle-class, with a number of international students from many nations, a small yet visible academically able population of Asian American students, primarily from Japan, as well as a visible number of African American and Mexican American and other Spanish-speaking students.

When I arrived to teach at that school, I filled a position that another black woman had left to complete her doctorate. There were no other African American teachers in the department at the time. My hiring along with that of several other black teachers took place within a politically charged environment: the late 1960s and the black power movement. African American families and communities had begun to question and challenge the poor and generally inferior quality of education their children were receiving. Schools remained racially segregated, given segregated and clearly demarcated housing patterns. Black students were often tracked in the lower ability levels, they experienced high dropout rates, and often graduated from high school functionally illiterate and unable to qualify for admission at colleges and universities as well as technical training institutions. They felt shortchanged. They had protested against racist practices and attitudes of teachers and administrators; they had also called for curriculum revision, black literature, and the inclusion of the experiences of African Americans and their contributions in the various content areas. The black community and students had also organized and demanded more black teachers.

At that time, the school was in the process of changing from a predominantly white school to a predominantly black school, with a growing number of students from Vietnam. While many of the middle-class white students began moving with their families to the suburbs, many white students remained: those who were working class and could not join the lemming-like white flight; those whose parents were committed to integrated schooling; and those whose parents decided to stay for a variety of other reasons. This was the nature of the crucible I entered as a new teacher, with an English major and a teaching credential from a graduate program in teacher education from the University of California system.

My first assignment of courses consisted of four classes of eleventh-grade English and one tenth-grade Advanced Placement (AP) course. Because students were tracked into different streams, my eleventh-grade courses included three that were regular track and one that was remedial, all of which were populated by largely black and other students of color. Regarding the AP course, there were no black students. It was here with the AP course that I first experienced the greatest resistance from a number of white middle-class students.

I remember it all so clearly. After having taught my first few lessons, I was informed that a number of students had been withdrawn from my class because of parental request. I was told by an administrator as well as student counselors that parents had been "concerned about my ability to teach [their children] what they needed to know to successfully enter college." Even among those who remained, there were those who were incredulous about my ability to speak articulately, comment critically on classic as well as contemporary literature. There were flash points regarding my rigor in grading essays and other written assignments—the subtext of which was how could I dare give them less than As? In the other regular and remedial courses, in which students of color were grossly overrepresented, parents were glad to see me. Many told me that they were glad that the person who was hired to fill the position was someone who cared, someone who had standards, someone who believed that their children could learn. Other black teachers who were hired during subsequent years were well received by the black community.

Those of us who were committed to the education of African American students in particular, and who were willing to take a stand against racism and be advocates of students as well as ourselves, decided to work together, to challenge inequalities and make changes in curriculum and teaching. Because we worked closely with parents as well as the parent advisory board, we were able to forge a strong relationship with parents who supported us and our teaching. The parents were there for us when we incurred criticism about our teaching methods in general, attitudes and style, as well as our use of material that deviated from the traditional curriculum and its canon.

By the end of my first year of teaching, I had been able to develop a rapport with most students, having earned a reputation of having high standards, making classes interesting, and being hard but fair. As a matter of fact, because the students in the tenth-grade course came to respect me, they asked if I could be their teacher for the eleventh grade—which I did. What followed was a struggle to which I will allude shortly. I was able to teach them in the twelfth grade as well. The result of this was that I had the opportunity to work with what came to be a group of students primarily white and middle-class, along with a small number of African American and Asian students who joined this core, for a three-year period. This sustained relationship created an unusual bond between my students (and their parents) and me. As a consequence, because of our ability to confront difference and work together, we were able to study rich and varied materials, inclusive of literature by and about people of color as well as women. Because of the trust that developed, I was able to use nontraditional material and be innovative in teaching and learning.

While I am proud of what I was able to accomplish with the AP courses as well as those for college preparatory students—those in which students of color, especially African American, Mexican American, and Native American were grossly underrepresented and often absent—it is my work with black students in particular that contributed most to my growth. As one who knew my "stuff," it was important that I learned in practice about the ideology of racism and discrimination within the context of the lived experiences of schooling from the perspective of students who had been marginalized by both institutional as well as personal politics and practices of teachers. Teaching in the particular school, during a particular historical time, within a particular political climate, enabled me to make sense of things like the interaction of race, gender, and class oppression and biases in a deeper way than I had previously understood given my individual experiences as a student.

Although as a black woman I myself had experienced racism—both overt and explicit, as well as covert and nuanced in the form of patronizing and condescending remarks about how I was "different from the others"—I had not been subjected to the same degree of oppression in my own education because I had always been in college prep as well as AP courses (as one of the exceptions). In retrospect, things became clarified: in my own elementary and high school experiences, I had almost always been the only or one of two or three black students in academic courses. During the school day, the only time I saw the majority of my black friends was in physical education, extracurricular activities, or elective courses. I had sensed something, but I had not known about tracking students according to perceived or tested ability groupings. All that I had known was that I had planned to go to college and that outside of my group of close friends, many black students were not planning to go. It was only after I entered the classroom as a teacher, armed with knowledge about tracking, and seeing its effects on the lived experiences of students, that I learned about what tracking meant. My work with black parents in terms of struggling against racist practices in testing, placement in courses regarding levels, discipline, counseling, and guidance led to strong solidarity with parents who became my advocates as I had become theirs as we struggled collectively.

The support of black parents was central. For it was not only white students and their parents, but also white teachers with whom I had to struggle in often sharp confrontations about racism and bigotry. I return to a struggle to which I alluded earlier. As I mentioned, my first-year courses were primarily eleventh-grade with one tenth-grade course. Because a particular group of eleventh-grade students responded quite positively to my teaching, they asked me if I would be their teacher for the twelfth grade. I said that I would like to, but that was not a decision I could make: that power resided with the department chair.

So, buoyed up by student interest and parental support, I talked with the department chair and shared with her my interest in teaching at least one section of twelfth-grade college preparatory English, as well as one eleventh-grade AP section, because the tenth-grade students who had remained in my course, as well as others who were eligible, wanted to take me again in the eleventh grade. Of course, I thought this was a reasonable request. And although I had not really expected both requests to be granted, I was not prepared for the department chair's response: she told me that she was not sure if I was qualified to teach the higher levels of either the college preparatory courses or the AP course in particular, and that I would need several more years of experience before she would consider it. I asked then if I could teach either the eleventh-grade AP course or a twelfth-grade college preparatory course. She replied with a pointed "No."

What ensued was a veritable war with many skirmishes. On my own, I had not really given it much thought—whether or not I taught all eleventh grade or not at that time. I had entered teaching with a commitment to public education, in an urban environment because of my commitment to teach in areas of greatest need: I had to teach where black people lived and in schools where they could afford to attend. I had not been particularly interested in spending my time teaching gifted, talented, or otherwise privileged (white) students—many of whom by virtue of their class and cultural capital would make it anyway. I had consciously chosen to teach in a large, urban inner-city school, one populated largely by students of color because I knew of the power of (mis)education and its potential to (dis)empower others. I knew that I had been an exception and that the education I had gotten was different from that which other African Americans had received. I came to know that my education had privileged me regarding opportunities and access that were not available to many others. Furthermore, given my family background, one in which service to others was stressed, I had developed a commitment to my community as a first priority in my professional and personal life. I wanted to teach black students as well as other students of color, as an insurgent educator; to be one who challenged, through her practice and belief in their ability to learn, racist notions about their alleged inferiority, disinterest in school, questions about their potential to contribute to society; and to make changes.

However, when affronted by the racism and what I later learned to be the privilege of the white female department chair, I decided to confront her and the department head-on. In doing my research, I learned that she, along with the other white teachers, allocated to themselves almost all of the college preparatory and AP courses. I had been given the tenth-grade AP course only because no one else wanted to teach it; they preferred the eleventh and twelfth grades, the college preparatory and AP courses in particular, which virtually assured that they would teach primarily white students. Further, because a number of the eleventh-grade college preparatory courses had a few black students, I could have them. And finally, regarding the one remedial section I taught, I had been given that class because I (a black teacher) "would be good with *them* because I knew how to work with *them*."

Detailing what happened as a consequence of my understanding about how I was perceived, the attitudes that persisted about black students and how they were treated, and the decision-making framework used by the chair and the other white teachers is outside the purview of this chapter. Suffice it to say, however, that I waged war. I worked closely with African American parents, counselors, and students; I raised the issue within the department regarding how course-load decisions were made and the racial politics as well as privilege, and the need for change in terms of the curriculum. To say we argued would be a gross understatement. The hostility was palpable and I was labeled an "arrogant troublemaker" "who *thought* she was smart," "did not know her place," and was "uncivil" because I spoke forthrightly and did not mince my words.

By the end of that school year, the chair was unseated. The department had become ungovernable, and the principal had to step in. We changed the manner in which course-load decisions were made; and the courses generally prized as the "best" were redistributed. And among other things, I was able to teach both the eleventh-grade AP course as well as one twelfth-grade college preparatory class. I taught in that system for 13 years, and while there is so much more that I could tell, I will end this story here.

Now, years later as a professor in a university in a school of education, the residues of earlier experiences with racism are reactivated as I strive to prepare diverse students for the teaching profession, work to address the particular interests of African American students and other students of color, and work with urban schools that continue to miseducate and undereducate large numbers of students of color. In this regard I strive to negotiate self-defined standpoints for my multiple selves—as an African American, as a woman, as one with a working-class background, as a professor, as a feminist, and as a critical pedagogue. I work in a context, the academy, in which few African Americans and other people of color have survived, let alone thrived. My race, gender, class, orientation to teaching, as well as my comportment still evoke responses that are raced, gendered, and classed. Here, too, in higher education, I find myself in a contested terrain regarding issues of identity, knowledge, power, authority, curriculum, teaching, and values vis-à-vis my relationship to the institution—my students as well as colleagues.

NEGOTIATING A SELF-DEFINED STANDPOINT AS A TEACHER

I will begin with reflections on the problematic of race and gender at the location of the academy. Magda Gere Lewis (1993, p. 156), in her work on the silencing of women in higher education, asserts, "In the academy, women find themselves inside institutions whose practices and intentions [have] been historically designed to keep them outside its concrete and theoretical forms." I would add that this is even more so for African American women. Perceived and often treated as intruders,

the African American woman is on display and her activities are often scrutinized and questioned: What is she doing? Is she doing what she is supposed to be doing? Why is she here? Is she qualified to be here? Further [assumptions are made that] her interests lie solely in the topics of racism, multiculturalism and cultural diversity and she is perceived as a professional ethnic with specialized knowledge and expertise in "minority" cultures. (Farmer, 1993, pp, 204–206; Blair and Maylor, 1993)

Patricia Williams (1991) alludes to responses of students as she recounts their reactions to her in light of their expectations of how a teacher should look, be, act, and dress, as they took license in critiquing her tone, attitude, and teaching. In narratives throughout her book, she describes conflicts over the "ideologies of style" (p. 22), student resistance, active and passive, anger and outright hostility at the "preposterous notion of her authority" (p. 96). Her student evaluations "deified, reified, and vilified her in all sorts of cross-directions" (p. 95) because she was different and her teaching style was different. She brought the study of conflict and controversy as it regards legal theory to the center of classroom discourse. She was challenging, and they felt uncomfortable.

Williams' experiences remind me of those of Anna Julia Cooper, one of the first black women graduates of Oberlin who went on to become principal of the Dunbar High School for black students in Washington, D.C. She too was vilified in a most scathing attack on her character (Hutchinson, 1981). In her case, it was because of her refusal to comply with the (all white male) school board's dictum that she make the school's curriculum primarily vocational. She refused to dilute the curriculum, to provide inferior education, and therefore insisted that her pupils take both the classical academic curriculum as well as the vocational, along with courses in music and art. She went against the grain, fought for quality education for black students, and in so doing paid dearly: she was dismissed under a cloud of scandal and her contract was unceremoniously terminated. She, like her contemporaries in the women's club movement, worked to organize and mobilize, committed to a life of service. Like other early black women educators, she lived and worked committed to a "lift and serve, uplift the race" mission, dedicated to service to her community (Perkins, 1988; Nobel, 1988; Etter-Lewis, 1993; Cole, 1994).

Today black teachers still experience conflict and are confronted with challenges to their competence by colleagues, administrators, and students—white students in particular. African American teachers continue to feel undervalued, their skills unacknowledged, their careers stunted, and their contributions marginalized. In their lived experiences as educators, they experience racism, ranging from apparently innocuous naive and sometimes patronizing attempts to acknowledge racial and cultural differences, to blatant and explicit manifestations of bigotry and hostility (Blair and Maylor, 1993, pp. 56, 61).

African American professors in higher education also recount similar experiences. Their research and scholarship are often observed with suspicion whether or not they depart from the mainstream (hooks and West, 1991). They also experience "negative and unfair teaching and course evaluations" (Foster, 1992). In addition, they incur rancor, hostility, and negativism when they take a stand against racism and discrimination. Further, when they serve as advocates and challenge the racist treatment of black students, voice their disapproval, and call others to task, they are often labeled as troublemakers (Blair and Maylor, 1993, p. 64).

In contending with racism and sexism, and the complex of challenges this brings on institutional and personal levels, African American women in higher education report that their experiences as teachers (and students), are emotionally draining (Andrews, 1993). In my informal talks with other African American faculty, recurrent issues come to the fore: the time and energy it takes to sustain a grounded sense of self and an equanimity to gird one's self against distractions and confinement in a permanent space of simmering rage. The daily insults are myriad. The experiences run the gamut from remarks and obvious shows of surprise about our ability to speak "so articulately"—to which I have on occasion reminded people that my first degree was in English and that I don't do "dis here dat dere," to comments about our "attitude" our "militancy" with *sotto voce* comments that we "should not be so sensitive and that we need to develop a sense of humor," to individuals taking the liberty to confide in us that they like us but find us so intimidating. In addition, our judgment is called into question, our ability to be team players is challenged when we insist upon addressing racism and sexism and make others uncomfortable in conversations and discussions, and our scholarship and research are questioned when they traverse the boundaries of traditional research questions, topics, and methodologies.

Further, African American professors, women in particular, perceive racism and sexism in promotion and tenure decision making, drawn on the axis of cultural values, attitudes, and normative behavior often based upon class. It should therefore not be surprising that for many of us, preoccupation with being fired, the awkwardness of relearning and making mistakes, issues of control, respect of one's peers, students, and administrators—all provide powerful disincentives for embarking upon engagement in developing self as a transformative educator (Shor and Freire, 1987, p. 53). To these concerns, Deborah Britzman (1992, pp. 153–154) adds problems unleashed by negative critique and tensions that become manifest when the political is coupled with the personal. When engaging in truth-telling in teaching and learning, examination of taken-for-granted notions and ideas, and contending with the canon and curricular transformation, African American women teachers must also contend with power structures, patriarchy, Eurocentrism, and class bias (Farmer, 1993, pp. 197–200). In so doing, African American teachers necessarily broach controversial issues and entertain conflict as part of teaching and learning, inviting students to journey to the edge of their comfort zones. Yet I know that while bringing the study of conflict to the core of the curriculum and teaching is necessary and that problematic things need to be discussed, it is not sufficient for the transformation of self and society. For far more is at stake than the mere change and adjustment of attitudes and beliefs through discussion. It is the issue of power, resources, and their distribution and allocation that needs to be redressed through pedagogical practices enacted in the classroom and open for consideration in the lived practices of individuals and groups. For teacher educators, this issue has particular salience, for it requires engagement in content as well as processes, examination of theory and practice, critical reflection on one's own attitudes, beliefs, practices, and relationships with self and others.

To educate for social transformation involves not only a sense of mission, but also a critical conception of practices. In a study of teacher reflection on conflict in their professional lives and the inscription of ethical dilemmas related to personal integrity, Nona Lyons (1990, p. 161) examines how knowledge and values are implicated in teacher attitudes, beliefs, and practices; reflected in their expectations of self and students. In her study, Lyons recounts a story of an African American high school teacher who experienced "dilemmas in teaching her world cultures course," a unit on South Africa and her attempts to make sense of a controversial situation: domination, oppression, control and inequality regarding the plight of black South Africans and issues of white privilege regarding race and class. The teacher had been confronted by (white) students who had wanted to hear "both sides." In discussing this situation, Lyons shares the following insights:

The teacher understands that dialogue about controversial material can polarize people. And in coming to terms with the orientation of adolescents who may not necessarily want to see the evil, ugliness, especially in terms of things important and close to them, involving their own families and themselves, she seeks to look at places to remove herself. This teacher recognizes that it is impossible to remain on the fence in discussing South Africa; yet, she also believes that a good teacher ought to be able to present certain scenarios for students so that they can find ways to say what they think, feel, and question. She looks for ways to get students to get closer to what they themselves feel and not react to her and how she feels.

This is the challenge that I face: how to create spaces in which my students and I can be and negotiate our own self-defined standpoints, argue for social change and transformation, enact a critical and democratic pedagogy, and at the same time sustain a community of learning, critical inquiry, fully cognizant of the sociopolitical relationships between dominant and subordinate groups within educational institutions, as well as within the larger society. As an African American professor, like the teachers Lisa Delpit (1987) alludes to, I also must struggle against the privilege of white students in a predominantly white institution and practice a critical and culturally sensitive pedagogy—one that affirms self, self-determination, the exercise of agency, the honoring of multiple subjectivities regarding black students and other students of color in particular—which is grounded in the development and cultivation of critical and creative thinking and writing abilities and skills through antiracist, antisexist pedagogy. Critical pedagogy is insurgent and it involves "interpellation of the unconscious ways in which authoritative ideas become infused with personal investment and thus become a part of who we are" (Britzman, 1992, p. 172), mobilizing deep investments, discursive positions, and contradictory identities.

Alluding to M. Bakhtin (1984), Britzman (1992, p. 152) states that "authoritative discourses signify the received and institutionally sanctioned knowledge that demands allegiance to the status-quo and authorizes stereotypes as if they were unencumbered by ideological meanings." In Britzman's view, antiracist and feminist pedagogues interrogate social change, social control, and radical agency, and address contextually dependent relations that affirm the power of lived experience. As such, an antiracist, antisexist pedagogical orientation attends to intersubjectivity and the making of sense regarding the relationships between knowledge and language that students bring to school and the discursive practices of the school as an institution.

The ethical issues implicit are articulated in the following hard questions which we must ask ourselves as educators:

We (as women) have to ask ourselves hard questions: how does what we do, see, or is there a part of what we do in our classrooms, in the articles we write, in the nonacademic activities in which we engage, that actively seeks to break down resistance to genuine acceptance of differences . . . and promote steps towards a better understanding of each other? What do our students learn from us, that helps their lives count in this matter? (McKay, 1993, pp. 279–280)

I, like other African American women professors engaged in this project, must acknowledge the importance of content with the reality that social relations of race, class, and gender reflect the larger political, economic, cultural, and social world. I must struggle daily on a number of planes to subvert the knowledge claims of white supremacy and the alleged universalism regarding its values and perspectives; challenge the derision of black humanity in academic discourse; challenge the refutation of self and community; repudiate the generalized disdain for black people; construct an oppositional social identity (Carty, 1991, pp. 16, 29; Casey, 1993, p. 142); and work for social change—corrective vision, eradiction of structures of domination and oppression, and the creation of spaces and places to be fully human with one's identify affirmed—without which changes in schools will be unable to bring about transformation in the lives of the majority of African American students.

In my pedagogy, as a woman who is raced, I must interweave critical examination of gender as well as other dimensions of difference. Yet I must do this in such a way that the study of "otherness"—self and other—is not done in such a manner that decontextualizes and delinks identities and their construction from oppression, exploitation, domination, and resistance (hooks, 1990). Such an approach to teaching and learning means that I must necessarily address the "perceived and real relations of students, educators and the curriculum to the experiences and histories of racism, sexism, heterosexism, Eurocentrism, and how these oppressive dynamics direct gendered and raced identities" (Britzman, 1993, p. 401). The subjugated knowledges, the linguistic, hierarchical structures of higher education must be connected in palpable ways to the lived experiences of students so that we construct understandings of racism and sexism in efforts to demystify things. These issues have particular resonance with the experiences of students of color in graduate programs, many of whom enter as mature adults, often having worked previously in other careers. Often they bring with them histories of having contended with institutional racism as well as sexism.

What is clear to me is that many adult learners, as in my own experiences as a mature person matriculating in a doctoral program, come to the university as mature adults, neither white, young, innocent, nor eager to conform (Johnson, 1993, p. 202). They bring a sense of self-worth that engenders confidence and authority. Their age and life experiences become important aspects of their character, which influence their relationships with fellow students—some of whom will be younger as well as of other cultural and racial groups—as well as with themselves. As an educator, one of my many challenges is to negotiate for myself as well as my students—with them—understandings about ways to grapple with the psychological, social, sexual, and racial spaces of the academy (Lewis, 1993, p. 177) in ways that challenge, nurture, honor differences, subvert silencing and envoice. How to do this is the challenge. To teach and promote growth, development, and learning for self as well as others within an institutional context that is raced, classed, sexed, and rich with a multitude of differences? How to be true to one's self, one's students? one's discipline?

Lewis (1992, p. 194) offers a compelling point of departure in this regard:

Before we can decide where we must go with what we know, we need to understand what it means to be educated against ourselves. . . . We need to learn new skills to see what is hidden, to hear the voices that have been silenced against their will, to create curriculum out of the invisible. . . . We need to live and teach from a place that refuses to displace dignity with efficiency. . . . We need to believe that our collective possibilities are diminished not enhanced by an educational process that does not honor the history, cultural, social realities, abilities and diversity of each group.

(White) feminist scholars who see a critique of racism central to their analytical framework as well as those of color, who define gender as one of the many ingredients related to systems of domination and control, necessarily argue for a multicultural orientation to teaching and learning. In quoting Caroline Sherrit, Britzman (1993, p. 27) cautions:

Don't presume that you can be multicultural without addressing issues of oppression and domination. Don't focus on cultural plurality if you're unwilling to deal with sensitive issues such as religion, gender, race, standardized testing, poverty and politics. Embedded in this discourse is an understanding that when we talk about race we are talking about our own racialized selves . . . when we talk about gender, it means talking about our gendered selves, how these are perceived, and understood in terms of social relations and power.

Similarly, consequences of a pedagogy that is antisexist means that one addresses the issue of gender regarding women and men, and assumes a critique of patriarchy in its varied manifestations—women's survival and issues of livelihood and welfare (Lewis, 1993, p. 157). Extending this argument means that an antiracist pedagogy must necessarily be translated into an education that includes the study of racial, ethnic, and cultural groups, their oppression, struggles, and resistance.

For me as an African American woman and educator, this means that my pedagogy argues for a critique of the gendered practices and structures of male supremacy, patriarchy, concerns of gender as a site of power, and addressing how the dynamics of patriarchy and male supremacy structure social relations between and among female and male students (Britzman, 1993, p. 25). In my teaching and relationships with students, I must strive to practice a pedagogy that engages all students as gendered subjects. What does this mean? It means attention to technologies of power in classroom dynamics: who is called upon, who is encouraged, who is coached and advised, who is invited to participate through speech, body language, and attitude, to enter the conversation. It means being cognizant of my own subjectivities and values that govern my teaching, modeling through my practices ways of examining and critically discussing issues and ideas using methods that are accessible to all students in terms of content as well as processes. In attending to these things, given who I am, gender and race impinge upon how I see myself and am perceived by students. The interaction of these two dynamics shapes my attitudes, speech, and actions; and they also influence how my manner of teaching is interpreted by students as they consider issues of knowledge, power, and authority manifest in our interrelationships.

As an African American, as a woman who sees gender as central and in so doing employs black feminist thought—grounded in self-definition, self-reliance, and agency in thought and action—I bring to my teaching an orientation that encompasses theoretical interpretations of black women's realities by those who live them (Collins, 1990). As Beverly Guy-Sheftall (1993, p. 77) argues, "Black women's studies emerged because of white women's racism and Black men's sexism and the fact that there was no room for the serious consideration and study of the lives of Black women." Therefore, I cannot pretend to be unconcerned nor can I pretend to be dispassionate about the experiences of African Americans in general and African American women in particular; nor can I ignore their particular experiences as teachers and educators. With this understanding, as I confront the politics of race, gender, and class in my teaching, within the classroom, I must interrogate the problematics of gender and race for women, men, people of color, as well as those who are European descendant. Regarding gender and the (de)essentializing of its meanings, my pedagogy must at once be a prism that refracts light in multiple bands, and at the same time a lens that simultaneously brings the foreground and the background as well as the periphery into focus. The differences in the experiences of women and the meanings of these differences must be critically examined in light of the following reality:

Women of color, lesbians, poor and working class women always knew that they were different from white heterosexual middle-class women and that these differences made them socially inferior and subordinate. Conversely, white heterosexual middle-class women took advantage of the privilege of their position to oppress and marginalize other women. (McKay, 1993, p. 272)

When we critically examine women's experiences in general, with attention to education in particular, my pedagogy must deconstruct notions of biologic sisterhood, universal women's experience, and generalized notions of femininity. As a teacher educator, this means that I must bring these issues to the center and core of what we do to prepare future teachers. In my courses this means engaging students in critical examination and reflection about what it means for multiple selves to confront teaching informed by antiracist, antisexist values as we study and practice curriculum development, classroom ecology, the selection of texts and audiovisual materials, exercise of pedagogical judgment, and sensitivity to discourse and language.

In developing a pedagogical orientation that theorizes race, class, gender, and their interconnectedness, I ground my teaching in the following proposition: that I enact and enflesh the following tenets:

• critique of the dichotomous/oppositional thinking by employing both/and rather than either/or categories of analysis

- acknowledgment of the simultaneity of oppression and struggle
- eschewment of the additive analysis of race, gender, and class; instead, acknowledging the multiplicative nature of the relationship between race, gender, and class
- reconstruction of the lived experiences, historical positioning, cultural perceptions, and social constructions of women, men, individuals, and groups of different racial and ethnic backgrounds
- development of a feminist framework which is rooted in the intersection of culture and class as an organizing principle. (Brewer, 1993, pp. 16–30)

My goal is to engage students in the search for an insurgent transformation of self and society (hooks and West, 1991) with attention to the many voices and their representations while attending to practical problems that emerge from the teaching/learning dynamic. In attempting to practice this transformative peda-gogy, in addition to contending with multiple dimensions of identity rooted in race, gender, and class, I as a constructed identity must inevitably address the issue of authority in teaching and learning. Through my practice, I must ever strive to transcend binary notions of power and its differentiations—authority/nurturance; authority over/authority with; authority/authorship; power as domi-nation/power as creative energy—and their manifestations in various social relations between and among students and teachers (Gore, 1993, p. 74).

Like Jennifer Gore, I see teaching as an enactment of a narrative in which "authority" refers to the power to represent reality, to signify, and to command compliance with one's acts of signification, a power that both teachers and stu-dents can exercise (p. 71). I strive to enact the creation of negotiations of authority *with* students instead of *over* them. Specifically, regarding my own identity as an African American woman, while I rigorously attend to the experiences of black women, I must also resist constructing and imposing a regime of truth about their experiences that negates the privileging of these experiences over those of other women, and men, as well as persons of different cultural and ethnic groups. When we address the specificities of gender in teaching and learning, we must attend to the context and the situatedness of identities and subjectivities of teachers and students as we seek to understand attitudes, beliefs, and practices as they reveal power in relationships.

GROUNDING IN TRANSFORMATIVE PRAXIS

A pedagogy inscribed with transformative values is predicated on the devel-opment of a "critical perspective" through which individuals can begin to see how social practices are organized to support certain structures. It is also "a process by which these understandings are used as the basis for active political interven-tion and agency directed towards social change with the intent to disempower relations of inequality" (Lewis, 1993, p. 15). In practice, this means starting with self and the examination of one's teaching, methods, processes, content, language, interactions with students, with the understanding that teachers and students are learners (Shor and Freire, 1987).

To create a community of learners in which the climate is open and conducive to dialogue and conversation, teachers must act in ways that students gain trust in them, and they in their students. This means that teachers must resist the urge to be in control and attempt to manage learning. There is a risk and a challenge here for teachers committed to transformative practice that abuts with the socialization of students that often renders them passive. Teachers face a dilemma in that if they do not assert their authority, they invite chaos, testing and acting-out behavior, and resistance by students. In response to teaching that is not based on the traditional approach of teacher as knower and banker of knowledge, students may doubt the seriousness of one's teaching and the course. They may believe that they cannot learn from other students and that they are not learning anything unless the teacher is doing most of the teaching. In this regard, teachers must be committed to "identifying and creating spaces of freedom to be, to learn, grow, develop and act" (Gore, 1993, p. 156) in ways that confront and negate pessimism, cynicism, and immobilization, to forge languages of possibility through the development of curriculum and learning activities that incorporate student understandings and language. Faced with these challenges, teachers must be prepared to negotiate processes that acknowledge the need for structure, begin where students are (Shor, 1992, p. 157), and yet provide occasions for learning that move them beyond what they know.

The transformative pedagogic project must argue for meanings that include instruction, social vision, and processes of knowledge production (Gore, 1993, p. 4), realized through the use of generative themes that problematize everyday life experiences and connect what is being studied and examined within a particular learning context and its activities. For teacher educators, this means making connections between what it means to be a teacher and a learner situated within particular historical, social, political contexts with attention to power relations. Problem-posing in classroom discourse therefore would address what it might mean within a clinical placement context (of university students working in classroom settings with high school students) of issues related to what it means to be a teacher—female, male, of a particular racial or ethnic group, of a given class— with students who are different from one's self and in multiple dimensions. How does one establish rapport where there is a distinct class divide? How does one establish rapport where there is a distinct class divide? How does the male teacher work effectively with a classroom of primarily female students? How does a Latina work with students who are primarily Anglo? How does a Native American male teacher conduct a class in the physical sciences when students enter the room surprised to find him there? How does one build trust? How does one create ways to include students actively in learning through the selection of topics and issues to be studied, decision-making regarding materials and processes, methods and nature of assessment and evaluation of student learning? How does one coauthor a learning environment?

Inscribed in an orientation to teaching that questions received knowledge and models student engagement in the construction and production of knowledge (Shor, 1992), challenges their sensibilities, and insists on risk-taking, the teacher must act responsibly in coauthoring a learning environment that considers student development, their vulnerabilities, and their own standpoints:

Many students enter our classes acknowledging the social existence of sexism, or racism [or heterosexism], or class privilege . . . yet, they often stop short of the necessary self reflection that might reveal how we ourselves might be complicit in practices that perpetuate the same social inequalities even as they make invisible and deny the social, cultural and economic benefits we might derive from our privileged positions. Practices complicit with creating social inequality are made invisible by students' comfortable indignation and outrage at social injustices that, nonetheless, allow them to displace such practices outside of themselves . . . even outside of our classroom to an abstracted OTHER called society. . . . In this context, both the agenda of the curriculum and the politics of feminist [and antiracist] teaching practice are potentially seriously disruptive of students' worldviews. . . . [A]s we strive to get them to move beyond depersonalization and guilt towards individual and collective responsibility for action, we must acknowledge their vulnerabilities as well as our own and the power to open and close minds. (Shor, 1992, p. 118)

I concur with Britzman that the teacher must be mindful of the consequences of exercising the power to engage in conflict. For "concepts which threaten to throw students into emotional and social disarray, are likely to be unpopular and viewed as yet another instance of the teacher's authority (with a pejorative connotation) if the teacher asserts the critical without regard to the threat its poses and its terror" (Britzman, 1992, p. 154). As a teacher acting upon my beliefs and my own subjectivities, I must be ever mindful of the power unleashed when we visit conflict and controversy in teaching and learning, and after "pedagogical encounters I must return to my plans, rethink my intentions and expectations, and (re)theorize the tensions emergent and their effects upon [all of] us" (Britzman, 1992, p. 151). I too must be prepared to visit those "involuntary places" (p. 151) where new meanings are created when I, like my students, learn and (re)learn about who we are as we struggle to become more.

What this means is that I must create an atmosphere that allows individuals to say unpopular things—"things combustible," for it is better to hear them than not. What one does not hear one cannot engage (Britzman, 1992, p. 155 [alluding to Hall, 1991]). In our experiences, raced and gendered, as teachers and students, striving to forge understandings and new meanings, at times we must listen to the disconcerting and disaffecting as a precondition to struggling for change (Fine, 1993).

I return to my challenges. I teach in a private, Catholic, predominantly white university, located in an urban metropolis, with working-class first-generation college students, along with a significant number of white middle-class commuters from the suburbs, and visible African American, Latina/o and Asian American populations. In the School of Education, students of color are distinctly underrepresented: most are enrolled in elementary and early childhood education programs; fewer still in secondary education, often with one or two in each class I teach, if any. Daily I ask myself how to prepare preservice teachers to interrogate their own beliefs and practices toward others. I invite them to examine self and others and the inscribed relationships. I invite them to join the journey to transformation with me as colearners. I invite the investigation of multiple standpoints, I insist on self-definition in the context of social agency, and I ponder ways to model my orientation to teaching in ways that are growth-promoting.

I ask myself, "How do I create ways to teach about teacher identity formation and construction in relationship to personal selves with other dimensions to our lives?" How do I engage them in critically examining notions of teacher authority within the context of different cultural, racial, ethnic, and gendered milieus? How, for example, do I share with them notions of authority that become problematic within various contexts, when acted upon uncritically: authority as something earned through trust building and evidence of trustworthiness; authority as something derived from fulfilling a position or a role (Delpit, 1987, p. 129); authority as something created through and as consequence of interaction with learners?

How do I remain true to my multiple selves as woman, African American, working-class, professor, teaching in ways that are in concert with my ethics, sense of integrity, and vision of social justice, and yet work in an engaging way with students who likewise bring their multiple selves to our classroom? How do I teach with authority and openness that invites inquiry, discussion, and critical examination of issues and ideas? How do I continue to struggle within a bureaucratic, patriarchal institution, in which other professors like me are newcomers, few in number, constantly on the edge, negotiating identities, and ever mindful of the critical spaces for oppositional identity and those offering possibilities of unity in commitment?

These are the things with which I continue to struggle—with myself, with students, with my colleagues—as I strive to create and recreate spaces and places for the exercise of agency. At the same time I must remain grounded in my knowledge and understanding of self at this particular historical, social, and political time as I work with students who bring diverse values, worldviews, and identities. Together we are forging self-defined standpoints that neither privilege, deny, nor erase those of others, while working toward the development of possibilities: community predicated upon subversion of structures of domination and control.

These challenges I embrace, fully aware of my own experiences as an educator, with the memories of African American women like Anna Julia Cooper, who defied the inauthentic authority of a racist, male-dominated school board and the unequal system it sought to preserve; the African American woman high school teacher in Nona Lyons' study, who wrestled with her own subjectivities in teaching about injustice; and the experiences of Patricia Williams, a university professor of law, who weaves legal theory with narratives of race, gender, and power in her teaching. I am alive in holographic imaging as I reaffirm what it means to be

African American, a woman, and a student and a practitioner of critical, antiracist, antisexist pedagogy.

REFERENCES

Andrews, Adrianne R. 1993. "Balancing the Personal and the Professional." In Joy James and Ruth Farmer, eds., *Spirit, Space and Survival: African American Women in (White) Academe*. New York: Routledge, pp. 179–195.

Bakhtin, M. 1986. *The Dialogic Imagination* (Trans. C. Emerson and M. Holoquist). Austin: University of Texas Press.

Bannerji, Himani et al. 1991. *Unsettling Relations: The University as a Site of Feminist Struggles*. Boston: South End Press.

Biklen, Sari Knopp and Pollard, Diane, eds. 1993. *Gender and Education*. Ninety-Second Yearbook of the National Society for the Study of Education. Chicago: Distributed by the University of Chicago Press.

Blair, Maud and Maylor, Uvanney. 1993. "Issues and Concerns for Black Women in Training." In Iram Siraj-Blatchford, ed., *Race, Gender and the Education of Teachers*. Buckingham: Open University Press, pp. 55–73.

Brewer, Rose M. 1993. "Theorizing Race, Class and Gender." In Stanlie James and Abena Busia, eds., *Theorizing Black Feminisms: The Visionary Pragmatism of Black Women*. New York: Routledge, pp. 13–30.

Britzman, Deborah. 1992. "Decentering Discourses in Teacher Ecucation Or, the Unleashing of Unpopular Things." In Kathleen Weiler and Candace Mitchell, eds., *What Schools Can Do: Critical Pedagogy and Practice*. New York: SUNY Press, pp. 151–175.

———. 1993. "Beyond Rolling Models: Gender and Multicultural Education." In Sari Knopp Biklen and Diane Pollard, eds., *Gender and Education*. Ninety-Second Yearbook of the National Society for the Study of Education. Chicago: Distributed by the University of Chicago Press.

Carty, Linda. 1991. "Black Women in Academia: A Statement from the Periphery." In Himani Bannerji et al., *Unsettling Relations: The University as a Site of Feminist Struggles*. Boston: South End Press, pp. 13–44.

Casey, Kathleen. 1993. *I Answer with My Life: Life Histories of Women Teachers Working for Social Change*. New York: Routledge.

Cole, Johnnetta B. 1994. *Conversations: Straight Talk with America's Sister President*. New York: Anchor Books.

Collins, Patricia Hill. 1990. *Black Feminist Thought*. Boston: Unwin Hyman.

———. 1991. "On Our Own Terms: Self-defined Standpoints and Curriculum Transformation," *NWSA Journal*, Vol. 3, No. 3, pp. 367–381.

Delpit, Lisa. 1987. "Skills and Other Dilemmas of a Black Progressive Educator." In Margo Okazawa-Rey, James Anderson, and Rob Traver, eds., *Teaching, Teachers and Teacher Education*. Cambridge, MA: Harvard Educational Review, Reprint Series No. 19, pp. 50–56.

Etter-Lewis, Gwendolyn, ed. 1993. *My Soul Is My Own: Oral Narratives of African American Women in the Professions*. New York: Routledge.

Faragher, John Mack and Howe, Florence. 1988. *Women and Higher Education in American History*. New York: W.W. Norton.

Farmer, Ruth. 1993. "Place but Not Importance: The Race for Inclusion in Academe." In Joy James and Ruth Farmer, eds., *Spirit, Space and Survival: African Women in (White) Academe*. New York: Routledge, pp. 196–217.

Fine, Melinda. 1993. "You Can't Just Say That the Only Ones Who Can Speak Are Those Who Agree with Your Position: Political Discourse in the Classroom." *Harvard Educational Review*, Vol. 63, No. 4 (Winter).

Foster, Michele. 1992. "The Politics of Race: Through the Eyes of African American Teachers." In Kathleen Weiler and Candace Mitchell, eds., *What Schools Can Do: Critical Pedagogy and Practice*. New York: SUNY Press, pp. 177–202.

Gore, Jennifer M. 1993. *The Struggle for Pedagogies: Critical and Feminist Discourses as Regimes of Truth*. New York: Routledge.

Guy-Sheftall, Beverly. 1993. "A Black Feminist Perspective on Transforming the Academy." In Stanlie James and Abena Busia, eds., *Theorizing Black Feminisms: The Visionary Pragmatism of Black Women*. New York: Routledge, pp. 77–89.

Hall, Stuart. "Teaching Race." 1991. In A. James and R. Jeffcoate, eds., *The School in the Multicultural Society*. London: Harper and Row, pp. 58–69.

hooks, bell. 1990. *Yearning: Race, Gender and Cultural Politics*. Boston: South End Press.

hooks, bell and West, Cornel. 1991. *Breaking Bread: Insurgent Black Intellectual Life*. Boston: South End Press.

Hutchinson, Louise Daniel. 1981. *Anna Julia Cooper: A Voice from the South*. Washington, DC: Smithsonian Institute Press.

James, Joy and Farmer, Ruth, eds. 1993. *Spirit, Space and Survival: African American Women in (White) Academe*. New York: Routledge.

James, Stanlie M. and Busia, Abena, eds. 1993. *Theorizing Black Feminisms: The Visionary Pragmatism of Black Women*. New York: Routledge.

Johnson, Elizabeth. 1993. "Working-class Women As Students." In Michelle M. Tokarczyk and Elizabeth A. Fay, eds., *Working-Class Women in the Academy: Laborers in the Knowledge Factory*. Amherst: University of Massachusetts Press, pp. 197–207.

King, Joyce E. 1994. "Dysconscious Racism: Ideology and the Miseducation of Teachers." In Lynda Stone, ed., *The Education Feminism Reader*. New York: Routledge, pp. 336–348.

Lewis, Magda Gere. 1993. *Without a Word: Teaching Beyond Women's Silence*. New York: Routledge.

Lyons, Nona. 1990. "Dilemmas of Knowing: Ethical and Epistemological Dimensions of Teachers," *Work and Development*, No. 2, pp. 159–180.

Marshall, Catherine. 1993. *The New Politics of Race and Gender in Education*. New York: Falmer Press.

McKay, Nellie. 1993. "Acknowledging Differences." In Stanlie M. James and Abena Busia, eds., *Theorizing Black Feminisms: The Visionary Pragmatism of Black Women*. New York: Routledge, pp. 267–282.

Minnich, Elizabeth; O'Barr, Jean; and Rosenfeld, Rachel, eds. 1988. *Reconstructing the Academy: Women's Education and Women's Studies*: Chicago: University of Chicago Press, pp. 139–154.

Nobel, Jeanne. 1988. "The Higher Education of Black Women in the Twentieth Century." In John Mack Faragher and Florence Howe, eds., *Women and Higher Education in American History*. New York: W.W. Norton, pp. 87–106.

Perkins, Linda. 1988. "The Education of Black Women in the Nineteenth Century." In

John Mack Faragher and Florence Howe, eds., *Women and Higher Education in American History*. New York: W.W. Norton, pp. 64–86.

Shor, Ira. 1992. *Empowering Education: Critical Teaching for Social Change*. Chicago: University of Chicago Press.

Shor, Ira and Freire, Paulo. 1987. *A Pedagogy for Liberation: Dialogues on Transforming Education*. South Hadley, MA: Bergin and Garvey.

Siraj-Blatchford, Iram, ed., 1993. *Race, Gender and the Education of Teachers*. Buckingham: Open University Press.

Tokarczyk, Michelle M. and Fay, Elizabeth A., eds. 1993. *Working-Class Women in the Academy: Laborers in the Knowledge Factory*. Amherst: University of Massachusetts Press.

Weiler, Kathleen. 1988. *Women Teaching for Change: Gender, Race and Power*. South Hadley, MA: Bergin and Garvey.

Williams, Patricia. 1991. *The Alchemy of Race and Rights*. Cambridge, MA: Harvard University Press.

9

Entre la Marquesina y la Cocina

José Solís

Yo quise ser, como los hombres quisieron que yo fuese: un intento de vida; un juego al escondite con mi ser. Pero yo estaba hecha de presentes, y mis pies planos sobre la tierra promisora, no resistían caminar hacia atrás, y seguían adelante, adelante, burlando las cenizas, para alcanzar el beso de los senderos nuevos.

Julia de Burgos
"Yo misma Fui Mi Ruta"

Morning entered the window of the bedroom where I slept in my grandparents' home in Caguanas, a *barrio* of Utuado, Puerto Rico. Besides, my sleep had long since been disturbed by the crowing roosters who had no respect for the dark; their morning song began long before sunrise, as if they were engaged in a competition to determine who could call on the morning light first. In any case, I would pull back the mosquito net from the bed and prepare for another day of adventures in childhood.

Abuela mami (grandmother mom) and Abuelo papi (grandfather dad), as we called them, had a relatively small home. The new concrete-walled structure replaced the old large wooden house. This new home had three bedrooms and a small extra room designed for their youngest son, Adrian, my uncle, one who didn't survive the Vietnam war. Size and space never seemed to trouble us, especially the children. It was family reunion time and there were eight married sons and daughters with a roster of grandchildren converging on *el campo* (the country, a reference used when speaking of Caguanas). It could have been any-thing, *Navidades* (Christmas), *Día de Los Reyes* (Three Kings Day), *Día de Pascua* (Easter), *Año Nuevo* (New Year's), someone's birthday, or just an occasion to get together. Regardless, we were together, and that's what mattered. For us as chil-dren there was space to run and explore. During the two or three days of reunion, time was filled with the thrill of playing with farm animals, fabricating our own fireworks, picking and eating fruits and vegetables from the mountainside farm, pitching marbles on the hard earth bordering the driveway leading up to the house, launching paper boats in the little, rich, red muddy streams (the result of a short Puerto Rican rain), bathing in the river, and so many more pleasing ex-periences, including enduring bee stings and mosquitos. But there was something peculiar about the geography that characterized our togetherness.

While whizzing like flies in and out of the house, screen doors slamming behind us, by then a distant voice of someone, usually an adult woman, shouting *no tiren la puerta* (don't slam the door), we (cousins and friends) found ourselves crossing borders. The critical consciousness of spaces was not present then as it is now. For us, it was simply the way things were. Notwithstanding, there was the in-nocuous impression that space had been mapped out, with the requisite borders delineating the possibilities and limitations of entry and participation. As children we could traverse this to some degree. You see we were border crossers, exploring the world. But our socialization had heretofore introduced us to and would pro-gressively forge us into compliant keepers of distinct spaces. Each of us identified places that we considered most endearing to us individually. I liked sitting on the flat-roofed house, scoping the hawks as they soared above in the Puerto Rican big blue skies of the country; or walking amid the vegetation, exhilarating myself with each inhalation of a thousand scents, aromas, and smells making their way simultaneously into me; or playing chase with my cousins on the farm. Others liked to hound the hens, tangle with the dog, or sleep, among other child-sanctioned activities. I don't remember thinking about how the girls felt or thought. The girls in the family seemed to be just fine. I mean, surely my grand-mother and aunts would remind the girls that this play or that was "boys' stuff." Yet, for the most part, there too was an allotment, not strict but apparent, between the girls who did stuff with the boys and those who sought other activity—I guess more conducive to the different expectations established for girls. But there was an understood convention, a body of tacit assumptions that, while not strict, made it nevertheless unequivocally clear that certain spaces conformed to specific groups.

La marquesina (the carport) was set up for playing dominoes. There was a table, usually in the middle of the floor, with four chairs, and maybe a radio or tape player. A large cooler was at hand, with the requisite 20-pound bag of ice; and there were limes, plastic cups, and gallons of Cutty Sark, J&B, and Don Q. This was "man" space. We played there too, though we were often reminded that they needed to concentrate and our disturbances might interrupt the match. I don't recall any animosity toward our presence, which was at best considered tolerable and not encouraged. Nevertheless, it was man space. Seated in four chairs facing one another, the men focused on the dominoes at hand. The space was restrictive in the social sense, or so I thought. How could one work their way into the space to get some attention, to engage? The space and dynamics of the dominoes game contributed clearly and carefully to a definition and determination of how such a geographical construction of space could legitimize the presence of the four players and the exclusion of any others from participation. It seemed something like trying to pass through some kind of force-field. This arrangement had a built-in discourse and activity that, given the strict rules of the game, excluded any nonplayer. Very little space was provided to partake in any other discussions that might unveil the complexity of togetherness and as such demystify the family's relationships. In man space they spoke of Puerto Rico's impending incorporation into the United States as the 51st state. Never was this a theme for any in-depth discussion other than the same narrowness with which space was defined in *la marquesina* generally. They talked of women and sports, and the headlines. Every so often one of us (border crossers) was asked to fetch a cold beer from the kitchen for one of them; or asked to go summon someone (a woman) from the kitchen to deliver one to them. And so we would zoom through free lands into another space and geography.

La cocina (the kitchen) was indoors. This was "woman" space. The space was considerably less defined in its restrictive configuration, though it too exemplified specific activity—but it was different to me. First there was the aroma of foods being prepared. For children burning calories as quickly as we consumed them, the kitchen was a haven where we were reenergized. There was so much stirring in the kitchen area—*abuela mami*, mama, and my aunts doing a thousand things simultaneously. There were *plátanos* (plantains) being peeled, the stripping of beans from their pods, rice being steamed, the grinding of fresh spices from the garden, plucking chicken feathers from the limp bodies of those funny dead white hens that would soon become a main ingredient in one of those beautiful Puerto Rican meals, the always-present aroma of home-grown coffee waiting to be sipped, and so much more. While the space was a kind of rainbow for the senses, just making it to the refrigerator for a drink of cold water was a frenetic run through a gauntlet of frenzied life. But there was something portentous about *la cocina*. We actually took part in the discussions. Yes, the children were spoken to and spoke in woman space. I guess maybe dialogue there seemed more obliging to me. There was talk of schools, and the neighbors, of illness, and friends, and sometimes of other women and men—but the talk of men and women was not in the same context as in man space. And yet here too I felt that there was something very particular about what the women knew and experienced that helped shape the discourse in the kitchen. Somehow this seemed again strange and restraining. Man and woman space had different talk that maybe had some-thing to do with the way space was manufactured, understood, and occupied. And again, maybe I came to understand that these borders were as much defense mechanisms for the survival of some inexplicable identity as they were parameters from which our identities were in part forged. These identities now however seem more like imposed abstractions of a reified culture whose existence is capacitated by the contingency of imposed cultural definitions truncating the creative and liberating potential of a people, particularly a colonized people.

So what made the dialogues in la cocina such a consolation? Maybe I had internalized the abstractions and as such acquiesced, accepting the tradition of woman space as nurturing and man space as something else. As children we were certainly being prepared for life in one of those geographies and the dialogues fortified the spaces. How to decolonize the spaces and as such our cognizance of one another across gender lines in Puerto Rico did not disquiet me then but it challenged a real part of my life as I became a public school teacher and then a university professor—and many questions remained. How could I promote the decolonization of Puerto Rico without decolonizing the abstraction of Puerto Rican women from our pedagogy? And how do we educate one another to discern that the process of decolonizing education means decolonizing ourselves and that this understanding might afford a contribution to the commitment necessary to struggle to liberate our nation? Paulo Freire reminds us that "liberatory dialogue is a democratic communication which disconfirms domination and illuminates while affirming the freedom of the participants to re-make their culture" (Shor and Freire, 1987, p. 99).

Given Freire's assertion, improved possibilities for decolonizing Puerto Rico are to be found in the pedagogical and political struggle to overcome the ubiquitous predisposition to manufacture identity through the abstractions of history and culture, abating experience as a reference, while promulgating culture as inertia. This means that the dialogue and different activities regarding decolonization must brave those borders that have traditionally placed feminism in Puerto Rico's independence struggle in a peripheral location, effectively reinforcing the marginalization of Puerto Rican women.

This chapter will examine how the abstraction of difference and identity reinforces a colonial pedagogy and as such limits the potentiality for a liberation of self and people. I will note how, as a Puerto Rican male professor, I am confronted with my own contradictions and limitations in my contributions to a decolonizing pedagogy and nation; how these limitations are transformed by my affirmation of the centrality of Puerto Rican women, not as an omniscient constituency of Puerto Rican colonialism, but in the redefining of centers and in the process of decolonization, as an autonomous reality impossible of substitution by any counterfeit assumptions. Finally, the chapter will briefly look at a couple of contemporary efforts to outline curriculum practices along nonsexist lines that argue for gender equity.

The critiques herein are driven by my concern with the relationship that what we say we want to do in Puerto Rico in the name of decolonization is obligated to insist upon decolonizing educational practice. In other words, as noted by Jennifer Gore (1993) in The Struggle for Pedagogies, to critically understand the pedagogy we argue for and the pedagogy of the argument. Striving to liberate ourselves is as much about the pedagogy in practice, about its process, as it is about the goal of liberation. To speak of one without invoking the other is to reinforce the generalizations that abstract and remove liberation from the process of liberating, which mystify education and sustain colonialism. The decolonization of our identity as a construct then requires mindfulness in the development of any emancipatory process. Among other things, this obliges us to examine how and why experience is abstracted.

DECOLONIZATION AND THE ABSTRACTION OF EXPERIENCE

The process of decolonization has conventionally been defined as that course of political transference of power from the colonizer to the colonized, effectively proclaiming the birth of a new nation-state. Invariably, the universalization of emphasis on political independence or sovereignty (if such is even the case for many of the ex-colonies) promotes the obfuscation of a transformative notion of decolonization. Amilcar Cabral (1994, pp. 39–56) in "National Liberation and Culture" notes:

The ideal for foreign domination, whether imperialist or not, would be to choose: either to liquidate practically all the population of the dominated country; or to succeed in imposing itself without damage to the culture of the dominated people—that is, to harmonize economic and political domination of these people with their cultural personality.

What Cabral did not account for was how the imposition of the colonizer was inextricably tied to and permeated the very fabric of the culture of the colonized. The proliferation of the values of the colonizer are manifest in the very life of production and religious and social habits manufactured simultaneously with the onslaught of colonial relations, impacting how the colonized view the colonizer and themselves—and these aspects of colonialism obscure the transformative possibilities of decolonization as long as the focus remains on the prerequisite of political independence alone. Since the cultural damage experienced by the colony outlives the transfer of political sovereignty, liberation from many of the "old habits" becomes considerably more difficult to accomplish, giving way to new colonizers in the form of, for example, the World Bank, the International Monetary Fund, for some even the United Nations, with its most recent patterns of U.S.-sponsored dictates; not to mention the persistence of sexism, racism, and classism, or other elitist substitutes for class.

I am a bit concerned by current discourses that assert a postcoloniality in the world today. I am compelled to assume that some of these affirmations are couched in some strict political allusions to decolonization. And yet there remain colonies, of the so-called classic type. From the standpoints of international law, economics, history, and politics, the colonial realities of numerous nations in the world today seem to have been passed over by the same reliance on a discourse manufactured by former colonizers and imported and internalized by too many scholars in hopes of naming a contemporary world differently, based on the experiences of some and the exigencies of contemporary imperialist idioms that have managed to co-opt much of the emancipatory element of language and, as such, international law. There is also, I believe, a compulsion to get on with the work of developing new discourses for the sake of intellectual exercise, at the expense of critically understanding the dangers embedded in this.

A simple understanding of Puerto Rico's history, for example, reveals the present colonial character of the country under U.S. domination. Interestingly, however, challenges to the official knowledge in academe on the topic of Puerto Rico are often quickly buried. To me this is, in one instance, evidence of how realities can be mystified even by those attempting to demystify colonialism, and also an example of how we so often find comfort zones in a critique of distant issues, since attention to the proximity of others might implicate us and demand that we change in real and personal ways.

Nevertheless, built into the sufficiency of the political transfer posture is an abstraction of the process of decolonization. Certainly the declaration of independence of a colony is a part of the decolonization process. However, to interpret this act in a totalizing manner reduces the significance and occludes the transformative potential of a decolonizing process: of "substituting one species of human with another," which is what Frantz Fanon (1994) referred to when he spoke of decolonization and which distinguished much of his concern with the transformation of "national consciousness" to "social consciousness." The concoction of Michel Foucault's notion that each of us is a site where "generalized operations of power press ineluctably on the subject," along with the Lacanian perspective that everyone is subjected to and colonized by the Law of the Father, and the postmodern assertion that all "I"s are colonized through irresistible interpellations—all these universalize and abstract colonization and as such decolonization (Watson and Smith, 1992, p. xiv). The likelihood of developing a decolonizing pedagogical project is virtually foreclosed by the inescapable condition of subjected colonized "I"s. Against this universalization of colonization, Puerto Ricans must then forge a pedagogical process of decolonization that redefines a strategy for advancing issues of gender, people, and place, not by placating the differences in the colony, but by enlisting these differences in the process of informing our effort to redefine culture.

While gaining independence is central to this struggle, the development of people committed to such a project will depend on whether we have been transformed by our own education of what decolonization means. In Puerto Rico, much of the debate regarding this continues to focus on the economic parameters of different status options. Again, the point is not to somehow abstract or downplay the import of economic analysis in developing and delivering an argument for decolonization. The point is, however, that in spite of the economic grip vis-à-vis federal transfers in Puerto Rico (e.g., food stamps, welfare checks, and social security) as a people we must reevaluate the argument of such a reading and its pedagogy, inasmuch as these advance decolonization in the broadest sense, and the mileage gained by restricting our efforts to the oversimplification of economic analysis as a pedagogical instrument. Among other things, this means that Puerto Rican educators need to engage in and develop projects that adhere to the principle of decolonization as "the substitution of one species with another." This includes the struggle to address notions of identity and our work to demystify gender.

The subjugation of identity is first consummated by the violent act of colonization—the domination and occupation of a people and their land. The processes that ensued—economic development projects, education and language of instruction, the establishment of legislative and juridical bodies under colonial rule, and the psychologization of consumerism of all that is of the colonizer's origin, as if somehow all of this was by fiat finer, more improved, developed, and modern—accelerated the colonial agenda responding to configurations designed by the colonizer. This process, however, informed the developments of resistance campaigns against the colonizer, nourishing efforts to differentiate between the colonizer and the colonized. Among these efforts was the appeal to a Puerto Rican identity.

The politics of a national identity has its roots in the equation of Western imperialist developments that engendered the antagonistic interactions between colonized and colonizer and can still be referred to as the "epistemology of imperialism" (Said, 1993, p. 308). One of the products of this line of thinking and being has been the development of a national essentialism. The characterization of a people was exacted and significantly defined in a laundry-list manner. While the colonizer and imperialist constructed an identity of themselves on the negation of the "Other," the colonized appealed to their history of traditions to resist. This has the effect of challenging the colonizer's legitimacy. Appeals to language, ancestry, physical attributes, dress, preferences for works of art, foods, literature, geographical location, and so on were all evaluated on the basis of their approximation to some pure national being, a kind of idealized form.

The point here is not to dismiss the fundamental importance of these in the context of developing a sense of cultural and national being and resistance, especially for colonized people. The point is that strict adherence to such qualifications are neither accurate nor reflective of the dynamics of cultural development and transformation—and as such can straightjacket the possibilities for developing a decolonization struggle predicated on a broader terrain of intellectual and political pedagogical endeavor aimed at national liberation.

Issues of language and other culturally distinguishing features, which do differentiate peoples and nations, need to be addressed in the context of calls for difference as this relates to the material and ideational development of a people and their contribution to the transformation of the tradition of domination. For example, I've often heard many Puerto Ricans tell me that "those Puerto Ricans in the United States are different." "Obviously they're different," I would respond, "but so are you and I." The implication advocates that somehow Puerto Ricans in the United States are a little less Puerto Rican. Granted the experiences and location wherein those experiences occur differ, bearing some significance on the development of identity; and this is certainly of considerable import as it plays into the exigencies of Puerto Ricans in Puerto Rico that Puerto Ricans in the United States, for example, need to return home to "get the yankee out." Nevertheless, in terms of the list of attributes noted above, such a notion of identity has proven problematic, since existentially how we exact who we are is as much determined by our reading of an identity as it is determined by external factors that identify us; the space for differences and debate thus prevails.

Again, such a position is also imbued with class undertones, since many unemployed and underemployed Puerto Rican migrants to the United States are the first victims of the mirage of colonial economic policies. The fact that they leave Puerto Rico does not endow anyone to make determinations about their position on the Puerto Ricanness spectrum, any more than the fact that many Puerto Ricans in Puerto Rico who position themselves high on the cultural scale go to Hollywood-made movies, wear Levis, drive Buicks, and have cable T.V. The facility with which such arguments can freeze a pedagogical project aimed at working for decolonization is obvious. Needless to say, the rejection of or resistance to artifacts and goods identified as colonial or belonging to the colonizers and their cultural imperialistic project constitutes an element of the broader opposition to a sustained colonial reality in hopes of fashioning new and different possibilities.

This opposition is couched in the perceived need to identify with that which validates self, culture, and nation in the colony. Such acts are constituted by the negation of the artificial—that is, the imposition of the colonizers' values that generate the meaningfulness of their goods, language, and habits. Simultaneously, and related to the side of the potentiality of liberation in the acts of resistance, attention is given to the constructive prospects of the colonized. Here meaning is created on the premise of national aspirations and need. Culture and its processes and products are infused and enlivened by the symbiotic environment where the imposed culture of the colonizer is transformed by resistance to it, and it is re-created to become an instrument of the liberation struggle. The linguistic, technological, and epistemological strategies of the colonizer are made into the blueprints for an architecture of decolonization. And yet our experiences remain consequential in developing ways to create identity that insists upon its liberation.

Granted different experiences yield potentially divergent identities. The problem with subscribing to experience as the determinant of identity is that what we experience is not, by logical requirement, necessarily defined unilaterally. Again, such a notion reifies the person or people, disengaging them from the definitions of their experiences in ways that might contribute to their own development and emancipation. Without a doubt, the colonialism experienced by Puerto Ricans is only known by Puerto Ricans. The colonialism experienced by Puerto Ricans in the United States is also only apperceived by those. Yet, understanding this, struggling with it in the context of the decolonization effort, should be seen as a challenge to transform decolonization from a merely political, linguistic, and procedural act to one that changes our conceptualizations of national liberation and as such ourselves as Puerto Ricans. This means, among other things, a precise examination of the abstraction of difference among Puerto Ricans.

It is beyond the scope of this chapter to elaborate on the abstraction of identity in Puerto Rico. However, in the context of developing some thoughts about my own pedagogical practices as a male Puerto Rican student of Puerto Rican feminism as central to the kind of decolonization that transforms place and people, I find it necessary to mention just a couple of general points about the abstraction of difference. The next section will spend a bit more time on this as it relates to Puerto Rican women.

Earlier in this chapter, I made references to some of the problems one encounters when attempting to generalize and define notions of identity in absolute terms. In some ways, similar issue can be taken with the abstraction of difference. For example, while all Puerto Ricans experience colonialism, not all experience it alike. A doctor in Puerto Rico, a professor, or a lawyer experience colonialism differently along class lines, but so too from one another. These experiences are certainly differentiated from those of the unemployed, or semiemployed farmworker, or from the urban dweller or the rural population, and differently between lighter-skinned and darker-skinned Puerto Ricans, and from male and female Puerto Ricans. There may be some who view in this differentiating a kind of subscription to some postmodern dismissal of a collective in favor of the primacy of the individualistic notions of subjectivities beyond which anything else seems imposed and artificial. But this need not be the case. Actually what is being attempted here is to note that experiences, inasmuch as they inform us, as we them, ideationally, of what, with, and why we identify as ourselves, need to be freed of their abstraction and relocated in the real world of the people living them. From this point we are in a better position to articulate how history and the creation and recreation of culture are both dynamic and developmental; not things that threaten our identity, but enrich our best possibilities for overcoming colonialism in its many forms.

The abstractions of difference and identity are in part grounded in an over-emphasized reliance on ideas that inform how we evaluate the concrete. This notion gives precedence to the ideational, similar to the hierarchical and mistaken binary divide assigned to theory over practice, thereby affirming that the idea of what culture is—that is, some preordained set of standards into which Puerto Ricans are cast—cannot become the basis for recreating culture in the context of a national liberation effort. Instead, the colonized are forced to regurgitate culture as a set of artifacts dictated to them. There remains then the need to proceed beyond the epistemological frame, which reduces difference and identity to simple binary constructs as in the case of models found in strict adherence—for example, to class or language, language or race, and race or gender—as strict positions for analyses.

In Puerto Rico, then, we need to pay close attention to how education reinforces those binaries at the expense of broadening the possibilities for understanding how these inform one another. For example, the decolonization of Puerto Rico requires the decolonization of Puerto Rican women—not after the fact but as a primary part of that which will define and from which decolonization will be evaluated. While the issues confronting Puerto Rican women here become pivotal, assertions of national interests cannot be considered independent priorities, since such claims only serve to reify liberation and any pedagogy aimed at overcoming sexism. The process of decolonizing and demystifying here can be upheld synonymously. There are then reasons to assert that decolonizing Puerto Rican women compels us to demystify the ways in which we have abstracted womanhood in Puerto Rico and feminism's struggle in the colony to develop pedagogical strategies.

PUERTO RICAN WOMEN, FEMINISM, AND DECOLONIZATION

The geographical configuration of space and the discursive activities that grew out of *la marquesina* and *la cocina* have the effect of mystifying experience and entrenching contradiction, inasmuch as the meanings of being, difference, and location in history and culture are strictly defined by the symbiosis of real, and at the same time, mythic space. The struggle for me as a male Puerto Rican committed to decolonization is not argued from the perspective of substantiating one discourse over another; nor of aggrandizing discursive lists of appreciable language to verbiage that continues to dominate and define legitimacy. Rather, my concern is threefold. First, how do our dominant conceptualizations of the Puerto Rican woman inform a decolonizing pedagogy? Second, what impact has this had on how Puerto Rican feminism is being advanced in its challenges to curriculum practices in education? And finally, how have Women's Studies and other feminist programs in Puerto Rico advanced practical pedagogical solutions to these issues?

In Puerto Rico, as in many cultures where the power of male dominance has organized and defined space and meaning of and for women, the stereotypical references to women are, without reducing this to a laundry list of confining particularities, most generally understood as those that are domestic and private. Puerto Rican women are persistently referred to in generalized ways that abstract their experience, an experience reduced to private spaces.

Women bear the burden of being "mothers of the nation" (a duty that gets ideologically defined to suit official priorities), as well as being those who reproduce the boundaries of ethnic/national groups, who transmit the culture and who are the privileged signifiers of national difference. The demands of the "nation" may thus appear just as constraining as the tyranny of more primordial loyalties to lineage, tribe or kin, the difference being that such demands are enforced by the state and its legal administrative apparatus rather than by individual patriarchies. (Kandiyoti, 1994, p. 377)

Although the history of Puerto Rico is replete with examples of women who struggled to work for the improvement of the conditions that characterized their realities (Acosta-Belén, 1986; Azize, 1979), official accounts of these remain imbued by the same demands noted by Deniz Kandiyoti. Nevertheless, while accounting for the strength of Puerto Rican women to resist domination through their activity and leadership in the development of campaigns for improved educational, labor, and living conditions generally in Puerto Rico, there remains a need to more critically address how these and other aspects of Puerto Rican women's experiences sustain colonialism and their domination by not broadening the analyses beyond the contributions women have made to change within the patriarchy. At the same time, there should be examination of the emancipatory possibilities of accounting for those aspects in a decolonizing pedagogy.

I will not address accounts of the roles that different social institutions have played in engendering and inculcating specific roles for women in Puerto Rico. As previously stated, let us note that the reference to the domestic applies to all those traditions so often reiterated in critiques against the domination and subordination of Puerto Rican women (work, leisure, academic development, sexuality, and art, among others). Even when some measure of change has occurred, it has generally been in response to certain conditions that oftentimes intensify colonialism. In the colony, most changes relevant to women's issues, though having their origins in the efforts and sacrifices of women, are swiftly co-opted and subverted by colonial powers that effectively neutralize their radical potentials.

The symbols of modernization and development manifested in different changes affecting the lives and labor of Puerto Rican women are often simultaneously affirmed in the same breath as the completion of superhighways, new shopping malls, or the expansion of U.S.-owned and -controlled industries in the colony (Kandiyoti, 1994, p. 380). Bound by the national context, Puerto Rican feminism is again reduced to its object status. A decolonizing pedagogy that hopes to reverse this has before it the task of working to redefine the centers of the national effort. My interest here, however, is to examine how identity grounded in generalizations and abstractions of Puerto Rican women impact the response from Puerto Rican feminists and the significance of this for a decolonizing pedagogy, with specific relevance for male Puerto Rican educators committed to national liberation.

In terms of their identity, abstractions of Puerto Rican women are as much a result of the tools of analysis that are called upon to explain Puerto Rican women as they are related to a reliance on the myths that become real(ized) vis-à-vis references to things such as natural law. Here resides the requirement to oppress, since Puerto Rican womanness is imposed by the traits of the myth-forming abstractions (ideation) actualized by the power of male dominance and colonialism. For example, more conservative elements may assert that Puerto Rican women have a greater responsibility for the home than, say, Puerto Rican men. This kind of argument situates women as the standard bearers of corporate identities and boundary markers of their communities, having a deleterious effect on the emergence of Puerto Rican women as makers of the movement for national liberation

(Kandiyoti, 1994, p. 388). A common response among Puerto Rican feminists to arguments of this kind draws from various elements of feminist discourse—for example, radical feminism, socialist feminism, Marxist feminism, and liberal feminism, to mention some. But herein is where the pedagogical and decolonizing challenge begins.

The experiences and identities of Puerto Rican women become totalized and compartmentalized in the same manner other identities are understood. That is to say, as in many other instances, the reification and objectification of people, and particularly women, facilitates and reinforces our understanding and expectations of Puerto Rican women by establishing a standard from which deviations should be calculable. The development of feminist discourse and decolonizing pedagogy in Puerto Rico then needs to struggle against such reification. Herein is located the significance of the interconnection between history and experience of Puerto Rican women. Identity constructed along male or female lines, where the center is determined on the basis of an ideationalized gender, has the effect of oversimplifying experience and as such the experience of being female is then naturally related to being feminist as if by osmosis, rather than a broader and less strict terrain—not just the effect of being female (Mohanty, 1992, p. 77).

While a central tenet of modern feminism has been the assertion that "all women are oppressed," such a position "implies that women share a common lot, that factors like class, race, religion, and sexual preference, etc. do not create a diversity of experience that determines the extent to which sexism will be an oppressive force" (hooks, 1984, p. 5). In other words, by not recognizing the differences between and among colonized women in a colonized nation, and the multifarious dynamics that differentiate Puerto Rican women from, say, white middle-class feminists of the United States, Robin Morgan's (1984) assertion of the globalism of sisterhood actually strengthens the subordination of the experiences of women in general and Puerto Rican women in particular and abstracts the possibilities for developing a decolonizing pedagogy that could derive social and political strength from Puerto Rican feminism. The globalization of sisterhood situates all women outside their particular historical context, ultimately suggesting some variety of transcendence rather than engagement in models for social change.

Further problematizing the possibilities for a Puerto Rican feminist decolonizing pedagogy, oftentimes the class, radical, and socialist arguments tend to establish parameters that define feminism in ways that disallow, or at best limit, the necessary incorporation of analyses other than their particular ones. Importing arguments without critically noting the limitations that this can have, and how this contributes to an abstraction of Puerto Rican women and the subordination of their experiences, hinders the developments of a decolonizing pedagogy. This can result in the establishment of a kind of homogeneity of women produced not on the basis of biological essentials, but rather through the psychologization of complex and contradictory historical and cultural realities. Such homogeneous representations have a particularly alienating effect on poor and working-class

Puerto Rican women, since their concerns are cast as a subtext under the generalization of woman-as-oppressed without the obligation to validate their particular realities as experienced in a colony. This kind of transcendence then evokes negative responses to feminist issues in Puerto Rico.

The complex relations between behavior and representation are either ignored or made irrelevant; experience is collapsed into discourse or visa versa. Second, since experience has a fundamentally psychological status, questions of history and collectivity are formulated on the level of attitude and intention. In effect, the sociality of collective struggles is understood in terms of something like individual-group relations, relations which are commonsensically seen as detached from history. (Mohanty, 1992, p. 82)

For example, a class analysis that defines feminism along a strict class line does not necessarily acknowledge the reinforcement of colonialism and racism in feminist discourse that avoids the importance of these in feminist critique. And yet, the class and race needs of the colonizers in today's world remain a significant part of their existential logic. Within such dynamics, "the cultural and class identifications call particular women to specific psychological and cultural itineraries that may collide and/or converge with itineraries of race and nation" (Watson and Smith, 1992, p. xiv). The formula of the psychology of being coupled with the biology of gender becomes the soul of womanness. Her experiences as a colonized woman of color are invalidated, or at best subordinated, by an official line. A feminist Puerto Rican pedagogy then needs to expand its points of reference to develop educational strategies built on the needs and aspirations of different sectors of Puerto Rican women. This then highlights the significance of a decolonizing feminist project that emphasizes the fundamental task of accounting for how different experiences relate to and reinforce and/or resist colonialism.

Some arguments assert that the metaphor of *la cocina* and *la marquesina* is class-specific, reflecting the experience of lower-class Puerto Ricans. The assumption of course is that somehow middle- and upper-class Puerto Rican women do not experience this kind of geographical positioning. This might be explained by such assertions that these women have access to a lifestyle that frees them of such categories. But acquiring cultural currency and cashing in on spaces not provided in other settings does not liberate them from the problem. Spaces for upper classes are also manufactured along gendered lines. First, these women usually hire a poor Puerto Rican or, generally, a Dominican woman to care for their houses and chores, paid for by the currency acquired by membership in a higher class. Second, sexism in these classes still groups and significantly determines and defines times and spaces for men and women. Additionally, for many Puerto Rican women, working outside the home has not meant a change in power relations in the home.

In Puerto Rico, women have always been viewed as a cheap source of labor. Working-class women in Puerto Rico have been working in and out of the home throughout the history of U.S. colonialism. In addition to working in their homes and in industries such as needlework, tobacco, and garments, working-class Puerto Rican women have also held much of the responsibility for others' homes. These variations on the theme of domination, however, are not defined by those middle- and upper-middle-class women enlisting the labor of the poorer Puerto Rican women. Rather, the options available to these women are the result of the spaces provided by the patriarchy of colonialism. The argument that working-class women occupy the objectified gendered spaces, and that somehow the answer is to rise above that low class, reinforces the myth that gender oppression is somehow class-specific. Additionally, such an argument accepts the liberal notion that the concern is with obtaining power and not questioning the oppressive relations of power in society.

As a metaphorical construct, *la cocina* and *la marquesina* could be substituted by any of a number of spaces that transcend class and reinforce the myths of gendered identity and women's oppression in Puerto Rico. Additionally, a radical analysis might merely articulate an assertion of radical politics as in the case of an emphasis on identity and feminist lifestyles, creating a false sense that one is engaged in praxis.

However, praxis within any political movement that aims to have a radical transformative impact on society cannot be solely focused on creating spaces wherein would-be radicals experience safety and support. Feminist movement to end sexist oppression actively engages participants in revolutionary struggle; and this is rarely safe or pleasurable. (hooks, 1984, p. 28)

And again, liberal feminist discourse tends to lack an emphasis on resistance to domination. This of course is consistent with the liberal belief that women can attain equality with men of their class without challenging the cultural basis of group oppression. (hooks, 1984, p. 20)

Furthermore, an essentialist reduction of oppression to the issue of gender suggests a kind of hierarchy of oppression, again implying an agenda for Puerto Rican feminists in a manner that reduces and abstracts their own experiences as women from a colony of the United States, with all of the classist, racist, and sexist realities that Puerto Rican women encounter daily—an encounter that white middle-class feminists of the United States, for example, do not experience.

Bonding as victims, white women liberationists were not required to assume responsibility for confronting the complexity of their own experience. . . . Identifying as "victims" they could abdicate responsibility for their role in the maintenance of perpetuating sexism, racism, and classism, which they did by insisting that only men were the enemy. They did not acknowledge and confront the enemy within. (hooks, 1984, p. 46)

There remains then a serious need to develop a feminist decolonizing pedagogy that critically examines feminism in the context of a colonized Puerto Rico—a context in which racism and classism, among other forms of domination, interact in order to sustain colonialism and as such to promote sexism. As noted by Margarita Ostolaza Bey (1989, p. 25) in her book, *Politica Sexual en Puerto Rico,*

In the meantime, regarding the question of focal importance in feminist debates over who the enemy is, the answer according to our analysis would be that it is the male dominant sexuo-gendered system and its sexist ideological content. To this enemy add its accomplices: colonialism and dependent capitalism and all forms of oppression that these generate, those that complement and reinforce one another.

And yet, it is not clear that here feminism accounts carefully and critically for the forms of domination that, say, white middle- and upper-middle-class women reinforce in ways that sustain the mystification of Puerto Rico's colonial situation, in particular as it is experienced by poor Puerto Rican women. Locating Puerto Rican feminism in its proper cultural and historical context aids in the demystification of colonial relations experienced by Puerto Rican women in ways that bring racism and classism into the discourse of sexism and the development of national liberation projects that assert the position that there can be no national liberation without the transformation of gender, race, and class relations.

Puerto Rican women are further disadvantaged in terms of having access to certain power structures that white U.S. feminists use to export their feminism to Puerto Rico. In another sense, however, Puerto Rican women have the power that comes from being who they are and in a position, as no one else, to forge a meaning of the struggle in their image and responsive to the concerns facing them and their nation. Feminism is not owned by those with the power to export it like a commodity seeking markets.

The educated Puerto Rican feminist is often viewed and critiqued by men and some other women as imitating white U.S. or imported feminism—clearly an indication of how some feminists have actually contributed to sustaining myths and abstractions of Puerto Rican women and their identity. There is in this as much a critique of education as of feminism. The object of the critique rests on a sense that education represents a part of one's life that is not by necessity a reflection of one's culture and its realities. Education remains a technical challenge for the acquisition of the colonizer's cultural capital. Credentialized, the colonized becomes admired and yet distanced. The affirmation that development and education are culturally constructed is not part of the lexicon of the colonized, and this has serious implications for a feminist pedagogical project.

This places a certain responsibility on Puerto Rican feminists for forging an agenda that has as its *modus vivendi* the realities of Puerto Rican women in a colony, and the anticolonial struggle, not subsumed by class or race analysis, but informing how class and race analyses are constituted, among other ways, as experienced and recreated by women working for national liberation (Mergal, 1991, pp. 3–4). The onus is also on Puerto Rican male educators to affirm that the responsibility of asserting decolonization in both pedagogical and political senses is impossible if not for the simultaneous transformation of our gendered subjectivities. Puerto Rican men committed to liberation then are compelled logically to struggle with our own sets of contradictions as we work to transform space and power and as such our conceptions and relations with Puerto Rican women.

The definitive constructs of gender and place, reinforced in my travels as a child from *la marquesina* to *la cocina* and back, informed my socialization in ways that accelerated a future of contradictions. The politics of this socialization taught me that women were somehow to be loved and hated, revered and humiliated, exalted and exploited, shared with and competed against—all simultaneously (Ostolaza Bey, 1989, p. 41). This dehumanizing contradiction, however, is analogous to any oppressor-oppressed relationship. It is through oppressing another or others that the oppressor understands his identity and gathers his strength. The reliance on oppression for his identity then commits the oppressor to a series of contradictions from which he is unable to liberate himself; and which in turn dehumanize him. As noted by Paulo Freire (1990, p. 42) in the *Pedagogy of the Oppressed*, "only the oppressed can free the oppressed; and only the oppressed can free the oppressor." Or in the words of Audrey Lorde (1993, p. 10), "the master's tools will never dismantle the master's house." Throughout my life as an educator, this socialization has constantly challenged me and my struggle to contribute to the decolonization of Puerto Rico—an effort whose meanings and significance continue to be transformed, among other things, by the work of Puerto Rican women.

This, however, is not to be understood as a reaffirmation of the universalization of oppression along strict gender lines. We are reminded that

women in lower classes and poor groups, particularly those who are non-white, would not have defined women's liberation as women gaining social equality with men since they are continually reminded in their everyday lives that all women do not share a common social status. Concurrently, they know that many males in their social groups are exploited and oppressed. While they are aware that sexism enables men in their respective groups to have privileges denied them, they are more likely to see exaggerated expressions of male chauvinism among their peers as stemming from the male's sense of himself as powerless and ineffectual in relation to ruling male groups [colonizer], rather than an expression of an overall privileged social status. (hooks, 1984, p. 18)

The point is that as a male educator the process of decolonizing education is synonymous with the process of decolonizing gender and nation. An attempt to subvert one while attending to another or others is equivalent to the abstraction of a decolonizing pedagogy. The development of educational programs that examine and contribute to transforming oppressive relations has become of central significance to various educational projects in Puerto Rico. Concern over gender and curriculum in schools has been the focus of many conferences, workshops, and curriculum development projects. The final section of this chapter will briefly examine some of these.

TOWARD A DECOLONIZING FEMINIST PEDAGOGY

During the summer of 1993, I had the privilege of meeting in Puerto Rico with different feminist scholars working in the area of education and gender. Much of the material I was presented reflected a profound commitment on the part of many Puerto Rican women and men to change educational practices that reinforced the subjugation of women. The generative theme of the work was gender equity in education, which included efforts to forge a nonsexist curriculum in Puerto Rico's education system. The corpus of projects developed over the past few years synthesized the history of inequality along gender lines in Puerto Rico, and there has been an attempt to develop projects that will reflect a more equitable educational experience. Numerous publications grew out of the many workshops, programs, and conferences held in Puerto Rico. This section will briefly highlight some of the ideas presented in two different publications, as these articulated a variety of concerns related to gender and equity in Puerto Rican education.

Included in the strategies outlined at a 1990 roundtable discussion on gender equity, sponsored by the Comisión de Asuntos de la Mujer (Commission on Women's Affairs, a governmental entity) were assertions that discrimination can be overcome only when the conditions that engender this are overcome (Zayas, 1990, p. i). Accounts of the tireless efforts of women to address gender in the curriculum were noted in the context of their failures to obtain the support of administrators (Azize, 1990, pp. 22–23). Concerns were raised and recommendations made for changes in teacher education and certification (Rodríguez, 1990, pp. 52–57). The Comisión de Asuntos de la Mujer and Pro-Mujer (the project for Women's Studies at the Colegio Universitario de Cayey) spearheaded much of the work on gender equity in the university curriculum. In March 1992, Pro-Mujer published *Hacia un Currículo No Sexista* (Toward a Non-Sexist Curriculum). The publication addressed different concerns related to gender in the introductory course of study in the social sciences, as well as Spanish and English.

Reflecting upon the literature provided me by Pro-Mujer, I kept two points of principal significance in mind. First, is the pedagogy of the argument consistent with the pedagogy argued for? And second, what were the political implications of these analytic strategies and principles (Mohanty, 1991, p. 55)? In other words, was political agency critically and carefully accounted for? Generally, I was compelled, after a more careful reading, to examine the different forms of domination reinforced by ideas that in one instance seemed to advocate a decolonizing pedagogy.

As I understand the effort, the goal is to create a nonsexist curriculum, one that asserts gender equity. At one level such an assertion appears universally acceptable, since opposition to equity of any sort would be perceived as an affront to the principles of empowerment. But might there not be conceptual differences between the notions of gender equity and nonsexist curriculum? First, inherent in any statement of equity are implications that reinforce the legitimacy of the status quo. To speak of gender equity is, in part, to recognize that, all things considered, the system and its institutions are either acceptable because they seemingly allow for such reforms or simply because the project for Puerto Rican feminists is to seek some kind of equity with men—equity in a male-dominant system, from a male-dominant discourse that promotes the exploitation of women, the poor, and reinforces a sustained colonialism in Puerto Rico. And again, equity arguments downplay the significance of the conflict at hand for Puerto Rican women.

The reliance on an equity paradigm additionally subverts the possibilities for such a pedagogy to be decolonizing. As mentioned earlier, to speak of a decolonized education as if issues of gender were somehow significant but peripheral is as much an abstraction and a contradiction as it is to believe that a nonsexist education can be promoted in a colonial context without attending to how racism, classism, elitism, and other forms of oppression advance sexism in a colony. We need to understand and develop programs that critically address the relationship of gender subordination to the history, education, and evolution under colonialism, and the interrelatedness of gender to colonialism and of colonialism to classism and racism in Puerto Rico. Such programs cannot be the exclusive domain of intellectuals or members of particular classes. A pedagogy of Puerto Rican women for decolonization must be forged from the efforts of persons, particularly women, with the objective to engage women and, in some instances, men in all walks of life in the process of curriculum development and implementation. The curriculum must be introduced as a living source of development and not a body of knowledge to be internalized and regurgitated. Equity as a modus operandi does not promote the necessary conceptual and practical constructs to critically approach those relationships and to forge an education capable of decolonizing. This educational project cannot not be additive, procedural, or technical. Changes that simply add to the curriculum, propose different procedural possibilities, or suggest technical variants are effective in contributing to decolonizing gender only to the degree that these respond to the framework of women's voices as they challenge colonialism. As ends, the additive procedural, and technical elements do not pose a threat to a sustained colonial patriarchy.

Feminism in Puerto Rico, as an educational project against sexist oppression, challenges not only *what* is taught but *how*, in the context of transforming domination. If equity were sufficient, the relationship that discourse has to practice would be violated, since practices result from choices and choices from values that are contextualized. In other words, the places and institutions that sustain certain sexist, classist, and racist practices and values would somehow, simultaneously, be reinforced and challenged by a discursive activity that finds them repulsive and oppressive. Finally, there is a classist undertone to a gender equity argument. Generally speaking, this position sees access to a share of the power held by men as the goal. The transformation of power arrangements and the relationship that this has to other forms of oppression in Puerto Rican society are not accounted for in an equity argument, and may actually reinforce sustaining colonial relations of macro and micro proportions.

The efforts to develop a nonsexist curriculum, in the document provided, gathers much of its argument from the developments of women's studies programs. The pedagogy here has historically concentrated on the voices of women and the exclusion of these from different areas of education, rather than on developing a feminist pedagogy. Two questions then might be asked of the effort to decolonize gender in Puerto Rico. First, what is a feminist pedagogy in Puerto Rico? Second, what makes a particular pedagogy feminist (Gore, 1993, p. 18)?

Part of the problem with contextualizing a feminist pedagogy is to be discovered in an understanding of the history of educational discourse. Educational discursive activity has historically been advanced from the notion that ideas or facts are the building blocks of educational discourse. Both, it has been argued, can be explained outside the realm of human interpretation—that is, human experiential and social environmental influence. In other words, educational discourse has, in some significant ways, reinforced the abstraction and colonization of experience and language.

The challenge to Puerto Rican feminism is made manifest from the possibilities that nonsexist or antisexist pedagogy has for the material and social transformation of the marginalization of women and place. "Our research efforts should locate these processes of marginalization and issues of AIDS, crime, illiteracy, and drug addiction in the context of Puerto Rico's reality and analyze them from a feminist perspective" (Mergal, 1991, p. 15). I would add other issues, including child care, domestic violence, and rape, to mention but a few. Yet what makes a particular approach feminist has to be defined or at least understood as such. Again, how does a feminist critique of issues differ from any other critique? And what are the implications for developing a decolonizing pedagogy upon such a different analysis? If our concern is to develop a nonsexist education, these issues seem significant given that the subordination of women remains a political and pedagogical project for national liberation of epistemological and linguistic significance that women alone, in some ways, can articulate. Clearly, this has implications for the development of culture and the struggles that will ensue.

The following items are part of what a pedagogy for decolonization premised on the voices of women should be:

1. It should be the product of Puerto Rican women from all sectors of the nation.

2. As such it will then encourage a critical appraisal of the colonial situation, forging the development of a popular culture capable of uniting women in a decolonization effort.

3. It should draw from the history of patriarchy in Puerto Rico to critically understand that sexism in Puerto Rico is related to colonialism and, as such, to be struggled against in the context of Puerto Rican women's realities. Global statements of gender oppression oversimplify the emancipatory potential of women in different places to liberate themselves and their people.

4. Puerto Rican men have a responsibility to understand that they are sexist by virtue of the privilege given them, regardless of attitude, in a male-dominant society. Puerto Rican male educators must also develop a curriculum premised on the notion that there is

no national liberation or decolonization without the transformation of our gendered subjectivities.

5. Every act and preparation for the development of a Puerto Rican woman's decolonizing pedagogy needs to consider the political and moral awareness of women and men in the nation. This will inform the effort to design and implement particular educational projects at any given time.

As a male educator I am challenged by a host of contradictions. For example, I would argue that there is no decolonizing pedagogy for Puerto Rico that is not understood as a political challenge to U.S. colonialism. I would assert that only by forging an independent Puerto Rico can we logically account for a pedagogy that is decolonized. However, there is no way we can affirm decolonization merely by changing the political relationship, though certainly sovereignty provides space that other relationships do not. It is then incumbent upon me to work to transform the pedagogical practices in Puerto Rico that contribute to discursive activities that reinforce colonialism. Puerto Rican male educators committed to the decolonization of Puerto Rico must come to terms with the position that it will be the Puerto Rican woman who will shatter her chains and break free from those who have engendered our dependency upon her subordination. This requires of us a great deal of self-critique and praxis. Struggling to defeat the enemy of colonialism without, we are challenged by Puerto Rican women to comprehend the colonizer within, and we recognize that she must fight against our socialized condition, if you will, to dominate her.

The development of antisexist curricula is, to me, synonymous with a decolonizing pedagogy. Among other things, this means that the very character of educational institutions needs to be transformed. Reliance on assumptions in contemporary education, for example, as in the design of expanded syllabi or canons, only reinforces the utilitarian and instrumentalization of education. The best critical test of our assumptions about education might be found in the exchange that creating and recreating knowledge with people outside academe could offer. The technification and mechanization of education continues to distance it from human interaction. Decolonizing pedagogy means, among other things, that the geography of traditional educational arenas where learning and teaching take place must be transformed. Higher education, for example, has insulated itself by assuming that what it attends to provides a sufficient position from which to name the world. This has entrenched intellectualism, nurturing the presumptuousness of radical scholars.

Without active involvement with communities of Puerto Rican women in clinics, neighborhoods, schools, offices, farms, factories, unemployment lines, and in the streets, feminism—like all other so-called transformative pedagogical discourse—is doomed to remain frozen by a language of transcendence. Action is prompted by knowing. But knowing alone does not compel one to act. When knowing is born from engagement with the world, and not merely contemplation, the transformation of the material, of the real, is a requirement for the promotion and advancement of human development. Contemplative knowing satisfies itself with itself, nothing needs to change, nothing does. Feminist pedagogy as a decolonizing project in Puerto Rico must challenge female and male educators to decolonize their own elitism and general assumptions about education. To decolonize our education means that we must begin to go outside our schools and universities to construct an education responsive to the realities of our people and not make our people responsive to an artificial set of educational standards that are, for the most part, imported and are severely limited in their ability to describe, explain, and prescribe a pedagogy of decolonization. This is an abstraction.

Whether in language, social sciences, natural sciences, or literature, the development of nonsexist curricula as decolonizing needs to engage with communities outside a university setting. Organizing groups of women and of women and men to study the development of education projects as these relate to their needs and aspirations might provide the pedagogical setting for decolonizing education to take place—that is, the pedagogy argued for becomes consistent with the pedagogy of the argument. While myths persist in reinforcing the formations of our identities, ultimately only by deconstructing those myths will we be able to travel in ways that engender a respect for and solidarity with difference and the transformative possibilities that present themselves when differences meet and struggle as power is redefined.

REFERENCES

Acosta-Belén, Edna. 1980. *La mujer en la sociedad puertorriqueña*. Río Piedras: Huracán.

———, ed. 1986. *The Puerto Rican Woman: Perspectives on Culture, History, and Society*. New York: Praeger Publishers.

Azize, Yamila. 1979. *Luchas de la mujer en Puerto Rico*. San Juan: Litografía Metropolitana.

———. 1987. *La Mujer en Puerto Rico*. Río Piedras: Ediciones Huracán.

———. 1990. *Estrategias para la Equidad por Sexto en la Educación* (Comision para los Asuntos de la Mujer). San Juan: Unidad de Investigaciones.

Burgos, Julia de. 1975. *Antología poética*. San Juan: Editorial Coqui.

Cabral, Amilcar. 1994. "National Liberation and Culture." In Patrick Williams and Laura Chrisman, eds., *Colonial Discourse and Post-Colonial Theory*. New York: Columbia University Press.

Centro de Investigaciones Sociales de la Universidad de Puerto Rico, Centro de Estudios, Recursos, y Servicios a la Mujer (CERES). 1986. *Participación de la Mujer en la Historia de Puerto Rico*. New Brunswick, NJ: Rutgers University.

Comisión para los Asuntos de la Mujer. 1990a. *Mesa Redonda: Estrategias para la Equidad por Sexo en la Educación*. San Juan: Unidad de Investigaciones.

———. 1990b. "Desarrollo de Curriculo y Equidad Educativa." *Mesa Redonda: Estrategias para la Equidad por Sexo en la Educación*. San Juan: Unidad de Investigaciones.

Comisión para los Asuntos de la Mujer, Oficina del Gobernador, Facultad de Educación. 1993. *Educación Y Género: Equidad, Justicia, Y Paz*. Río Piedras: Universidad de Puerto Rico.

Fanon, Frantz. 1994. "On National Culture." In Patrick Williams and Laura Chrisman, eds., *Colonial Discourse and Post-Colonial Theory*. New York: Columbia University Press.

Freire, Paulo. 1990. *Pedagogy of the Oppressed*. Trans. Myra Bergman Ramos. New York: Continuum.

Gore, Jennifer. 1993. *The Struggle for Pedagogies: Critical and Feminist Discourses as Regimes of Truth*. New York: Routledge.

hooks, bell. 1984. *Feminist Theory: From Margin to Center*. Boston: South End Press.

Hostos, Eugenio María de. 1969. *Obras Completas*, Vol. XV. San Juan: Editorial Coqui.

Kandiyoti, Deniz. 1994. "Identity and Its Discontents: Women and the Nation." In Patrick Williams and Laura Chrisman, eds., *Colonial Discourse and Post-Colonial Theory*. New York: Columbia University Press.

Lorde, Audrey. 1993. "The Master's Tools Will Never Dismantle the Master's House." In Laurel Richardson and Verta Taylor, eds., *Feminist Frontiers III*. New York: McGraw-Hill.

Mergal, Margarita. 1991. "Las Mujeres, el sujeto popular y las Nuevas Formas de Lucha en Puerto Rico." Ponencia en la conferencia, Sobre la Realidad Colonial Puertorriqueña: Aquí y Allá. Chicago: unpublished paper.

Morgan, Robin, ed. 1984. *Sisterhood Is Global*. Garden City, NY: Anchor Books.

Ostolaza Bey, Margarita. 1989. *Política Sexual en Puerto Rico*. Río Piedras: Ediciones Huracán.

Pro-Mujer. 1992. *Hacia un Curriculo No Sexista*. Cayey: Proyectos de Estudios de la Mujer Colegio Universitario de Cayey, Puerto Rico.

Rodríguez, Carmen. 1990. "La Equidad como Problemática." In *Mesa Redonda: Estrategias para la Equidad por Sexo en la Educación*. San Juan: Unidad de Investigaciones.

Said, Edward. 1993. "The Politics of Knowledge." In Cameron McCarthy and Warren Crichlow, eds., *Race, Identity, and Representation in Education*. New York: Routledge.

Shor, Ira and Freire, Paulo. 1987. *A Pedagogy for Liberation: Dialogues on Transforming Education*. South Hadley, MA: Bergin & Garvey.

Talpade, Chandra Mohanty. 1991. "Under Western Eyes: Feminist Scholarship and Colonial Discourse." In Chandra Mohanty Talpade, Ann Russo, and Lourdes Torres, eds., *Third World Women and the Politics of Feminism*. Bloomington: Indiana University Press.

———. 1992. "Feminist Encounters: Locating the Politics of Experience." In Michele Barrett and Anne Phillips, eds., *Destabilizing Theory: Contemporary Feminist Debates*. Stanford, CA: Stanford University Press.

Valle Ferrer, Norma. 1979. "Primeros fermentos de la lucha feminina en Puerto Rico." *Revista del Instituto de Cultura de Puerto Rico*, Vol. 22, No. 84 (July-September), pp. 15-19.

Watson, Julia and Smith, Sidonie. 1992. "De/Colonization and the Politics of Discourse in Women's Autobiographical Practices." In Sidonie Smith and Julia Watson, eds., *De/Colonizing the Subject: The Politics of Gender in Women's Autobiography*. Minneapolis: University of Minnesota Press.

Williams, Patrick and Laura Chrisman, eds. 1994. *Colonial Discourse and Post-Colonial Theory*. New York: Columbia University Press.

Zayas, Yolanda. 1990. "Introducción." In *Mesa Redonda: Estrategias para la Equidad por Sexo en la Educación*. San Juan: Unidad de Investigaciones.

10

Deconstructing Mainstream Discourse Through Puerto Rican Women's Oral Narratives

Lourdes Torres

Learning how to listen to the voices of others is of vital importance as teachers are increasingly confronted with classes of students from diverse national, racial, and ethnic origins. This context can be problematic for teachers who lack experience with persons outside of their own racial and/or ethnic identity group. Even after educating themselves about men and women from different groups, teachers often rely on stereotypes as they relate to unfamiliar others. After a lifetime of exposure to print and audiovisual media that either abound in negative images of people of color, or render them invisible, one-dimensional generalizations are not easily unlearned.

In this chapter I will explore Latina representations of self in oral narratives of personal experience produced by Puerto Rican women. The discourse of Latinas about themselves is obviously different from the narrow representations of Latinas most white Americans encounter in the media, one body of dominant discourse from which knowledge of others is acquired. I briefly describe basic characteristics of mainstream representation and then introduce the discourse of Puerto Rican women of different generations to explore how these women construct their multiple, sometimes contradictory, subjectivity through language. The study documents how internalized sexism and racism are inscribed in the narratives of Latinas at the same time that their voices engender resistance and self-determination. The approach to listening to the voices of Puerto Rican women through discourse analysis of everyday talk rejects monolithic, static representations of women of color in favor of a more complex, multifaceted reading.

MAINSTREAM CONSTRUCTION OF LATINO MEN AND WOMEN

We interact with diverse systems of representation as we construct our perceptions of self and others. For persons living in homogeneous contexts, the media may be the exclusive means through which to encounter others who are outside of personal networks. Thus the mass media is a powerful tool in the shaping of society's prejudices and biases. According to C. Clint Wilson and Félix Gutiérres (1985, p. 67) the media make frequent use of stereotypes to "quickly bring to the audience's collective consciousness a character's anticipated value system and/or behavioral expectations." Stereotyped images serve to foster or reinforce prejudiced viewpoints and racist attitudes.

Since its inception, Hollywood has perpetuated an unfavorable portrayal of Latinos/as. In the first two decades of American movies, Latinos were presented in denigrating films, featured as rapists and murderers in productions such as *Tony the Greaser* (1911) and *The Greaser's Revenge* (1914). In the 1930s and 1940s, the few Hollywood pictures that featured Latinos presented them as irrational and with hot temperaments. Latinas were typically portrayed as lascivious sex objects. The 1960s featured Puerto Ricans in updated "greaser" films. For example, *West Side Story* (1961) remains for many the only media portrayal of Puerto Ricans ever seen. The movie emphasizes violent, knife-wielding street kids, and the two major parts for women represent the two sides of the whore/virgin dichotomy. Reinforcing a pattern that continues today, Latina women are presented as sex objects or as passive doormats, mainly attending to the needs of family, husband, and children.

In Charles Ramírez Berg's (1990) analysis of stereotypes of Latinos/as in Hollywood, he finds that the portrayals of woman can be classified in four main types. The first type, "the half-breed harlot," appears especially in westerns: women are presented as lusty, hot tempered, and oversexed. "The female clown" is featured in the Mexican spitfire series, where women are presented as goofy Ricky Ricardo counterparts; they are silly and bumbling—for example, Carmen Miranda and others. "The Dark Lady" character is a mysterious, virginal, distant, reserved, and alluring sexual figure. Another stereotype, which also appears in many of the Latino-produced movies, is the long-suffering mother. Rosa Linda Fregaso (1993) examines some of the contradictions of the mother role in two recent films, *La Bamba*, a Latino-made movie, and *Boulevard Nights*, an Anglo-made film. Both portray the mother as the cause of a son's downfall.

In summary, as Richie Pérez (1990) suggests, the mass media approach to Puerto Ricans (and other Latino/as) features three strategies: exclusion, dehumanization, and discrimination. For the most part, Puerto Ricans are just not presented as part of the American culture. When they appear, they are portrayed in an offensive manner. In most films women figure in the virgin/whore dichotomy; they are basically one-dimensional, sexualized or passive, primarily presented as bearers of meaning instead of makers of meaning (Ramírez Berg, 1990,

p. 293). Since the 1980s, which brought more Latino/a involvement in film production, some positive perspectives on Latinos/as have emerged from Hollywood
in films such as *Zoot Suit* (1981), *The Ballad of Gregorio Cortez* (1982), *La Bamba*
(1987), *The Milagro Beanfield War* (1988), and *Stand and Deliver* (1988). Unfortunately, even in films produced by Latino/a producers and writers, the women
represented are one-dimensional, stereotypical, and simplistic.

More complex readings of the portrayal of women in the mainstream Hollywood films are possible; nonetheless, even when produced by Latino males, the
general tendency in films remains: the complexities of women's lives remain unex-
plored and their reality simplified.

The mass media is not the only source of monolithic and racist representations
of Latinas. Another example of denigrating discourse can be found in the social
science literature about the Puerto Rican. Much of the early literature follows
along the lines of works by Oscar Lewis such as *La Vida: A Puerto Rican Family
in the Culture of Poverty—San Juan and New York*, which presents Puerto Ricans
as a defeated, morally deficient population. More recent "pseudo" social scientific
works, like Linda Chavez's *Out of the Barrio: Toward a New Politics of Hispanic
Assimilation* (1991), continue to perpetuate a view of the Puerto Rican as a welfare
prototype, condemned to a life of violence, poverty, and misery. Fortunately,
more complex interpretations of Puerto Rican life in recent works (i.e., Rodríquez,
1989; Comas-Díaz, 1988, 1989; Walsh, 1991; and the Language Policy Task
Force, 1982, 1988) contest this perspective.

METHODOLOGICAL APPROACHES TO WOMEN'S
NARRATIVES

Because the mainstream images of Puerto Ricans and most people of color are
so limited and biased, students and teachers who wish to learn about marginalized
communities are truly challenged. When people of color are included in school
curriculum at all, although not as overtly racist, the representations presented are
often as one-dimensional as what is offered in the media. As Deborah Britzman
et al. (1993, p. 188) state, "newly represented cultures appear on the stage of
curriculum either as a seamless parade of stable and unitary customs and
traditions or in the underdeveloped form of particular heroes modeling roles."
The complexity of peoples' lives is entirely lost. Another problem that occurs
when a dominant group tries to understand people from different ethnic or racial
groups is that they may interpret the whole construct of ethnic identity as a
question of individual choices rather than as collective experience intimately tied
to social structures and economic forces (Sleeter, 1993, p. 165).

Britzman et al. (1993, p. 189) recommend that multicultural studies should
commence with an understanding that the representation of ethnic and racial
identities are "overburdened" with interpretations and meanings that learners
have experienced in the course of their lives. We cannot really choose these
meanings, especially if they are part of dominant discourses of the media and

education, but we must challenge and transform them. Since reality is mediated through these systems of representation, we must constantly construct and re-construct our understanding through interaction with such systems. It is not that any one system of representation is complete or better than another, but rather we come in contact with many readings and form our views based on these presentations, our interpretations of them, and our own interactions with people.

These numerous readings condition our expectations about, for example, members of ethnic groups with whom we have not had a lot of contact. Despite our good intentions, often it is the racist representations that are deeply ingrained in our psyche. As Mari Matsuda states (1993, pp. 25–26):

At some level, no matter how much both victims and well meaning dominant-group members resist it, racial inferiority is planted in our minds as an idea that may hold some truth. The idea is improbable and abhorrent, but because it is presented repeatedly, it is there before us. "Those people," are lazy, dirty, sexualized, money grubbing, dishonest, inscrutable, we are told. We reject the idea, but the next time we sit next to one of "those people" the dirt message, the sex message is triggered. We stifle it, reject it as wrong, but it is there, interfering with our perception and interaction with the person next to us.

Given this reality, it is challenging to listen to others without projecting onto them a monolithic understanding based on our preconceived expectations. One approach to this is to study speakers' discourse and consider how people represent themselves in oral narratives. Through their stories, Puerto Rican women actively construct their lives and formulate images of themselves. By focusing on their perspectives in a given moment, I do not want to create yet another stable, unitary identity, but I wish to highlight the contradictions and complexities of their discourse and representation of self. While the narratives of Puerto Rican women reflect the internalization of dominant discourse, they also exemplify how women resist messages of passivity and inferiority received from the dominant and home cultures.

I do not intend to present the *puertorriqueñas* as the unique source of truth or the producer of the master narrative, but rather explore some of the contradictions in their language around sexism and racism in their lives and that of their communities. Studying the discourse of Puerto Ricans offers one means of shattering recurrent myths and stereotypes about Latinas in the dominant culture.

My framework for analyzing oral narratives is derived from Teun van Dijk's (1984, 1987, 1993) work on the racist stories majority group members tell about minority persons. Insight into community norms and biases can be reached through an examination of topic development, argumentation, semantic and pragmatic strategies, and other discourse properties (Torres, 1992).

The data presented are obtained from a larger study on Puerto Rican life in a New York suburb (Torres, n.d.). I interacted with and interviewed community members of all ages over a period of two years. I recorded interviews only after becoming acquainted with the participants of the research. These lasted approximately two to three hours and focused on the general topic of Latino/a life in New York. For the purposes of this chapter, I will discuss only the Puerto Rican women's narratives. First-generation women are those who were born and raised in Puerto Rico and came to the United States as adults; they tended to be in their 50s and 60s when I interviewed them. Second-generation woman were born and raised in New York and were in their late teens or early 20s at the time of the interviews.

PUERTO RICAN WOMEN'S DISCOURSE ON GENDER

When examining the oral narratives of women of different age groups, there are apparent generational differences in how women talk about themselves and their communities. However, the stereotypical image of the passive Latina woman is absent even in the narratives of women from the oldest generational group. Conversely, even in the stories of the youngest members of the community, the internalization of patriarchal discourse is manifest.

Older women seem more likely to explicitly sanction sexist behavior from men. The narratives of first-generation women are replete with traditional ideology concerning rigid sex role differentiation. Notions of *machismo*, whereby males have unlimited sexual freedom in spite of their marital status, are commonplace. For women, it seems that behavior is guided by the ideal of *marianismo*, which is built on the veneration of the virgin Mary, and implies that the woman should sacrifice the self for her man and family. Accordingly, women should be passive, and since they are presumed to be spiritually superior to the man, they should be able and willing to endure all suffering induced by the man (Comas-Díaz, 1988). Narrative A was offered by a women in her 50s, born and raised in Puerto Rico, who came to the United States as a young adult.[1]

Narrative A

1) right here there is one

2) that Jesus she already has seven children

3) she has seven

4) and she is with her husband

5) and he isn't around

6) because when he comes

7) he comes to beat her up

8) he has all those kids nervous and all

9) but also the woman has to make herself respected

10) because men are like children

11) yes, no, men are stronger than women

12) but we mentally we are stronger than them

13) and women must teach them

14) because they are children

15) one has to show them one's way

16) no this isn't like this

17) it's like this

18) it's like this

19) and sit down

20) not fight or anything

21) but because she let herself like that

22) and has more and more children

23) it's not like that

In this narrative, occasioned by a discussion of marriage, the storyteller essentially blames women for the situation they are in. Before she began the story, the narrator was contrasting her own successful marriage to the conjugal problems her adult children and some of the neighbors were having. In lines 1 through 8 she describes the situation of a young neighbor who has seven children and is abused by her husband. In lines 9 through 23 the narrator evaluates that situation, basically criticizing the woman and excusing her husband. In lines 5 to 8 she lists the husband's aberrant behavior: he is frequently absent, when present he beats his wife, and he makes his children nervous. Line 9 begins with the connective "but," signaling a concessive clause, which undercuts the aforementioned behavior as the narrator states that it is the woman who must make herself respected. This idea is supported in lines 10 through 18, where the narrator infantilizes the husband as well as all men, absolving them of any responsibility and insisting that it is women who must educate them since women are mentally stronger than men. This is a slight variation of the *marianismo* philosophy. In line 21 the concessive connective "but" again begins a statement that undercuts male responsibility, and in the rest of the story the narrator again faults the woman for letting herself be abused. She is also held solely responsible for continuing to have children (line 22), since the husband's role as a father remains invisible.

Through negative evaluation of the woman, lack of evaluation of the man, and frequent use of moves of concession (clauses introduced by "but" occur three times, in lines 9, 12, and 21) women are held singularly responsible for their situation. While a totalizing agency is assumed on the part of the woman, male agency in creating and maintaining a violent context is neither examined nor its absence noted. While women's strength is alluded to in the narrative, it is basically a negative strength to be used solely in the service of controlling male transgressive actions.

Other narratives of the first generation more positively negate the stereotype of the passive Latina. A main difference between the two generational groups is the degree of evaluation offered by second-generation women. While first-generation women tell stories that show much strength and resistance, they are more muted in their overt criticism of the male. Among traditional Puerto Ricans, aggression of any type is taboo, especially for women (Comas-Díaz, 1988). This lack of explicit commentary, however, does not mean that women necessarily conform to the status quo. Narrative B was told to me by a first-generation, 58-year-old woman who had come to the United States as a young adult with her husband. This story was part of a string of narratives about her physically abusive father who controlled the family through violence.

Narrative B

1) And one day he threw me out of the house

2) because he took my sister

3) in the Bronx, yeah

4) he took me

5) and and he took my younger sister to hit her into, against the wall

6) because he was like that

7) then I got up to take her away from him

8) mama didn't dare

9) but I dared

10) and and god what was that for

11) when, I "look [formal] leave that girl alone

12) how can you [formal] hit her against the wall?"

13) and he went and let her go

14) and he put her on the floor

15) and he gave me a punch, over here (points to her head)

16) that left me crazy

17) and he told me,

18) "and now you [informal] get the hell out of here right now"

19) and I took and I went out into the hall

20) and mama said,

21) "You [formal] are not going

22) the one that's leaving is him

23) come in here he is the one that's leaving"

24) and he said,

25) "I'm not leaving"

26) what happened, later he got to thinking

27) then it was that he left for Puerto Rico, remember?

28) and he said that between my mother and me we had hit, we had hit him in the face

This narrative contests the stereotype of the passive Latina and demonstrates the contradiction of accepting sexist behavior and at the same time defying it. The terms of address are indicative of the power relations in the narrative. Even in the heat of the argument the narrator and her mother refer to the father and each other with the formal you (lines 11, 12, and 21) while the father uses the informal you (line 18) when speaking to his daughter. Minimal evaluation typifies this story and this is especially ironic considering the dramatic content being conveyed. For example, the narrator understates the rationale for the father's repeated violence. "He was like that" (line 6) is the only comment on his behavior. Also understated is the narrator's defiant move against the father, and the mother's final siding with the daughter against the father. Curiously, she also leaves without comment the father's ludicrous resolution of the story (line 28). This narrative, typical of the discourse of older women talking about males, demonstrates the tendency toward few external evaluations of males, demonstrates the tendency toward few external evaluations of males, while simultaneously conveying women's strength and resistance to male aggression.

One might expect that the younger generation of Puerto Rican women would react more overtly to male domination given the different geographic, generational, social, and cultural experiences they have had. Unlike their mothers, they have grown up in a context where they have available more options and representations of what being a woman means. Indeed younger women, born and raised in the United States, have a more direct articulation when referring to male-female relations, although many of the characteristics found in first-generation discourse obtain in their language as well. Narrative C, told to me by a 21-year-old Puerto Rican women, captures this dichotomy. The narrative occurred in a discussion on relationships between the sexes; it was occasioned by a reference to my experience working at a shelter for battered women.

Narrative C

1) I have a friend like that

2) as far as that, ugh that disgusts me

3) I have a friend who lives on the next block

4) where I live now

5) and she is a real pretty girl okay

6) um her boyfriend is a real son of a bitch

7) he is machismo up to his ass I'm, I'm serious

8) he takes

9) if she goes outside okay

10) and talks with another guy as a friend nothing else

11) he—that's another thing that my boyfriend understands

12) that I have a lot of friends okay

13) it's not that I'm gonna lay all of them

14) but it's that

15) I just always been more friends with men

16) for some reason I feel that I get along with them better

17) understand, so he understands that

18) that other guy doesn't

19) if she goes outside

20) and a guy comes

21) and talks, as a friend nothing else

22) when she goes upstairs

23) he beats her up

24) she had on glasses for an entire week

25) because she had them all black okay

26) she has bruises a—forget it

27) she must have them everywhere

28) because he beats her up

29) but um she stays with him right—

30) I saw her at the doctor's one day right

31) and I started to talk with her

32) I said to her,

33) "What do you plan to do about him?

34) you know, do you like it when he beats you up?"

35) I mean cause I'm pretty sure

36) some women like it

37) come on, why would one stay?

In contrast to the language of first-generation women, in narrative C we notice the direct evaluation of male, sexist behavior, specifically in lines 6 and 7. There is also more explicit language about sex or the possibility of sexual encounters— for example, in line 13 the speaker uses very colloquial language to refer to sex.

In this story the narrator sets up a contrast between two types of women, those who get abused and those who do not. In lines 11 through 17 she interrupts a narrative about her friend who is a victim of physical abuse, to suggest how she is a different type of woman: she knows how to deal with men, both her boyfriend and others. In line 34 she reproduces a comment she made to this woman, asking her if she enjoys the beatings. She closes the narrative by blaming the victim (lines 35–37), suggesting that some women must enjoy getting beaten, otherwise they would not stay in the situation. While the narrator recognizes her right to live free from violence, her analysis is individualistic; and the ultimate responsibility for gender arrangements rests with the woman. Like the narrative by the first-generation speaker, this woman feels that it is each woman's obligation to teach her man to respect her, as the present narrator has done with her mate. At the same time, unlike narratives A and B, this speaker forcefully condemns male sexist and violent behavior.

In narrative D, an 18-year-old woman explains her reaction when her uncle tries to molest her. The woman defends herself physically and is able to get away from the man. She expresses her right to resist male sexual aggression; however, her discussion of the event uncovers community perceptions of sexual abuse and the bind it creates for women. In lines 1 through 26 (not reproduced here) the narrator told how as a little girl her uncle tried to rape her and she kicked him and ran away, but did not tell anyone. In the following portion of the narrative reproduced here, she explains how she defended herself when he tried to assault her again a year ago.

Narrative D

27) um recently, recently, about a year ago . . .

28) he tried again

29) and this time I was with Junior

30) I took a knife

31) this time I took a knife

32) and I told him

33) "you touch me

34) and you're going to have

35) you are going to be dead

36) because you are in my house

37) and I can say

38) that you got in my house"

39) and I told him

40) "please get out of my house

41) because if you don't leave

42) my, my bomb will explode

43) because my aunt never knew . . . you know

44) if she finds out

45) that you are here

46) that you weren't supposed to be here

47) you are supposed to be working

48) and she finds out

49) that you are here

50) and I almost had to stop you

51) but, you will be here bleeding

52) and she will see the proof

53) that you are alone with me

54) and you tried something"

55) because she wouldn't believe it

56) I am sure

57) that she would say that the woman
      that is a woman

58) that she got um, you know

59) right away they blame you

60) and I don't go for that

61) I told him . . .

62) it's better

63) that you leave

64) you know and with the knife in my hand

65) because if not, he would have, you know . . .

66) I was actually . . . that day I was really scared

At the same time that she expresses her fears and her efforts to defend herself, she documents that if she is attacked, the community may think that she instigated the encounter. She continually discusses the evidence that makes it clear that she is being victimized. She comes right out and states that her aunt will not believe her because the assumption is that it is always the woman's fault if she is assaulted and/or abused (lines 55–59).

The discourse of Puerto Rican women indicates that younger women raised in the United States have more options and are reinterpreting sex-role expectations within the culture. Still, women are understood to be ultimately responsible for consequences of their sexuality and what occurs to them because of this sexuality. In narrative D, for example, there is no discussion about bringing charges against the uncle for attempted rape, or holding him accountable in any way, since the case is interpreted as an individual, family matter. In my sample, a social analysis of women's rights is not developed at this point for this speaker or any of the second-generation Puerto Rican women.

DISCOURSE ON RACE

The discourse on race in the narratives is another site where contradictory messages are conveyed. While the Puerto Rican women of both generations express a consciousness about discrimination suffered by their ethnic group, also expressed is a denigration of black people, which reveals the internalization of American, dominant group norms or the norms learned in Puerto Rico. While historically many Puerto Ricans have denied the existence of racism on the island, discrimination against black Puerto Ricans has long been documented (Gordon, 1949, 1950; Rodríguez Cruz, 1965; Blanco, 1975). Given the context of intense racial mixture that has given rise to a population that is approximately 70 percent of mestizo ancestry, and the racial variation present in many Puerto Rican families, some have claimed that racism is unlikely. However, ample economic, political, and social evidence suggests the existence of a racially based social hierarchy on the island. While the temptation exists to conclude that racism has only become a problem due to influence from the United States, Maxine Gordon documents that the unequal treatment of blacks and Indians already existed in Spanish colonial times. Gordon (1950, p. 297) states: "The Puerto Rican Negro or mulatto justly fears the prejudice of many *Americano* outsiders. But many Puerto Ricans deny him equally effectively (though less overtly), protected by the dictum 'We have no prejudice here.' "

Like other Latin American countries, Puerto Rico's racial classification is not dichotomous, rather there is a range dependent on a skin-color spectrum that runs from black to brown (*trigeño*) to white. Face and hair features, as well as class and social position, also figure into the hierarchy. Aspects of this racial classification based on physical features are outlined by Lillian Comas-Díaz (1989, p. 182):

Racial differences are expressed according to gradations of colors and traits. For example: *mulato* is the equivalent of mulatto; *jabao* is light-skinned, but with features that indicate Black ancestry—equivalent to Black "yellow"; *grifo* is with Caucasian features but has frizzled/kinky hair; *trigeño* is olive skinned; and *negro* or *prieto* is Black.

U. S. racial ideology, based on a dual system where one is either white or nonwhite, undoubtedly also influenced Puerto Rican consciousness about race on the island and especially in the United States (Rodríguez, 1989).

Today in urban areas of the United States, Puerto Ricans and African Americans often live side by side. While some writers (Rodríguez, 1989; Flores, 1985) stress the Puerto Rican affirmation of their African roots visible in the music, arts, and language of Puerto Ricans in this multicultural context; others (Fuentes, 1992) point out that friction exists between Latinos and blacks in places like New York City where the two groups are frequently competing for scarce resources. Both points of view are valid and this contradiction is captured in the language of many of the narratives.

Narrative E was produced by a first-generation woman aged 60 who came to the United States when she was in her late teens. She was active in community politics in New York, particularly in the Latino/a struggles to secure equal rights in housing and education. In the following narrative the speaker denies that she is prejudiced; however, her comments reveal a racial bias. She answered a question about the relationship between blacks and Puerto Ricans in New York with the following narrative (which is not translated in the Appendix).

Narrative E

1) There's always that little bit of resentment

2) and it all comes from the way we are classified

3) you pick up a newspaper

4) says the black and Puerto Ricans, the black
and Puerto Rican, the black and Puerto Rican

5) and some of us do not wish to be classified
like that

6) I don't like it

7) I don't resent the blacks

8) and I could live next door to a black

9) *que es Latino* (who is Latino) very comfortably

10) cause I don't think of him as a black

11) I think of him as a Latino

12) and that's the thing you have to understand

13) in Puerto Rico, in Puerto Rico *un negro
es puertorriqueño primero* (a black is Puerto Rican first)

14) *y después tú le puedes decir negro, jabao,
mulato* (and then you can call him negro, yellow, mulatto)

15) *lo que te de la gana* (what ever you want)

16) but first I'm a Puerto Rican

17) and that's the thing that ties us

18) that we live in peaceful coexistence, the blacks and whites in Puerto Rico

19) because first we are Puerto Ricans

20) that unites us

21) and then you can classify me

22) cause then I am not blind

23) I can see who is black and who is white

24) all my daughters are married to black men, black Latinos

25) *porque* (because) we don't think of them as black

While the speaker initially acknowledges resentment toward blacks (line 1), she displaces this resentment by not expressing its subject and then minimizing it (a little bit); a few lines later (line 5) she generalizes her uneasiness about getting linked with black people, but still uses an undefined subject, "some of us." Finally, she takes a position in line 6, but concerned with self-presentation and the management of inferences, this move is quickly followed up with a denial that she resents blacks (line 7). The rest of the narrative attempts to rationalize her position. An apparent concession that she could live next door to a black in line 8 is undercut in line 9, where she specifies that she is talking about black Puerto Ricans.

Since the speaker is invested in differentiating Puerto Ricans from blacks, she must deal with the contradiction presented by black Puerto Ricans. She does this basically by favoring an ethnic classifying system as opposed to a racial system when it comes to Puerto Ricans. After revealing that Latinos/as who are black are not really blacks at all, but Latinos/as (lines 8–11), the narrator contrasts the racial system in the United States with that of Puerto Rico (beginning with line 13). According to this speaker, the connection through ethnicity or culture supersedes racial differences and allows for unity. She suggests that good relations between blacks and whites on the island are attributed to the denial of race as a primary identifier. She emphasizes this type of thinking by repeating it three times in lines 16 through 20, alternating first person singular and plural pronouns in her references. Then she offers the specific example of her own family, where apparently the racial characteristics of her sons-in-law are denied so that they may be accepted as Puerto Ricans (lines 24–25).

This contradictory discourse around race is manifested in second-generational narratives as well. While second-generation speakers are more direct in their discussion of ethnic prejudice as well as sexual oppression, like first-generation speakers they articulate biased sentiments toward people of color. However, they do speak out clearly against prejudice against Puerto Ricans. Narrative F presents the conclusion of a story by a young speaker who tells of being denied a job because she is Puerto Rican. She stated that she was trained by one woman and then the head employer refused to hire her when she interviewed her and noticed that she is a Puerto Rican. The narrator's aunt convinces her to take the case to court, where she is vindicated and must be hired. The following comments offer her evaluation of the situation.

Narrative F

1) well, they had to give me the job

2) and they almost didn't give it to me

3) I was so good at the job

4) that they used to give me the keys to close the place

5) so uh so that she understands

6) that just because one is Puerto Rican . . .

7) does not mean that one . . .

8) that one cannot have confidence in a Puerto Rican

9) because sometimes, we are better

10) than the same class of them . . .

11) that's the truth

The narrator criticizes whites for not trusting Puerto Ricans (lines 6–8). When given a chance she proves to be a valued employee, the one entrusted with closing the store (lines 3–4). In her evaluation of the situation, according to the narrator, the employer learns that Puerto Ricans can be more responsible than whites themselves (lines 9–10). The speaker believes that her personal experience and the moral of the story can be generalized for the entire Puerto Rican community. She progresses from using first person singular pronouns (1–5) when discussing her specific story, to an indefinite pronoun (7–8) as she generalizes her experience, and then she concludes with a first person plural pronoun form (line 9) when she defends her community.

While in many narratives there is a recognition of racism and discriminatory practices against Puerto Ricans in the United States, this sense does not unproblematically transfer to other oppressed groups of American society—for example, African Americans. The prestige stratification system according to color is played out in intimate relations as well. In a conversation about her present boyfriend, the same second-generation speaker who told the last story also produced narrative G.

Narrative G

1) my boyfriend now is black

2) he is a negro

3) but he is real light skinned

4) I don't care that he is black

5) because he treats me like a queen, understand

6) he knows how to treat me well

7) he is very jealous

8) because obviously I am white

9) you know, light skinned and all that

10) but as far as that goes

11) for me it doesn't matter what race
you are, you know

In lines 1 and 2 of narrative G, this speaker emphasizes race by stating in two ways that her boyfriend is black. In line 3 she uses a concessive clause to explain why he is acceptable. She feels she must justify her relationship further and emphasizes how well he treats her (lines 5 and 6). Perhaps feeling that even more explanation is warranted, she further explains that his great treatment of her and his jealousy is understandable because of the race difference between them (lines

7–9). Apparently, in her mind, the difference in their skin color dictates that he should be honored to be dating a lighter skinned woman. The color hierarchy described before is obviously referred to here, although in lines 10 and 11 the speaker claims that race is not an issue for her.

In their talk about both sex and race, Puerto Rican women reveal contradictory, complex positions as they verbalize their understanding of their lives and their communities. A unitary, prototype Puerto Rican woman cannot be projected onto the discourse of the community. Puerto Rican women are alternatively, and/or concurrently, passive and active, dominant and submissive, racist and committed to fighting injustice. The women's stories confound the monolithic portraits of Latinas in the media and other dominant discourses. Their words suggest that learning and teaching about Latinas, as any other marginalized group, entails the rejection of static models and the development of active listening skills.

NOTE

1. All of the narratives were originally produced in Spanish; see Appendix to this chapter for original text. In the Spanish version of this story and all other narratives, dialectal phonological processes are preserved.

APPENDIX

Narrative A

1) aquí mismo hay una
2) que bendito ya tiene siete hijoh
3) tiene siete
4) y está con el esposo
5) y no está
6) polque él cuando viene
7) lo que viene es a dale pela
8) tiene to esos neneh nervioso y eso
9) pero también la mujer tiene que darse a respetal
10) polque el hombre es como un niño
11) sí, no, el hombre es mas fuerte que la mujer
12) pero nosotras en mente somos mas fuerte que ellos
13) y mujer tiene que enseñale a elloh
14) polque elloh son niños
15) uno tiene que enseñale la manera de uno
16) no esto no eh así
17) es así

18) es así

19) y sentalse

20) no pelaer ni nada

21) pero como ella se dejó así

22) y tener mas que muchachoh y muchachoh

23) no es así

Narrative B

1) y un día me botó de la casa

2) porque cogió a mi hermana

3) en el Bronx, sí

4) me me cogió

5) y y cogió mi hermana pequeña para darle en contra la pared

6) porque él era así

7) entonces yo me paré para quitársela

8) mama no se atrevía

9) pero yo me atreví

10) y y bendito para que fue eso

11) cuando yo "mira deje esa muchacha quieta

12) como Ud. le va a dar con la pared?"

13) y vino y me la soltó

14) y la puso en el piso

15) y me ha dao un arevé a mi por aquí encima

16) que me dejó loca

17) y me dijo,

18) "y ahora te me largas de aqui ahora mismo"

19) y cogí y me salí al jol

20) y mama dijo,

21) "Usted no se va

22) el que se va eh él

23) entre pa dentro es él que se va"

24) y él dijo,

25) "yo no me voy"

26) lo que paso, después se puso a pensal

27) y entonces fue cuando se fue pa Puerto Rico, ¿te acuerdas?

28) y dijo que entre mamá y yo le le habían dao le habíamos dao en la cara

Narrative C

1) yo tengo una amiga así

2) as far as that ugg eso me da un asco

3) yo tengo una amiga que vive en el próximo bloque

4) donde yo vivo ahora

5) y ella es una muchacha bien linda okay

6) um el novio de ella es bien hijo de la
   gran puta

7) el es machismo hasta el culo I'm, I'm
   serious

8) él coge

9) si ella sale pa fuera, okay

10) y habla con otro muchacho de amistad na mas

11) él—eso eh otra cosa que mi novio entiende

12) que yo tengo muchos amigos okay

13) no eh que me la voy me voy a tirar a to

14) pero eh que

15) I just always been more friends con loh hombreh

16) for some reason I feel that I get along with them better

17) entiende, so él entiende eso

18) el otro muchacho no

19) si ella sale pa fuera

20) y un muchacho viene

21) y le habla de amistad na mas

22) cuando ella vaya pa arriba

23) le cae encima

24) ella estaba con unoh espejelos por una
    semana entera

25) porque lo tenía to negro okay

26) tiene bruises a—forget it

27) she must have them everywhere

28) because él le cae encima

29) but um se queda con él verda—

30) yo la vi en el doctor un día verdad

31) y empecé a hablar con ella

32) yo le dije

33) "¿qúe tú piensas hacer de él

34) tú sabe, a ti te gusta cuando te cae encima?"

35) I mean cause I'm pretty sure

36) a algunah mujereh le gusta

37) come on, ¿por qué se va a quedar?

Narrative D

27) ehte recientemente, recientemente, hace como un año atra . . .

28) trató de nuevo . . .

29) y esta vez yo ehtaba con Junior.

30) cojí un cuchillo

31) ehta veh coji un cuchillo

32) y le dije

33) "tú me llegas a tocar a mí

34) y tú vah a tenel,

35) vah a ehtal muelto

36) poque tú ehtáh en mi casa

37) y yo puedo decil

38) que tú te metihteh a mi casa"

39) y yo le dije

40) "pol favol vete de casa

41) poque si tú no te vah

42) se me, se me explota la bomba

43) because mi tía nunca supo . . . you know?

44) si llega a saber

45) que tú ehtás aquí,

46) que tú no estabas supuesto de estar aquí

47) tú estás supuesto de estar trabajando

48) y llega a saber

49) que tú estás aquí

50) y casi pueh yo te stop

51) pero, vas a estar aquí sangrando

52) y va vel la prueba

53) de que tú estás solo conmigo

54) y tú tratahte algo"

55) because ella no lo creería . . .

56) yo estoy segura

57) que ella diría que esa la mujer esa eh

una muher

58) que ella se puso eh, you know
59) right away lo culpan a uno you know . . .
60) y I don't go for that
61) yo se lo dije . . .
62) "mah vale
63) que tú te vayah"
64) you know y con el cuchillo a la mano
65) porque si no, me hubiera you know . . .
66) I was actually . . . that day I was really scared

Narrative F

1) pueh, me tuvieron que dar el trabajo
2) y de poco no me lo dieron . . .
3) era tan buena en el trabajo
4) que me me daban las llaveh a mí para cerral el sitio
5) because así eh que ella aprenda
6) que sólo pohque unc eh puertorriqueño . . .
7) no quiere decir que uno . . .
8) que uno no puede tener confianza con un puertorriqueño
9) because a veceh, nosotroh somoh mejoreh
10) que la misma clase de elloh . . .
11) that's the truth

Narrative G

1) mi novio ahora es moreno
2) el es negro
3) pero el es bien clarito
4) no me importa que el es negro
5) porque el me trata como una reina entiende
6) el sabe tratarme bien
7) es bien celoso
8) porque claro yo soy blanquita
9) tu sabe clarita y to eso

10) pero as far as that goes

11) para mi que no tiene que ver que raza tu eres, tu sabe

REFERENCES

Blanco, Tomás. 1975. *El prejuicio racial en Puerto Rico.* New York: Arno Press.

Britzman, Deborah P.; Santiago-Válles, Kelvin; Jiménez-Múnoz, Gladys; and Lamash, Laura M. 1993. "Slips that Show and Tell: Fashioning Multiculture as a Problem of Representation." In C. McCarthy and W. Crichlow, eds., *Race, Identity, and Representation in Education.* New York: Routledge.

Chavez, Linda. 1991. *Out of the Barrio: Toward a New Politics of Hispanic Assimilation.* New York: Basic Books.

Comas-Díaz, Lillian. 1988. "Mainland Puerto Rican Woman: A Sociocultural Approach." *Journal of Community Psychology* 16 (1988): 21–31.

———. 1989. "Puerto Rican Women's Cross-Cultural Transitions: Developmental and Clinical Implications." In C. T. Garcia Coll and M. L. Mattei, eds., *The Psychosocial Development of Puerto Rican Women.* New York: Praeger.

Flores, Juan. 1993. " 'Qué Assimilated, Brother, Yo Soy Asimiao': The Structuring of Puerto Rican Identity in the U.S." *Journal of Ethnic Studies* 13: 1–16.

Fregoso, Rosa Linda. 1993. "The Mother Motif in *la Bamba* and *Boulevard Nights*." In A. de la Torre and B. M. Pesquera, eds., *Building with Our Hands: New Directions in Chicana Studies.* Berkeley: University of California Press.

Fuentes, Annette. 1992. "New York: Elusive Unity in La Gran Manzana." *Report on the Americas* 26 (September): 27–33.

Gordon, Maxine. 1949. "Race Patterns and Prejudice in Puerto Rico." *American Sociological Review* 14: 294–301.

———. 1950. "Cultural Aspects of Puerto Rico's Race Problem." *American Sociological Review* 15: 384–392.

Language Policy Task Force. 1982. *Intergenerational Perspectives on Bilingualism: From Community to Classroom.* New York: City University of New York.

———. 1988. *Speech and Ways of Speaking in a Bilingual Puerto Rican Community.* New York: Centro de Estudios Puertorriqueños.

Lewis, Oscar. 1966. *La Vida: A Puerto Rican Family in the Culture of Poverty—San Juan and New York.* New York: Random House.

Matsuda, Mari J. 1993. "Public Response to Racist Speech: Considering the Victim's Story." In M. J. Matsuda, C. R. Lawrence III, R. Delgado, and K. Williams Crenshaw, eds., *Words that Wound: Critical Race Theory, Assaultive Speech, and the First Amendment.* Boulder, Co: Westview Press.

Pérez, Richie. 1990. "From Assimilation to Annihilation: Puerto Rican Images in U.S. Films." *Centro Bulletin*, Spring: 8–27.

Ramírez Berg, Charles. 1990. "Stereotyping in Films in General and of the Hispanic in Particular." *Howard Journal of Communications* 2 (Summer): 286–300.

Rodríguez Cruz, Juan. 1965. "Las Relaciones Raciales en Puerto Rico." *Revista de Ciencias Sociales* 9: 373–386.

Rodriguez, Clara. 1989. *Puerto Ricans: Born in the U.S.A.* Boston: Unwin Hyman.

Sleeter, Christine E. 1993. "How White Teachers Construct Race." In C. McCarthy and W. Crichlow, eds., *Race, Identity, and Representation in Education*. New York: Routledge.

Torres, Lourdes. n.d. "Puerto Rican Discourse: A Sociolinguistic Study." Unpublished manuscript.

———. 1992. "Women's Narratives in a New York Puerto Rican Community." In Lana F. Rakow, ed., *Women Making Meaning*. London: Routledge, Chapman and Hall.

van Dijk, Teun. 1984. *Prejudice and Discourse. An Analysis of Ethnic Prejudice in Cognition and Conversation*. Amsterdam: Benjamins.

———. 1987. *Communicating Racism: Ethnic Prejudice in Thought and Talk*. Newbury Park, CA: Sage Publications.

———. 1993. "Stories and Racism." In D. K. Mumby, ed., *Narrative and Social Control: Critical Perspectives*. Newbury Park, CA: Sage Publications.

Walsh, Catherine E. 1991. *Pedagogy and the Stuggle for Voice: Issues of Language, Power, and Schooling for Puerto Ricans*. New York: Bergin & Garvey.

Wilson, C. Clint II and Félix Gutiérrez. 1985. *Minorities and Media: Diversity and the End of Mass Communication*. Beverly Hills, CA: Sage Publications.

PART IV

Curriculum, Canon, and Syllabi: Who's Teaching What and How

11

Education in Community: The Role of Multicultural Education

Terence O'Connor

Mother: It was always said and written that every Gaelic youngster is hit on his first school day because he doesn't understand English and the foreign form of his name and that no one has any respect for him because he is Gaelic to the marrow. There is no other business going on in the school that day but punishment and revenge. . . .
Son: What you say is amazing and I don't think I'll ever go back to that school but it's now the end of my learning.
Mother: You're shrewd in your early youth.[1]

Across the street from the school, a mobile home and a small house stand next to each other. Several shingles hang awkwardly on the side of the house. A plastic deer poses in front of the mobile home. This marks the beginning of a small Indiana town, one reminiscent of the movie *Hoosiers*, 40 years later. At the crossroads in the center of town, three of the eight buildings are closed. The others look worn out. Sitting at the stop sign, I wonder if the school would really be better off connecting its curriculum to this little town.

It is not the first time I have had these doubts. How would linking the curriculum to street culture help children in a city block? How would we make learners ready for the global marketplace by focusing on lifestyles in the mountain hollows? It seems easier to argue that schools would serve students better by standing against these tawdry communities, offering a way out of their parochialism.

Hoosiers have given up on the local community. Over the last 25 years, they have moved their children away from their towns and into consolidated buildings. Schools have left their neighborhoods; teachers are no longer part of the town family; lessons do not prepare students for life among friends or local government. The genius of building a national education system around local schooling has yielded to a cosmopolitan faith.

For many Americans, progress toward a modern world meant moving from the isolated world of small communities to a single, great society.[2] Schools became public demonstration sites, where educators could model the new social order. Students were to be trained as national citizens. Lessons were aimed to deliver a common curriculum. Degrees were marketed as entrance requirements to the national labor force. The results are obvious. Today, schools serve as models of an illusory national culture, training children to participate in a grand cosmopolitan society that, in the end, has room for only a few.

The idea of a great society has so captivated the public imagination that signs of its failure to create an effective school system are ignored. The alienation that had come to pervade student and teacher lives was obvious in the works of early social scientists like Karl Marx, Max Weber, and Emile Durkheim (each of whom took this transition from local community to the great society seriously). The sense of disempowerment, apathy, and antiintellectualism that has grown in modern schools was anticipated in Charlie Chaplin's *Modern Times* and Aldous Huxley's *Brave New World*. Giorgio Morodor's use of rock music in his remake of Fritz Lang's silent film *Metropolis* carries this critique across the generations. Our faith in schooling for a great society has blinded us to the loss of human dimensions naturally woven into learning in local communities.

The most shocking and cruel examples of the effects of separating schools from community can be found in the stories of colonized people. Native American children were taken from their families and raised in the lessons of the Euro-American school. They describe the fear and loss this education brought into their lives.[3] Similarly, Africans were drawn away from their bush schools and put into mission education that stripped them of their abilities to fit into their homes. The tragic loss of connections between school and social life in colonial Africa were clear to the famous anthropologist Bronislaw Malinowski, but he also had the genius to see the same problem in America.[4] African Americans, he claimed, confronted the same disjuncture. Even today's schools create a similar sense of cultural confusion and defeat.[5]

Malinowski explained that such problems were likely if education was not tied to culture in three ways. First, he argued that the school should be built on the fundamental birthright of the child to the cultural experiences into which he or she was born. Second, the school must mold the child with appropriate experiences, those tied to the events and concerns of children within their communities. Finally, the school should provide the student with the appropriate skills and capacities to enter the adult world; it must deliver a charter of citizenship. Schools that broke these basic connections under the pressure to deliver lessons from the colonial empire inevitably miseducated these youth, preparing them for neither the village nor the metropole.

The discontinuities facing Africans 50 years ago remain relevant to Afro-Americans, Latinos/as, rural poor, women, and other communities of color in today's modern society. The birthright to a rich life grounded in their heritage has been frustrated by schools that delegitimize the culture and identity of their communities. The second break occurs when public schools attempt to mold students of color around experiences that idealize the narrow norms designed in the image of elite groups. The third break is apparent at graduation. Limited opportunities for minorities in modern social institutions mean schools offer false hopes for the future. Most students must learn to work out their lives on the farm or in the neighborhood, without help from the schools. These ruptures between everyday life and the public schools of the great society have made modern education both alienating and miseducative.

John Dewey saw the conflicts between a single, great society and people's reliance on local community to define meaningful social spheres as a pervasive problem of modern society.

The invasion and partial destruction of the life of the latter [little community] by outside uncontrolled agencies is the immediate source of the instability, disintegration and restlessness which characterizes the present epoch. Evils which are uncritically and indiscriminately laid at the door of industrialism and democracy might, with greater intelligence, be referred to the dislocation and unsettlement of local communities.[6]

The disruption created by the colonial nature of American schooling has made public education a crippling force in our communities. The separation of education from real involvement in personal and social life undermines cultural voice, contributing to the oppression of whole communities and the reproduction of inequities throughout the country. It has become difficult to imagine the proper role of public schools within local communities.

Until the myth of modernism is replaced, multicultural education cannot connect schooling to cultural lives. The rhetoric of multicultural education has avoided this central point. To conservatives, the local community is of little import. Society's curriculum is defined by elite cultural productions; other cultural forms are less deserving of inclusion in the legitimated canon. Liberals also devalue the centrality of local life. They attempt to define the national culture more broadly than conservatives but still place their trust in the great society.[7] Curricular and pedagogical reforms have failed to create authentic learning connected to the themes and concerns of the neighborhood. Even many radicals have described the school as sites of struggle for a just, equitable, but common modern social institution. Resolving the conflict between local community and the great society is the core problem for constructing nonalienating, truly multivoiced education.

Educators need to forge a vision of how schools could cultivate local communities if they are going to engender principles of democracy in education and life. They need to reinvent classrooms that draw on the powerful human relations preserved in families and neighborhoods. They must link learning to everyday lives if they are ever to show how diversity in public education is a pillar of progressive societies. Educators must learn how to sit at the crossroads in a small town or at a stoplight in an urban neighborhood and consider how their work is part of the daily life of these communities.

RECOVERING THE LOCAL COMMUNITY

John Dewey's defense of the local community failed to turn social theorists away from an infatuation with grand scale models of social order. Only in recent years have postmodern theorists begun to promote views of society that celebrate the central role of local communities in the life of the public. Debunking great society's universalistic claims, postmodernists turn to community-based narratives and the wisdom of daily lives as the legitimate ground for social living.[8] Local tradition becomes the personal source for engaging in social action. Henry Giroux, for example, develops these new directions into a "border pedagogy" that challenges educators to recover local cultural lives and bring reinvigorated people together in a pluralistic democracy.[9] A revised understanding of culture and community is beginning to mark out new ways to make multicultural education the source of authentic learning and democratic citizenry.

Local communities are social relationships that emerge from regular encounters between people. They include a variety of groups: couples, families, peer groups, work groups, clubs, even villages and small tribes. What these different groups have in common is that people are responsible for direct, face-to-face interactions with each other. This personal contact creates the human scale by which people gauge their lives.

Local communities have always maintained patterns of teaching and learning suited to these relationships. Before modern society emerged, the local community had the primary role in the production and transmission of knowledge. Intellectuals had vital positions in traditional cultures and small communities.[10] Native education systems handed down folk wisdom on every aspect of village life.[11] Proverbs, riddles, games, and songs have all served as educational instruments among illiterate people in small villages.[12] These informal ways, Dewey and others concluded, provided the kinds of dialogue primarily responsible for an individual's intellectual growth.[13]

The reason this local dialogue is so critical to our lives is not readily apparent when we use classic views of culture. If individuals simply learn to assimilate a static set of uniform norms, beliefs, and values, it hardly matters whether we receive these from television, school, or momma. This view of culture is wrong, however.[14] Culture is constructed, not received. Because mass culture—whether television programs or school curricula—is constructed outside the experiences of the individual, it is elusive. Unable to test, reflect upon, or reinterpret this information, individuals "lose the right to know what they know, the right to be human."[15]

Cultural construction demands participation, and local communities are the principal organization for social participation. They provide the foundation from which people advance or defend their culture. The educator who works within these relationships inspires growth of both child and community. The schoolmaster who drills the student in the mass culture of the great society, says architect Hassan Fathy, kills the soul and destroys the tradition of individuality.[16]

Local communities offer the critical structure for cultural participation because they require individuals to make choices. At those moments when they construct culture, people must decide whether to maintain a tradition, modify it, or begin another altogether. Far from being static, traditions are continually evolving through countless decisions. A culture is at risk only when this dynamic falters and individuals are not capable of making choices that thoughtfully extend traditions. Individuals become alienated and lose a sense of identity when they no longer know how to make cultural choices. This is the case when cultural invasion by the great society substitutes foreign, elitist traditions by delegitimizing local ones.

A self-determining pedagogy transforms tradition and engenders empowering identity formation and cultural practices. Folklorist Barre Toelken explains that people responsible to a local community for their actions must both be conservative and retain some expected cultural practices, and innovative, revising these practices to suit personal and changed social needs.[17] Individuals must be able to reflect back on past traditions and decide which themes are important and which practices are practical. At the same time, they must be able to translate tradition's intentions to new circumstances, creating new or alternative forms of expression.[18]

These twin pressures require what, in educational jargon, are roughly called critical thinking skills. Conserving skills are enhanced when students learn how to research their communities and uncover historical, mathematical, literary, and scientific dimensions of their heritage. These skills help students use academic knowledge to assess the strengths and weaknesses within the community's traditions. Students learn to decide which parts of the community are sound and critique those that are not.

Students also need to learn how to bring innovation to their communities. Creative skills allow them to look for new ways to combine scientific, literary, or artistic ideas with existing traditions. Students who invent thoughtful applications of new ideas keep local traditions fresh and vibrant. School subject areas offer powerful points for individual and community growth. Through these twin skills, thoughtful choice leads to cultural transformation.

Unfortunately, students cannot be expected to develop these skills within the distant and disconnected traditions of the mass society. The subtle and complex skills involved in analysis and innovation are intimately bound into local communities, where social bonds make people responsible for their actions. For subject matter to become meaningful, it must help the student use these twin thinking skills to make good cultural choices in a community where their decisions matter.

The organization of learning around critical construction of the local culture is the fundamental beginning of public education, but not its endpoint. A pluralistic society gathers its strength when schools assure that local traditions are in skilled hands. Public schools that promote diversity must also provide some means to bring these differences together into a larger, cooperative society, one not reliant on the false image of the great society's common culture. The public must be defined as a polyvocal conversation rather than a single culture. This notion acknowledges that there are always multiple legitimate voices involved in fashioning public discourse and institutions. Democratic structures resolve the parochial forces that threaten to tear a society apart by defining public arenas in which multivoiced dialogue is possible. Developing in students the ability to bring their heritage into a democratic, pluralistic public sphere is the ultimate goal of public education that begins with the local community.

USING LOCAL COMMUNITIES FOR MULTICULTURAL EDUCATION

When we understand children as cultural beings growing within local communities, it is evident that multicultural educators must break schools away from the denatured, pseudo universalized framework of standardized education. To counter the hegemony that has marginalized and debilitated local communities, public education must be reconnected to local communities. The broken links described by Malinowski need to be restored. By training students in the cultural skills that improve their groups' traditions, such education prepares them to join the public discourse with confidence in their heritage.

Obviously, traditional school patterns are unequal to this task. Teachers cannot adapt a uniform curriculum to the many different backgrounds brought into the classroom. No single set of truths can be written into textbooks. No standardized evaluation instrument is politically neutral in intent or effect. Educators who attempt to include multiculturalism within these traditional approaches are caught within contradictions that will inevitably work against their best efforts. This has been the unfortunate history of over 25 years of mainstream multicultural education in this country.

The resolution of this contradiction is not to encourage teachers to do more but to suggest we learn how to do it differently. In rejecting teacher-centered approaches to great society curriculum, educators must turn to student-centered approaches. Students gain cultural skills through problem-solving classroom activities. They sharpen social skills in productive dialogue with peers and community members. They learn how to contribute to the public good by producing valued resources. These approaches view the schools' role as enhancing local culture by developing its human resources.

The dominance of teacher-centered, great society pedagogy has obstructed the development of progressive alternatives.[19] In the first half of this century, educators used community-centered projects as a medium for developing social and intellectual skills.[20] In some cases, schoolwide programs would send students into the community to survey existing structures. Teachers would facilitate student groups working to address identified needs.[21] These educators clearly understood schools as institutions committed to community building. By the 1950s, such programs were lost by the pressures to drive schools toward national goals and standardized methods.

By the late 1960s, the energy bound up in community-centered education became briefly popular in a method called cultural journalism.[22] *Foxfire* magazine set off an enthusiastic movement across the country to restore pride in local regions by having students write about the folklore of their relatives and neighbors. Today, the Foxfire Fund is moving beyond cultural journalism and developing a systematic approach to teaching all subject areas at all grade levels.[23] Connection to the community remains one of the core practices of this student-centered, democratic pedagogy.

While Foxfire teachers would agree that much needs to be rediscovered from the lost tradition of engaging local communities, their insistence that the classroom be tied to community offers a critical advancement over other liberal reforms. Whole language, cooperative learning, and thematic cycles concentrate on classroom practices without explicit ties to the community lives of the students. Lisa Delpit warned that for students of color these new procedures used uncritically may only serve to further discourage their efforts to learn the rules for school success.[24] Multicultural educators can turn these methods into just and effective classrooms when they also allow students to have learning activities that help them become valuable contributors to their home communities.

Because such classrooms engage children in the skills essential to any cultural discourse, they have the potential to restore marginalized communities to full rights in a democratic society. As the initial sites where students learn to step outside their home communities, democratic classrooms teach children how to bring their cultural voice into a common public arena. The teacher unites the goals of multicultural education with the normal processes of good learning.

To use local communities to create truly multicultural schools, educators must rediscover how to organize classrooms around the life of their students' communities. Such a profound shift in pedagogical approach necessarily reinvents alternative strategies at every level of teaching. There are guidelines from progressive educators, like Foxfire teachers, that offer some credible directions. The following sections introduce some ideas as starting points for reflecting on how to create classrooms that are truly multicultural.

Preparing the Lesson

Preparing teacher-centered lessons means getting the curriculum in order: What lessons will I teach in what order? Considered as a static list of subject matter, the curriculum may be ordered but it is not likely to be effective. Since effective lessons are linked into the life experiences of the students, the first job of a good teacher is to find these connections.

Victims of an overly formalized curriculum, we have lost the sense of how academic subjects contribute to the community's store of knowledge and the students' quests to solve their problems. Literature has become a canon of authors rather than storytelling done well; mathematics is reduced to formulae rather than a way of making sense of the world. Instead, we should be looking for the way in which our subject matter helps students see the world anew, leading to vigorous problem-posing. We should transform our curriculum from a static list of unfamiliar "facts" to an organic process. History can lead to a historical understanding of people's lives; writing becomes a skill for thinking; social studies develop sociological imaginations. A teacher who searches for the real uses of a subject area will be far better prepared to engage students in appropriate learning processes.

The more a teacher is able to learn about culturally different ways of applying these subject areas, the better he or she will be at anticipating alternative ways the subject area works as a problem-solving tool. This familiarity can be gained by studying ways in which various communities already utilize these disciplines. How do they tell stories or use numbers or analyze events? Thus prepared, the teacher is ready to meet the students, whatever their background.

A good teacher also attempts to discover student knowledge and learning styles before committing to the work of learning. Traditional teaching materials are geared toward the child who fits all the averages. Yet nationality, race, age, gender, and social background have given different personal biographies for each one. Each looks at the world differently. Teachers must be ready to turn these differences into opportunities for intellectual cross-fertilization during learning activities.

Teachers should also look for patterns in how students' lives are woven into the community. Are they expected to contribute ideas? What type of intelligence is valued (and what type is undervalued)? Do students see others utilizing these skills? Interviews, discussions, and brainstorming about where students encounter this subject area in their community can reveal to the teacher the context within which students expect to use their knowledge. A teacher who hopes to help an individual grow must discover how the community expects its members to participate.

Inventories of the physical, economic, political, health, recreational, social, aesthetic, or moral systems in the community can indicate its need for further knowledge. This early understanding of students and their communities helps orient the lesson toward practical paths of growth that will be naturally sustained by the community. It orients the teacher to the best directions for engaging students in ways of using subject matter to contribute to their cultural groups. This orientation makes it possible for the teacher to lead any student into activities that will strengthen his or her voice at home and in the larger public.

Facilitating the Lesson

Whereas the traditional classroom begins a unit by introducing new material, the student-centered classroom begins by generating student motivation to learn. Familiar with the students' orientation and confident in using the discipline, the teacher relies on his or her familiarity with the subject area to decide what is the next intellectual step for students. From this decision, the teacher initiates a learning cycle by creating an occasion that requires additional knowledge. For Dewey, the teacher's job is to construct a situation where students, unable to solve the problem with their current knowledge, work to gain the knowledge needed to resolve the situation. In Paulo Freire's problem-posing method, the teacher uses pictures, plays, stories, or other media to reveal to learners the themes that pervade their community's intellectual life.[25] Revealing the inadequacy of these themes is the first step in working to develop better ones.

Beginning instruction through problematizing the taken-for-granted worlds of the students gives the teacher every opportunity for linking learning to community. Identifying the community's needs becomes the center of relevant learning as students are taught how to survey and reflect on community life. Learning directions emerge when students define themselves as potential contributors to the culture. The teacher's opportunity to introduce formal subject matter emerges throughout this culturally relevant learning.

For multicultural educators, examples of local racism, sexism, and classism provide points through which to challenge the thematic worlds of overly parochial communities. The broader notions of democratic public life in a pluralistic society offer new avenues for growth. Problematizing these issues helps students learn how to incorporate in their community ideas about how to participate with others in the larger society.

Once begun, the teacher's role is to facilitate personal growth and sustain a social environment in which this growth can flourish. The first task prepares the students in the cultural skills required by the community. The second promotes the arts of democratic living that are critical in a pluralistic society.

The process of questioning, studying, dialoguing, and decision making that make up an individual's learning engages the same conserving and transforming abilities that a cultural performer uses in choosing how to construct a tradition. The teacher understands that his or her job is to facilitate children's development as they experience education, helping improve abilities that are weak. In the facilitator's role, the teacher is better able to respond appropriately to each individual's background and intellectual habits. This attention to multicultural diversity is central to the craft and not a mere supplement to regular teaching responsibilities.

The choice not to rely solely on lectures as an instructional method does not mean the classroom is organized around individualized instruction. Active learning settings depend on social relationships to support learning. School sociologists have described how group interactions lead to successful classroom communities.[26] Learning groups provide a social structure that catches students up in the activities of the classroom, offering guidance during learning cycles. Student decision making makes them responsible for directing the curriculum toward their own needs. Democratic, cooperative learning groups are one of the most effective learning organizations for designing educational environments that respond to diverse student backgrounds.

In these classrooms, teachers encourage dialogues that bring students with different backgrounds into common conversations. There is not one correct history; there are multiple histories. There are multiple and diverse literatures, mathematics, and sciences. Multicultural teachers show students how to enter into these multivoiced conversations. As students discover their own heritage, they find they can contribute its voice to these pluralistic conversations. In this setting students will be forced to confront the complexities of multivoiced conversations and, with teacher modeling and guidance, gain the skills of listening to and learning from alternative insights into the questions of civilization.

Multicultural education's aims to promote cross-cultural communication, cultural transference, and public equity are basic to the life of these classrooms. Opportunities for border crossing arise as part of the everyday business of group learning.[27] Democratic politics as part of the process for understanding multiple positions within a subject area are mixed into the school day. It is through these lived practices that students learn how best to counter the narrow, hegemonic approaches to knowledge that disempower, anger, and silence students in traditional classrooms. Working in democratic settings, students learn how to avoid reproducing the prejudice, hate, and injustices built into existing social stratifications in our society.

Assessing Knowledgeable Performances

Efforts to establish student-centered, democratic classrooms are contested by the powerful gatekeeping role of standardized examinations. Threats of failure repel teachers from community-centered pedagogy, since this knowledge is absent from tests and other assessment tools that do not include knowledge of particular local communities. This pressure keeps multicultural education marginalized.

Since an engaged learner has a better chance of success than a student who finds schooling to be meaningless drudgery, students in democratic, community-centered classrooms are not usually at risk in examinations. They have continually improved their understanding of literature, mathematics, science, or social studies. Performance on a single exam can be treated as a singular problem, not a learning goal. A more honest evaluation of learning must be constructed to measure accomplishments throughout the learning cycle. Authentic assessment poses no real obstacle to community-centered learning.

Evaluation points occur during many occasions of the learning process. Students have moments of insights; groups discover solutions. These are the natural moments to document. By exploring these documents with the teacher, students do not drift off task but rather gain guidance at precisely the moments when they are ready to reflect and make decisions. These audit trails mark the normal flow of students throughout the various phases of the learning cycle. Derived from student efforts, this form of assessment easily accommodates to cultural and personal learning styles.

At some phase, students judge their abilities as complete and adequate enough to step beyond the safe confines of the classroom and act as contributing members of the community. Then, the community itself plays its normal role as evaluating audience. Students must learn to properly anticipate their standards, aligning their work with the cultural expectations of the community. Where multiple communities are involved, the class must explore how to design its work for a multivoiced, pluralistic audience. In short, this kind of evaluation, like the rest of the community-centered approach, flows within the structures of the surrounding community.

In this final phase, teachers help students become more skilled at creating culturally appropriate projects by anticipating problems that might arise in any cultural performance. They guide students in formulating strategies for dealing with these problems when they occur. The classroom is a safe place to respond to the community's real feedback. It is in such an environment that students can learn how to modify culturally inappropriate efforts or products whose ethnocentrism leads to confusion or injustice. These are some of the most powerful skills that a student who is attempting to use knowledge to work with others may learn.

From preparation through evaluation, student-centered teachers can organize learning to connect with the cultural life of the local community. These strategies do not require additional, supplementary activities to include minorities in a prefabricated curriculum. Rather, they build upon existing diversity by drawing authentic learning into a pluralistic enterprise. They illustrate how multicultural education can step beyond the school's traditional dream of a single, modern culture and build authentic learning through developing the abilities and potential of all students.

PREPARING MULTICULTURAL EDUCATORS

Teacher preparation has long been organized to produce colonial agents for the great society. Radical critics have struggled to break its dedication to elite culture and insist on preparation for a more democratic public.[28] If we are ever to include all students in the life of the schools, however, educators must be able to deal with student differences as an integral part of everyday learning activities. This means that multicultural education must convince teachers to abandon teacher-centered methods that maintain the myth of the great society. It must show teachers how to restore authentic learning by establishing relationships within the local community, while defining ways to build the national discourse that brings diverse communities and individuals together.

The loss of community in the modern school reveals itself through symptoms of alienation, hostility, silence, and resistance. Racism, sexism, and classism persist as ugly responses to the inability of the great society to confront its contradictions and social order. For multicultural education to commit its energies to training teachers how to treat these social ills with patience, sensitivity, and acceptance promotes a false charity. Local communities, battered and neglected as they may have become, provide the basis for methods that can turn students into thoughtful, confident contributors to their homes and to our pluralistic democracy. If multicultural education aims to truly restore the cultural lives that bring diversity to a progressive society, it must press teacher education programs to push educators beyond the comfort of an impersonal, detached school system. Teaching programs must redirect educators toward methods that reach out to the communities that students bring to the school. Not until professional education programs show teachers how to honor this birthright will schools learn how to restore the humanity and justice at the heart of authentic learning.

NOTES

1. Flann O'Brien, *The Poor Mouth* (London: Picador, 1975), p. 34.

2. Thomas Bender, *Community and Social Change* (Baltimore: Johns Hopkins University Press, 1982).

3. Forrest Carter, *The Education of Little Tree* (Albuquerque: University of New Mexico Press, 1976).

4. Bronislaw Malinowski, "The Pan-African Problem of Culture Contact," *American Journal of Sociology*, Vol. 48 (1943), pp. 649–665.

5. Nathaniel McCall, *Makes Me Wanna Holler* (New York: Random House, 1994), pp. 17–21.

6. John Dewey, *The Public School and Its Problems* (Chicago: Swallow, 1954 [originally published in 1927], pp. 211–212.

7. Tomasz Szkudlarek, *The Problem of Freedom in Modern Education* (Westport, CT: Bergin and Garvey, 1993), pp. 91–95.

8. Pauline Marie Rosenau, *Post-Modernism and the Social Sciences* (Princeton, NJ: Princeton University Press, 1992), pp. 82–85.

9. Henry Giroux, "Border Pedagogy in the Age of Postmodernism," *Journal of Education*, Vol. 170, No. 3 (1988), pp. 162–181.

10. Paul Radin, *Primitive Man as Philosopher* (New York: Appleton, 1927).

11. J. A. Majasan, "Traditional Education and Its Possible Contribution to Modern Educational Techniques," *West African Journal of Education*, Vol. 19, No. 3 (October 1975), p. 423.

12. Barbara Kirshenblatt-Gimblett, "Introduction," *Keystone Folklore Quarterly*, Vol. 22, Nos. 1–2 (1975), p. 15.

13. Dewey, *The Public School and Its Problems*, pp. 218–219; and Robert Redfield, "Culture and Education in the Midwestern Highlands of Guatemala," *American Journal of Sociology*, Vol. 49, No. 6 (May 1943), p. 647.

14. James Clifford and George Marcus, eds., *Writing Culture* (Berkeley: University of

California Press, 1986); and Renato Rosaldo, *Culture and Truth* (Boston: Beacon Press, 1989).

15. Henry Glassie, *Passing the Time in Ballymenone* (Philadelphia: University of Pennsylvania Press, 1982), p. 652.

16. Hassan Fathy, *Architecture for the Poor* (Chicago: University of Chicago Press, 1973), p. 27.

17. Barre Toelken, *The Dynamic of Folklore* (Boston: Houghton Mifflin, 1979), pp. 32–43.

18. Cornel West, *The American Evasion of Philosophy* (Madison: University of Wisconsin Press, 1989), p. 230.

19. Kathe Jervis, and Carol Montag, eds., *Progressive Education for the 1990s* (New York: Teachers College Press, 1991).

20. Joseph Hart, ed., *Educational Resources of Village and Rural Communities* (New York: Macmillan, 1914).

21. Roberta LaBrant Green, "Developing a Modern Curriculum in a Small Town," *Democracy and Education*, Vol. 7, No. 3 (Spring 1993), pp. 29–35 [originally printed in *Progressive Education*, March 1936].

22. Kathryn Olmstead, "Touching the Past, Enroute to the Future," *Eric Digest*, March 1989 (ED 308 057).

23. The Foxfire Teacher Outreach program's magazine, *Hands On*, offers the best source of ideas about the Foxfire Approach.

24. Lisa Delpit, "The Silenced Dialogue," *Harvard Educational Review*, Vol. 58, No. 3 (August 1988), pp. 280–298.

25. See John Dewey, *Experience and Education* (New York: Collier, 1963); for Freire, see Ira Shor, ed., *Freire for the Classroom* (Portsmouth, NY: Boynton Cook, 1987).

26. Richard Schmuck and Patricia Schmuck. *Group Processes in the Classroom*, 6th ed. (Dubuque, IA: Brown, 1992).

27. Henry Giroux, *Border Crossings* (New York: Routledge, 1993).

28. Henry Giroux and Peter McLaren "Teacher Education and the Politics for Engagement," *Harvard Educational Review*, Vol. 56, (August 1986), pp. 213–238.

12

Core Culture and Core Curriculum in South Africa

Neville Alexander

In a rapidly changing South Africa, the central task of specifically educational reconstruction is to design a curriculum that will promote the unity and accommodate the diversity of a population that is destined either to lay the foundations for a model of multicultural harmony or become one more bloody twentieth-century example of ethnic conflict, fragmentation, and "cleansing." As I hope to demonstrate in this chapter, this project can only succeed, other things being equal, if a core curriculum is derived in a particular process from the concept, and let me add immediately, the reality, of a *core culture*.[1] Above all, that curriculum will have to be owned by the body of teachers and educators, who can become its owners only be means of such a process.

In order to point to the crucial significance of the education system in a context where nation building (whatever one's critique of this particular concept) is clearly the order of the day, let me begin by quoting an author whose work, though it has been helpful to me in my own recent researches into the evolution of a core culture in South Africa, tends in a very different direction from mine. E. D. Hirsch, Jr. (1988, p. 73), in his well-known work *Cultural Literacy*, asserts that "at the heart of modern nationhood is the teaching of literacy and a common culture through a national system of education." And S. Alisjabana (1975, p. 287) has made the same observation about the closely related issue of standard languages, which, he says bluntly, are mainly the product of compulsory education.

Such statements, trite as they might seem today, demonstrate that at the superstructure level of discourse and consciousness, few if any social institutions and agencies are more important in the modern world than the generally under-rated preschool, primary school, and secondary school. For this reason, the re-designing of teacher education on the basis of radically new approaches to multicultural pedagogy is crucial to the success of any large-scale and long-term projects of social transformation.

MULTICULTURAL EDUCATION

A brief problematization of multicultural pedagogy has to suffice in this chapter. In South African, many of us who are involved in liberatory pedagogy became suspicious when we noticed the alacrity with which the former ideologues of apartheid grasped at the theory of multicultural education imported from Britain, the United States, and later also from the European mainland. It soon became obvious that as apartheid as a political and economic strategy began to disinte-grate, many of the race- and class-based privileges bestowed on white South Africans by the ill-gotten wealth of colonial conquest and capitalist exploitation could be salvaged via the reification of "cultures" and the de facto hierarchization of the human carriers of these. In short, it became obvious to us that multicultural education, as interpreted by the establishment in South Africa, was simply an elegant variation for apartheid, a kind of neoapartheid. Some general critiques of the assimilationist and accommodationist potential and consequences of theories of multiculturalism have begun to see the light of day in South Africa (see, for example, Heugh, 1993, 1994a). While it was clear that these assimilationist ver-sions of multiculturalism were predicated on the existence of ethnic minorities in a context dominated by a usually Euro-oriented majority, it was also clear that this theory was eminently transplantable to South African soil because of the peculiar power relations in this country.

For it is a fact of no mean significance that despite the black majority population in South Africa, the white minority constitutes a social majority by virtue of the concentration of economic and politician power in white hands. The most recent statistics throw some light on this statement.

About one-third of blacks are unemployed, compared to 3 percent of whites. Most black households earn less than R800 a month, and many lack electricity and plumbing, while white families earn from R3600 to R9000 a month. Although blacks made up 75 percent of the country's 40 million people, they own just 15 percent of the land, control 2 percent of the capital and hold only 2.4 percent of managerial jobs in business. (*Sunday Times* [Johannesburg], April 10, 1994)

This list of antinomies cold be lengthened almost at will. Indeed, the picture is much bleaker than it implies. Blacks actually only "occupy" rather than own 15 percent of the land and between 30 percent and 40 percent of blacks are illiterate in any language, a devastating handicap in a modern industrial society. The point of the juxtaposition is simply to underline the fact that in practice the black majority in South Africa is in the position of a subordinate minority on whom the desires, values, and standards of the white minority generally speaking have been imposed.

In effect, therefore, the application of the conventional model of multicultural education reduces, in South African, to the continuation in practice of a neo-apartheid system. In the generic model, space is made for dealing with aspects of minority culture as a separate entity, while perpetuation of the majority's hege-monic scheme ensures that the space provided remains no more than a decorative forum for the appreciation of folklore. I subscribe to the general position adopted by authors such as T. Skutnabb-Kangas and J. Cummins (1988) and J. Tollefson (1991) among others on the question of multicultural and intercultural education as practiced in Europe and North America. In the words of T. Skutnabb-Kangas and J. Cummins (1988, pp. 126–127),

the overt goals of multicultural education can be realised only when policy makers, edu-cators and communities acknowledge the subtle (and sometimes not so subtle) forms of institutionalised racism that permeate the structure of schools and mediate the interactions between educators and students. In other words, unless it becomes "anti-racist education," "multicultural education" may serve only to provide a veneer of change that in reality perpetuates discriminatory educational structures.

These insights have merely reinforced the suspicion that radical educators in South African have always had about reified concepts derived from the historical experience of European peoples. The fact of the matter is that notions of culture, language, nation, and so on based on that experience are shot through with racist hubris and with indifferent sociology and even worse anthropology when applied to non-European contexts. What has happened almost imperceptibly is that the-ory and model have been conflated—that is, generalized, abstracted experience (theory) is confused with the manifestation or application of experience in a par-ticular sociohistorical context (model). Consequently, instead of European theo-ries of the nation, language, and culture influencing non-Europeans' perceptions and understandings of their situation, European models were, and still are, im-posed in such a way that reality is constructed in accordance with these. General sociocultural and political-economic perceptions as well as specific pedagogical (and other socialization-related) practices are determined by such models.

THE INVENTION OF ETHNICITY

Two relevant examples from the sphere of language throw some light on these assertions. Many non-European social theorists have intuitively rejected the Ri-sorgimento notion (see Lemberg, 1967) of a monolingual nation. For while this notion indeed corresponded to a few Western and Central European situations, the global norm is quite different: most nations are multilingual. In the words of Debi Pattanayak (cited in Constable, 1993, p. 16), the concept of a nation state is built round unitary symbols, one language, one culture, one religion and so on. This is how the nation state is conceived of in the European plan. Their one language is the national language. This is an entirely inadequate concept. It is inappropriate both to European countries, as they have discovered to their great cost, and even more so to the developing countries. National monolingualism is a complete myth. New identities are emerging on the one hand, yet on the other there is a drive towards greater unity as exemplified in the concept of the EEC [European Economic Community].

Similarly, many Southern African (and other) historians, basing themselves on the insights and methods of a seminal paper by Terence Ranger (1983), have shown how ethnicity was created in Southern African by an ensemble of missionaries, colonial administrators, and entrepreneurs in the course of the nineteenth and early twentieth centuries (see Vail, 1991). Leroy Vail demonstrates clearly how the economic imperatives of colonial modernization, especially the demands of deep-level mining and plantation-style farming, brought about the system of forced migrant labor by means of which the African males of the surrounding territories became "available" for ethnic mobilization. The authors maintain that the emergence of ethnic identities in Southern African can be traced to the same kind of "crisis of modernization" that gave rise to nationalist movements in Europe during the eighteenth and nineteenth centuries. As in the case of those movements, intellectuals and petit bourgeois strata played the decisive role. In Southern Africa, it was particularly the white missionaries and their predominantly male converts, the so-called mission elite, who determined the content of these ethnic identities by, for example, reducing the African languages to writing and by recording the respective heroic epics, myths and customs of the "tribe."

In this way, many of the ethnic groups that are taken as self-evidently real today were virtually invented. Vail's conclusion, which now has the status of conventional wisdom, is that "ethnicity is not a natural cultural residue but a consciously crafted ideological creation" (p. 7).

In line with this kind of research, Patrick Harries (1988), in another pivotal article, suggests that what the missionaries and other agents of colonialism did was to impose a kind of Cartesian perceptual grid on the African reality in order to make sense in terms familiar to themselves of what they experienced as a Babylonian confusion of tongues. Indeed, he took the matter to the point of absurdity when "albeit tongue-in-cheek, he maintains that in the case of the controversial ethnograpy of the Tsonga we have to deal with a classic instance of ethnic differences whose roots may be traced to an obscure linguistic debate between two Swiss missionaries" (see Alexander, 1989:24).

CULTURE AND CULTURES

It ought to be clear, therefore, that we have, in the South African context, for both historical and general theoretical-epistemological reasons, more than enough justification for questioning the sole authentic status of the notion of discretely existing cultural entities or cultures. We have to dig even deeper though. Modern theories of culture and cultural studies have similarly called into question the Cartesian notion (see Bohm, 1980, p. xv) of culture. Stuart Hall, (1990, p. 225), one of the most exciting contributors to this debate, has put the matter very clearly in a recent article:

Cultural identity . . . is a matter of "becoming" as well as of "being." It belongs to the future as much as to the past. It is not something which already exists, transcending place, time, history and culture. Cultural identities come from somewhere, have histories. But, like everything which is historical, they undergo constant transformation.

This Heraclitean approach to social phenomena is essential if we are to liberate ourselves from the straitjacket of Cartesian constructions, which are both the product of and the legitimation for the global system of domination and exploitation. We have to get back to the profound reflections of a Raymond Williams (1976, p. 500), who reminded us that culture is "a noun of process" and that Josef Herder was the first author to use the term in plural.

Some thought leads us to the inevitable conclusion that it is essential and theoretically completely tenable that we adopt a wave-particle approach à la Heisenberg to the question of culture (and, incidentally, to derivative and related social concepts). In other words, it is obvious and also explicable that under certain conditions people perceive ("live") their culture as a state, a thing, a definable entity, whereas under other conditions they experience it as a flux, an ever-changing stream mixing with many other similar streams. It is a relationship that is analogous to that between Euclidean and relativity mathematics—that is, the former is correct at certain levels but inadequate at other levels of magnitude. To take an example from South African history, the Cartesian conceptualization is obviously insightful in a case such as the first encounter (in 1487) between the exploring Portuguese mariners under Bartholomeu Dias and the KhoiKhoi herders near Mossel Bay on the South Cape coast. On that occasion, indisputably, two quite distinct, historically unconnected cultures came into antagonistic contact. On the other hand, to adopt the same approach to the situation that arose some 150 years later when the Dutch trader/raider Jan van Riebeeck was bartering with some of the descendants of the men and women of Dias' Angra dos Vagueiros near Mossell Bay would simply lead to a subtle falsification of the historical record, since these two cultures had by that time to a certain extent become interdependent.

We have, in Williams' (1979, pp. 500–501) terms, to equip ourselves with an analytical approach that allows us "to see both structural and historical dimensions"; we have to see "tradition as both operative continuity and contemporary formation and try to discover, in terms of our goals, the most appropriate connections between that which is 'residual' and that which is 'emergent.' " In the global village, in which all of us live today, it is no longer tenable to pretend that cultures coexist (peacefully or otherwise) without constant interpenetration and consequent mutual adaptation. Herder's move from "culture" to "cultures" represented a reduction of vision from the global to the national, and even to the parochial, scale and was carried into the colonial world by missionaries and others, as I have indicated. This was a move that was latent in the ideological requirements of capitalist competition. On the other hand, the colonial era itself, together with the revolution in communications, inherently pointed in the opposite direction and while Gordon Childe's (1953) conclusion that "cultures are becoming culture" was too simplistic, it does compel us to reflect on the relationship between "culture" and "cultures."

Recent studies by authors such as Edward Said are pointing the way forward. In his most recent work on the subject, Said (1994, p. 15) makes the point that

we have never been as aware as we now are of how oddly hybrid historical and cultural experiences are, of how they partake of many often contradicting experiences and domains, cross national boundaries, defy the police action of simple dogma and loud patriotism. Far from being unitary or monolithic or autonomous things, cultures actually assume more *foreign* elements, alterities, differences, than they consciously exclude. Who in India or Algeria today can confidently separate out the British or French component of the past from present actualities, and who in Britain or France can draw a clear circle around British London or French Paris that would exclude the impact of India and Algeria upon those two imperial cities?

What ought to be abundantly obvious is that in the global village, most states tend to be multiethnic and that inevitably under the conditions of modern life there is a confluence of different cultural streams in such societies. The major premise of my call for a reconsideration and a "verbalization" as opposed to a "substantivization" of concepts such as culture (see Bohm, 1980) is the hypothesis that under these circumstances what I call a core culture evolves. It is based on the interaction, interpenetration, or perhaps interfluence of all the relevant currents. The precise definition of the core at any given moment depends on the changing relations of domination and subordination in the given social formation. The tributary cultures do not, and should not, disappear. Instead, they continue to swell the common pool and themselves change in certain respects and continue to be tolerable as long as they do not subvert the need and consequent desire for a degree of commonality. Should expansive socioeconomic or sociopolitical pressures arise or build up in these tributary spaces, the result is inevitably ethnic conflict and a separatist or centrifugal dynamic.

This has been the practical experience in South Africa. Theories and learned analyses that used to be buried in academic tomes read by a handful of "bats of erudition" are now the stuff of journalistic virtuosity (see Giliomee, 1994; and de Villiers, 1994). Modern South African history can be summed up at the ideological level as a contest between primordialist and situational theories of ethnicity and of collective identities in general. The ideologues and theorists of the white minority tended to legitimate their own power-political segregationist and apartheid strategies in terms of divinely ordained autochthonous racial and ethnic givens, whereas the publicists of the national liberation movement were inclined to trivialize ethnicity and racial prejudice or try to deride these as a Machiavellian divide-and-rule conspiracy hatched in the think tanks of the white minority.

Crucial to the more dynamic process-oriented approach to the question of culture implied in my hypothesis is the need to see the tributaries not only as flowing and thus changing at all times but also as open to interfluence with other tributaries, either directly or via the common pool of the core culture. This is much more than the usual notion of (democratic) tolerance and mutual respect. It implies an active appreciation of the peculiar traits or qualities of "the Other" as of equal value to "one's own" and as being worthy of emulation. It recognizes the contingent character of the subject—that is, the accident of birth and of particular socializations. It involves an understanding of the catastrophic potential inherent in difference or diversity construed in an antagonistic mode, but gets away from the patronizing tendency of dominant groups to see difference in terms of mere folklore and exoticism.

By way of practical illustrations of these propositions in the South African context, I refer to the fact that on the basis of the gradual industrialization of the country, beginning with the mineral discoveries in the last quarter of the nineteenth century, such a core or mainstream South African culture has evolved and is continuing to develop. In all sectors of South African society, elements of African, European, and Asian origin have flowed together and wherever the dominant white-minority strategies have not deliberately tried to keep these apart or where these strategies have failed to do so, a peculiarly South African amalgam has been the result.

Thus, for example, in the sphere of religion, the African Independent (or Ethiopian/Zionist) churches represent such a confluence. While they remain separate from the established churches for doctrinal and linguistic reasons, they are sufficiently close to these to partake of a common (Christian) ethos and common practices in such a way that they are perceived as being in the mainstream. Proof of this is the fact that more and more the established churches have had to slough off their European garb in ritual, hymns, and litany and adapt to the African constituency they hope to "save." In this sector, on the other hand, non-Christian monotheistic and other theologies have remained tributary and respected—that is, accorded full rights of proselytization. Indeed, in the latest (interim) constitution, freedom of religious belief is guaranteed in the Bill of Rights.

Similar centripetal tendencies can be observed in virtually all sociocultural spheres, notably in music, drama, dancing, and poetry. Whatever the merits or demerits of works such as *Sarafina*, for example, they represent a real merging of traditions, rhythms, and patterns that have their origins in different hemispheres. The most recent example of this is the adoption of both *NKosi sikelele iAfrika* and *Die Stem* as South Africa's national anthems. All of these manifest the phenomenon of mainstreaming through confluence rather than through the domination of Euro- or Afro-elements. This dynamic is typically South African, even if largely urban, and undoubtedly derives from the peculiar relationship of a white minority of European descent wielding overwhelming economic and political power, balanced and kept in check by an overwhelming black majority of African descent, which is fast acquiring a pool of skills and purchasing power enabling it to set up a countervailing force. In a paradoxical manner, this relationship, instead of closing off actually opens up channels of communication between groups forcibly held apart by slavery, colonialism, segregation, and apartheid.

CORE CULTURE AND NATION BUILDING

The nation-building project in newly independent colonies or in countries such as postapartheid South Africa is predicated upon this openness. Summing up the profound writings of Amilcar Cabral on the quest for a national culture by national liberation movements, Karen Press (1989, p. 23) writes that

the validity of . . . tradition as a weapon of culture resistance is undeniable. The difficult task facing a liberation movement with revolutionary goals is to accept such forms of resistance (often quite spontaneous) on the part of the oppressed people, while simultaneously initiating a move beyond dependence on these traditions.

At the level of cultural policy, this means that a core of common cultural practices, beliefs, customs, and such has to be allowed to become manifest and to develop unhindered—a core that is derived from all the different social, regional, and language groups. In a multilingual country such as South Africa, this means, for example, that songs or stories that at present are peculiar to, say, Nguni-speaking people or to Sotho-speaking people will become generally known either in the original or in translation. This is no different from what the Christian church has done in regard to the Bible and many hymns in multilingual countries and, indeed, worldwide. Through translations of these into all the languages of the people, a common basis for communication among Christians—a veritable bridge of metaphorical discourse—was established with the potential of eventuating in genuine sisterhood and brotherhood. The emergence of a sense of national consciousness and national identity based on such a conception of a core culture is completely tenable in a country such as South Africa. Parenthetically, it needs to be said that such a national consciousness does not imply a national chauvinism. However, this is a separate subject, which we cannot explore in this chapter.

Unity and solidarity, born in the struggle for liberation through common political and economic action, have to be and are reinforced by means of increasing the openings of what are still seen as closed circles of culture based on language, color, and sometimes religion or even region. A genuinely developmental approach would open the existing boundaries between the ethnically conceived cultures, or subcultures, in order to permit as gradual or as rapid a convergence of customs, practices, beliefs, institutions, and so on, as suits the requirements of an emerging South African/Azania free of all oppression. An excellent practical example is the quite unproblematic way in which the culinary culture of South Africa has come to be knit together out of African, European, Asian, and American strands into an indefinable fabric that appears different, depending on the angle of vision from which one perceives it. In this regard, two of the key issues that have to be addressed are language policy and early childhood educare.

THE CORE CURRICULUM

With that we come to the question of multicultural education strategies and specifically to the evolution of a core curriculum in a multilingual or multiethnic society. The first point that has to be cleared up is the distinction between a core curriculum and a national curriculum. The latter is clearly directed against the centrifugal tendencies of educational systems in any large country. It attempts to ensure that there is a common basis from which norms and standards can be derived and that enables the citizens to move relatively freely between different parts of the country without their children having to start from scratch after every such move. This is the explicit rationale for projects such as the Core Knowledge Foundation in the United States (see Hirsch, 1988). As against this, the core curriculum, in my use of the term, reflects and promotes an evolving core culture that is itself constituted by the pooling of different cultural streams from which the citizens of the country derive. Whereas the national curriculum has as its point of departure the socioeconomic project of sustaining an existing nation, the core curriculum, in my usage of the term, is predicated on the nonexistence of the nation or, more positively, the fact that the sociocultural bonding of the nation is as yet very weak. Paradoxically, in South Africa, the term "core curriculum" has always signified what I refer to as the "national curriculum." Elements of what I refer to as the tributary or border aspects of the curriculum (see below), did exist, and in fact still exist, in the apartheid curricula, but these were quite explicitly intended to reinforce racial consciousness and social divisions among the people.

It is axiomatic that in a more democratic, postapartheid South Africa, the Euro- and whitecentric curriculum and syllabi are going to have to disappear. Antecedent developments in this connection were engendered in the decades-long struggle against Bantu education and against apartheid educational structures more generally. Numerous studies on this general subject as well as on specific aspects of it have been published since the mid-1980s. Virtually nothing, however, has been published on the curriculum development initiatives to which those struggles gave rise. Initially, the most important of these emerged in the domains of preschool educare and in adult and worker education, for the simple reason that these were areas beyond the control of the apartheid state. Although there were many important differences among all of these projects, they were usually characterized by bottom-up processes, some of which, it has to be admitted, were quite self-delusory, since most aspects of the process were often conceived of, initiated, or refined by the intellectuals who coordinated the projects concerned.

By way of example, I will refer briefly to a project that was specifically oriented toward the development of a curriculum in the preschool field for a postapartheid South Africa. The Vumani Pre-School Project came into being in 1984 and began working with educare workers (in workshops) about approaches to the care and education of children and about the making and use of education resources. Only in 1991 did the project workers feel sufficiently confident to venture on to the thorny terrain of formal curriculum proposals and a training course for educare workers based on these proposals. (Educare workers include teachers, cooks, and cleaners in Vumani's definition.) The following excerpt from the information brochure on the training course gives a good indication of Vumani's approach, one that in fact enjoys wide popularity among educare workers in South Africa.

Our philosophy is that of seeing a common South African/Azanian community in the future. We believe that a society free of racism, sexism and all inequalities can be created through consensus by adults who are involved with education and care of young children. This must also be done with the active participation of parents and teachers by instilling in young children a sense of self worth and respect for all human beings.

The training of people who work with young children must be situated within the social, economic and political context of South Africa. . . . It is important that a body of knowledge be created that promotes the understanding of the growth and development of young children in our context.

To this end we have actively involved ourselves in analysing existing pre-school curricula together with parents, teachers and many people concerned with the education and care of young children. Through our workshop programme and seminars as well as our fieldwork we have begun to develop an approach to curriculum and training which will meet the needs and problems particular to our context.

Teaching methods and resources have been and will continue to be developed in order to empower educare workers with the skills they need to contribute to the nation building process we believe needs to take place for a united, democratic South Africa/Azania.

Further to Vumani's approach, they stress that "all children should have access to all the cultures alive in our country and should share the stories, games and songs of those cultures." Their bottom-up, participatory democratic stance is made explicit in the course outline: "The development of a progressive and relevant educare curriculum should take place through the active participation of teachers, parents and children along with other skilled persons (educationists, psychologists, musicians and so on)."

Space does not permit more detailed reference to this program or to others in the educare field. Suffice it to say that antibias and multilingual approaches are widespread in this field and that coordination, unfortunately accompanied by a strong centralization tendency, is at present taking place. Despite numerous problems of coherence, articulation, and especially of overall conceptualization of the curricula, the preschool field in South Africa is a model of a democratic curriculum development process. Many efforts are now being made to ensure that this process does not become bureaucratized in the wake of a more legitimate post-apartheid government.

In the field of adult education, especially adult literacy, and the reentry of out-of-school or out-of-age children and workers (especially trade-union) into education, similar developments are strongly in evidence. In this respect, the recent work of associations such as the National Literacy Co-operation (NLC), the South African Association for Literacy and Adult Education (SAALAE), as well as A Secondary Education Curriculum for Adults (ASECA) and the Primary Open Learning Pathway (POLP), all of which have developed along similar lines to those I have pointed to in educare, is of great significance. ASECA (1993, p. 3), for example, stipulates the following, among other things, in regard to language policy:

ASECA does not value English above other South African languages, particularly the languages that have been marginalised by apartheid. ASECA affirms the learner's right to choice of language medium for education, and supports the principle of affirmative action with regard to languages whose status was reduced under apartheid. . . .

In the short term English will be the only language medium and course choice available within the ASECA curriculum. However, ASECA will ensure that its tutors are multilingual in the sense that they understand or are versatile in the mother tongue of the learners that they are working with. During face-to-face contact, tutors will also be encouraged to use whichever language is most appropriate for the explanation of concepts and issues to the particular audience they serve.

Similarly, POLP has developed for the 2 to 3 million out-of-school children of South Africa

a self-paced syllabus which can be used to integrate children after a minimum of 2 years into the formal standard 3. This syllabus focuses on literacy and language in the mother tongue, English and numeracy, while covering subject content through integrated themes. . . . [It] can be used in a multi-literate, multi-age classroom . . . and emphasises the building of the child's self-image. . . . [It] has trained paraprofessionals to work with these "street" children and with those in informal settlements and from hostels. . . . [It] is networking to see whether certain modules being designed for the teacher training programme should be portable between training for formal teachers, educare workers and adult literacy teachers.

The Congress of South African Trade Unions (COSATU) and some of its major affiliates, especially the National Union of Metalworkers of South Africa, have been a dynamic source of innovative curriculum development in the general sphere of adult education. As in the other cases, the issue of teacher education or teacher development is seen to be pivotal. As intimated already, one of the ways in which the massive POLP justifies the special training for community educators is precisely that these trained educators (25,000 of them) will swell the ranks of well-trained teachers and at the same time introduce directly and indirectly into colleges of education innovative methods of teacher education. This relates particularly to mentoring as a preservice and inservice method of developing teaching skills as well as to such vital skills as working in multilingual classrooms and multilingual schools.

It is particularly in the area of language policy in education that the issue of multiculturalism is being confronted in South Africa. Because of the particular manner in which the transition to democracy is taking place in South Africa, there is much ad hoc experimentation and adaptation in the schools (mainly formerly white, coloured, and Indian) that have suddenly been opened to all children. In a nutshell, in South Africa today, formerly white educational institutions are filling up unused or underutilized capacity (through which the jobs of white teachers are threatened) with limited numbers of black children, who in turn are being pushed out of overcrowded and underresourced schools in the black townships. In the extreme case, entire schools have been taken over by black children who have to make their way by bus, train, and car over long distances from townships to the abandoned white schools. More generally, black children constitute highly visible minority islands in a sea of white, coloured, and Indian children. In only a very few cases, as in some New Era Schools Trust (NEST) sites and at other private schools such as Sacred Heart Convent in Johannesburg, is there some more justifiable proportionality among the children. The real issue, however, is not the ratio of color groups but rather the fact that the dominant language at all these schools is English, sometimes Afrikaans, and that in most cases the black children come from academically deprived backgrounds, which places an added burden on their shoulders. If ever the concept of an educational handicap had a concrete meaning, this is the perfect context in which to study its effects.

Discussing at length the many different strategies adopted by teachers and (the racially defined) education departments to address this problem would be counterproductive, since most of these end up in abject failure, frustration, and increasingly tense intergroup relations. Indeed, South Africans are fortunate, viewed in the historical perspective, that this phenomenon is still in its infancy—that is, that there is probably still enough time to bring about fundamental changes in the strategies used to address these vitally important issues. It ought to be more useful to consider the proposals and practices of one project where a comprehensive long-term approach is being advocated.

PRAESA

Such a project is PRAESA (Project for the Study of Alternative Education in South Africa) at the University of Cape Town. PRAESA represents the culmination of more than two decades of antiapartheid experience and its theorization in the educational sphere. Its point of departure is the proposition that this antiapartheid experience will be the main source of educational renewal in a more democratic South Africa—that is, next to the reform of the existing apartheid institutions and comparative educational theory (international experience). Because of its long-term perspective of radical social transformation, PRAESA has focused on language policy and primary school curriculum development. It advocates three fundamental changes in the conceptualization and structuring of education in South Africa, two of which have major implications for teacher education and development—the deghettoization of education and multilingualism in education and primary-school curriculum development:

1. *Schools (education) should be taken out of the ghetto.* All new schools should be located in "educational zones" to and from which all learners will travel (or walk). In the South African context, busing of (usually) black children to (usually) white schools is strongly opposed in PRAESA because of its prejudicial consequences. The present ad hoc stumbling into this particular option is considered to be a disaster that has to be prevented. PRAESA has consequently commissioned research in metropolitan and semirural contexts in order to arrive at the urban planning and other socioeconomic implications of this approach. Because of the widespread perception of opportunities for change, it is thought that this approach to the deghettoization of education in South Africa is likely to be considered seriously. (For more details concerning this proposal, consult Alexander, 1993; and Smit and Hennessey, 1994.)

2. *The ghetto should be taken out of education.* This means quite simply that all South African schools should become multilingual in their social composition as well as in their pedagogical practice. Single-medium-language schools are considered to be deleterious in their overall sociopolitical consequences, since they tend to enhance and entrench ethnic divisiveness. PRAESA is experimenting with, observing, and analyzing various models of multilingual schooling in South Africa and in other multilingual countries in order to place before the emerging provincial and national educational authorities carefully researched proposals in regard to the restructuring and eventual transformation of South African education.

This proposal has many important implications for materials development, textbook production, teaching methods, and teacher education. Depending on the language constellation in a particular region, most teachers will in the future be required to know with high levels of proficiency at least three languages, one of which will always be English. Teaching in a multilingual classroom and using three (in some cases even more) languages, will necessarily influence teaching styles and strategies adopted by these teachers. Versatility, creativity, metalinguistic interest, and sensitivity as well as a general disposition to be tolerant of diversity will become the hallmarks of the new South African teacher. Because of the felicitous historical fact of the overwhelming numerical preponderance of black Nguni- and Sotho-speaking people, these attitudes are already very widespread among South African teachers. However, very few English- and Afrikaans-speaking South Africans have any knowledge of the African languages and at least two generations will have to pass until these South Africans are comfortably trilingual.

The findings of PRAESA and of the National Language Project (NLP) as well as of a few academics working in the field of language in education are now being published (see Heugh, 1994b). It is abundantly obvious, though, that the success or failure of the new system will depend in the first and last instance on whether or not a core of committed, skillful, culturally sensitive, and tolerant educators will be forthcoming from the colleges and faculties of education. It is in this connection that the numerous teacher-training initiatives in the nongovernmental organization sector are going to be of great significance in the next five to ten years.

3. The third major thrust of PRAESA's intervention is in the area of *primary school curriculum development*. Although secondary and tertiary-level curricular developments are not ignored in the project, it has explicitly concentrated on preschool and primary initiatives. In summary, PRAESA is trying to bring together all curriculum development initiatives relating to the primary school with a view to establishing a democratic, bottom-up curriculum development process owned by primary schoolteachers themselves at a moment in South African history where such a strategic move is not only likely to be considered seriously but is in fact deemed to be essential if the old order is not simply to be dressed up in a new jacket.

Essentially all the many different microinitiatives in materials development, language teaching, teacher education (mostly inservice training), integrated studies approaches, early literacy, and numeracy strategies are being challenged to indicate where on a notional map of the new primary-school curriculum they locate themselves. This map, however, is being drawn by these initiatives themselves. They are already finding one another and are to be encouraged to articulate more systematically with one another for greater effectiveness, coherence, and economy. PRAESA organized the first national South African conference on primary school curriculum initiatives in July 1994, at a time when the new government (of "national unity") was gearing up to move in a new, antiapartheid direction. The objectives of this conference are stated as follows:

- To review and assess primary school curriculum policy initiatives.
- To involve teachers, students, parents, and all other educators in curriculum changes.
- To highlight valuable but isolated curriculum initiatives.
- To facilitate communication among relevant curriculum initiatives.
- To explore all emerging ideas and to map out options and guides for curriculum change in:

    Language policy in primary education

    Teacher development

    Core curriculum and accommodating diversity in the curriculum

    Math, science, technology, and other subject areas.

- To highlight the continuity between educare and primary schooling.
- To identify priority areas for short- and medium-term research in regard to the above (and other) issues.

The conference and the process of consultation that has preceded it are seen as the beginnings of the recomposition of the core curriculum in South Africa. This is not only for the primary school domain but for all education eventually, because of the ripple effect that changes in basic education invariably have. It is assumed that in this process, teachers, parents, other educators, and professionals will, quite organically, arrive at the core curriculum for South Africa derived from African, European, Asian, and the universal modern industrial cultural streams. This is based on the perception that in South Africa such a core culture has been evolving over a period of more than a century of capitalist development and that all the people of South Africa have access to this core culture regardless of the language(s) they speak. From the foregoing analysis, it is clear that the examination of any sector of social life bears out this contention: in sports, religion, music, dance, theater, eating habits, dress, and in education itself, the overlapping area of commonality, as in a Venn diagram, is large enough despite deep-seated class, racial, and gender conflict to constitute the base for building a new nation— that is, for promoting national unity and a national identity. The educational system, as elsewhere in the modern world, is the most effective instrument of socialization for this purpose. Hence the core curriculum will and should reflect this evolving core culture. Because of the peculiar balance of power that exists in South Africa, the chances are that the eventual core curriculum will be neither Eurocentric nor Afrocentric. Judging by the fragmentary but by no means insignificant curricular developments hitherto, it is already obvious that the curriculum in the next few years is bound to become "a theatre of contested community expectations and aspirations" (see Moore, 1992, p. 1)

Reference to Venn diagrams leads me to suggest that the most appropriate metaphor for our understanding of the multiple identities, which all modern people invariably have, is that of every individual being at the center of a concentric universe where the concentric circles represent any number of possible and actual identities. Overlapping lines connect up the sum of individuals in the world in kaleidoscopic ways so that one is always many more things than the immediately perceived persona. Said (1994, p. 408) makes the same point very clearly:

No one today is purely one thing. Labels like Indian, or woman, or Muslim, or American are no more than starting points, which if followed into actual experience for only a moment are quickly left behind. Imperialism consolidated the mixture of cultures and identities on a global scale. But its worst and most paradoxical gift was to allow people to believe that they were only, mainly, exclusively, white, or black, or Western, or Oriental. Yet just as human beings make their own history, they also make their cultures and ethnic identities. No one can deny the persisting continuities of long traditions, sustained habitations, national languages, and cultural geographies, but there seems no reason except fear and prejudice to keep insisting on their separation and distinctiveness, as if that was all human life was about. Survival in fact is about the connections between things.

The core curriculum, it is assumed, will tend to promote unity among all the people of South Africa. It is vital, however, that the total curriculum provide the space and the mechanisms for the expression and accommodation of the tributary aspects of South African culture. By this I mean that the special interests of self-defined groups (other than so-called racial groups) should be legislatively provided for in the educational system. An average of say 75 percent core and 25 percent tributary space and time across the curriculum, treated with the necessary flexibility, would suffice initially. The actual space/time proportion for any subject area or for a particular region will obviously have to be negotiated between the interested parties or stakeholders. Under no circumstances could this proportion simply be dictated by some educational authority from above. Once the principle has been accepted, its implementation should be undertaken with utmost pragmatism. It is quite conceivable, for example, that subjects such as mathematics as well as most of the natural sciences will not be presented differently from the way in which they are taught today, except that illustrations will be indigenized where appropriate and the specific contributions of Europe, Africa, and Asia will be highlighted. In practice, this might mean, for example, that 25 percent of the history syllabus in the higher primary or in the secondary schools could be reserved for the particular contributions, say, of Muslims to South African history. "Muslims" could be replaced by other categories, such as "the people of the Western Cape" or "Nguni-speaking people" or "Europeans."

At first, there will be much confusion and hesitation as well as painful philistinism, but this is the only way to go if a new, radically transformed South Africa is to emerge in the twenty-first century. In history, for example, an open public debate about what constitutes South African history and the different approaches to it will have to be conducted during the next few years. It will be necessary to tolerate for many years contradictory interpretations of South African history in the same textbooks in order to make it possible for all to walk across the bridge between the past and the future and, incidentally, to introduce students to the problems of historiography. Similar strategies will confront educators in one degree or another in all disciplines.

Educational and administrative mechanisms will have to be devised to make possible in as natural a manner as possible the teaching and learning of core as well as tributary elements of the total curriculum in multicultural (i.e., multilingual) South African schools. Numerous strategies are feasible, ranging from peer groups learning with or without extramural assistance where teachers are not themselves competent, through portfolio (workfile) approaches to more elaborate research projects. All the tributary syllabi would be assessed by means of the same criteria that are used to assess the core syllabi.

The crucial contest, in my view, is going to be between the tendency of government departments to bureaucratize the curriculum development process and the inherited tradition of grassroots democracy in the liberation movement. In this regard, teachers' unions; parents', teachers', and students' associations; as well as education nongovernment organizations are going to have to create strong lobbies and mobilize social movements on specific issues of the curricular canon, as well as on the appointment of educators and the management of educational institutions, if the many gains that were made in the 1980s are to be retained and built upon.

In spite, or perhaps because, of the ad hoc character of the present transition to democracy in South Africa, it is possible that the contest between democratization and bureaucratization of the curriculum development process will eventuate in a constellation that affords maximum, if not optimal, space to grassroots initiatives, which will ensure that no new orthodoxy obstructs the process of constant transformation, which alone is the guarantee of life. Certainly, the titanic battles that are already being waged between the mandarins of the old order and the young lions and lionesses of the emerging dispensation, muted though they are at present, are of global significance. For it is abundantly obvious that the former are inclined to be satisfied with a slightly modified racial capitalist order, while the latter are inspired by the asymptotic vision of a raceless society that, in often very inarticulate and confused ways, they equate with what at present appears to be no more than a hopelessly utopian vision of a classless society.

NOTE

1. From among the many possible and acceptable definitions of culture, I choose the rather elaborate and descriptive but, in my view, very useful definition offered by Chung and Ngara (1985:71–72):

[The] culture of a society can be analysed in terms of four basic elements—the economic-technological element, the social-communicative structure, the ideological sphere and the aesthetic element. By the economic-technological element we refer to a society's level of technological development, its implements of work, its mode of production. The social-communicative system comprises the social structure, language, social classes and social relations, the manner in which the individual is socialized, customs and accepted canons of behaviour. The ideological element subsumes religion, philosophy, superstitions, attitudes to and views about life. The aesthetic component includes artistic productions such as dances, literature, crafts and sculpture. . . .

Culture is partly determined by environment and historical conditions. A community's system of values, its implements of work, its diet, etc., will to some extent depend on historical and ecological factors, on climate conditions and on what is available in the locality. As time passes, conditions also change: new things are acquired and old things relinquished. With the passage of time a community interacts with other communities, assimilating new values, its own ways of living and [of] doing things to other communities. Culture is therefore dynamic, not static.

REFERENCES

Alexander, N. 1989. *Language Policy and National Unity in South Africa/Azania.* Cape Town: Buchu Books.
———. 1993. "Take Education Out of the Ghetto—and the Ghetto out of Education." *Weekly Mail.*[Johannesburg], February 12.
Alisjabana, S. 1975. "Some Planning Processes in the Development of the Indonesian-Malay

Language." In J. Rubin and B. Jernudd, eds., *Can Language Be Planned?* Honolulu: University Press of Hawaii.

ASECA. 1993. *Appendices for August 1993.* Cape Town: SACHED.

Bohm, D. 1980. *Wholeness and the Implicate Order.* London: Routledge and Kegan Paul.

Childe, G. 1953. *What Happened in History?* Harmondsworth: Penguin.

Chung, F. and Ngara, E. 1985. *Socialism, Education and Development: A Challenge to Zimbabwe.* Harare: Zimbabwe Publishing House.

Constable, P. 1993. "Language planning for the soul: Interview with Debi Pattanayak." *Bua,* 8(4).

Giliomee, H. 1994. "Apartheid May Be Dead but Racial Fears Are Flourishing." *Cape Times,* [Cape Town], April 14.

Hall, S. 1990. "Cultural Identity and Diaspora." In J. Rutherford, ed., *Identity: Community, Culture, Difference.* London: Lawrence and Wishart.

Harries, P. 1988. "The Roots of Ethnicity: Discourse and the Politics of Language Construction in South-East Africa." *Africa Affairs,* No. 346 (January).

Heugh, K. 1993. "Tongues Tied: Can We Take Language Policy Statements at Face Value?" *Bua,* 8(3).

————. 1994a. "Disabling and Enabling Implications of Language Policy Trends." In R. Meshtrie, ed., *A Reader in South African Sociolinguistics.* Cape Town: David Philip.

————, ed. 1994b. *Multilingual Strategies for South African Schools.* Cape Town: Heinemann.

Hirsch, E. 1988. *Cultural Literacy: What Every American Needs To Know.* New York: Vintage Books

Lemberg, E. 1967. "Nationalismus. Definitionen, Tendenzen, Theorien." *Moderne Welt,* 8(3).

Moore, B. 1992. "The Curriculum: A Theatre for Liberation." Address prepared for "Drama Ties," National Drama in Education Conference, Adelaide. Unpublished mimeo.

Press, K. 1988. "Towards a Revolutionary Artistic Practice in South Africa." Unpublished B.A. (Honours) dissertation, Centre for African Studies, University of Cape Town.

Primary Pathway. 1994. "The Primary Open Learning Pathway" Initiative. *National Conference on Primary School Curriculum Initiatives Newsletter,* No. 2 (April).

Ranger, T. 1983. "Missionaries, Migrants and the Manyika: The Invention of Ethnicity in Zimbabwe." Paper delivered at an International Conference on the History of Ethnic Awareness in Southern Africa. Charlottesville, VA, April 7-10.

Said, E. 1994. *Culture and Imperialism.* London: Vintage.

Skutnabb-Kangas, T. and Cummins, J. 1988. *Minority Education. From Shame to Struggle.* Philadelphia: Multilingual Matters.

Smit, W. and Hennessey, K. 1994. "Education Cluster Project." Unpublished mimeo. University of Cape Town.

Tollefson, J. 1991. *Planning Language, Planning Inequality: Language Policy in the Community.* London: Longman.

Vail, L., ed. 1991. *The Creation of Tribalism in Southern Africa.* Berkeley: University of California Press.

Villiers, I. de. 1994. "de Bestaan 'n groter Suid-Afrikaansheid?" (Is there a larger South Africanism?) *Rapport,* April 3.

Vumani Preschool. 1992. "Training Programme Project." Cape Town: Unpublished mimeo.

Williams, R. 1976. "Developments in the Sociology of Culture." *Sociology* 10(3).

In an impassioned reiteration of the necessity for dialogue in all liberatory struggles, bell hooks (1981, p. 28) insists, with Paulo Freire (as we hear him in the second epigraph) that "language is also a place of struggle. . . . The oppressed struggle in language to recover ourselves—to rewrite, to reconcile, to renew." The cultural voice, the articulate self that resists attempts to silence it, is also gregarious, reasonably flexible, and unavoidably multivocal. This is to say, the speaking and writing subject is capable of revealing more than one way of being in this world. In fact, individuals at various points in their lives seek out opportunities to develop competence in secondary discourses, to be part of their repertoire that normally includes the home discourse as the primary way of seeing reality, of valuing, and of using language.[1] Indeed, perhaps the most inevitable sight of cultural sharing and cross fertilization, aside from what human beings produce as cultural artifacts, is in their language behavior. As Henry Louis Gates (1992, p. xvi) observes, "mixing and hybridity are the rule, not the exception."

I would like to suggest that while individuals from the economic and political margins of society must and do resist attempts from the center to mold them into conformity and to silence their cultural voices, they also come into public arenas, such as university classrooms, wanting not only to claim a space for the values, the ideas, the cultural constructs—that is, the discourses of their cultures of origin—but also to claim the right and the ability to appropriate the discourses associated with public power.

The purpose of this discussion is to explore the ways in which strategically constituted student interaction in a culturally diverse classroom can encourage students' facility in the written discourse of the classroom, which is sometimes referred to as formal print code (Hartwell, 1982, pp. 49–50). Particularly, I will argue that the classroom with a culturally diverse population is, perhaps ironically, better suited than more culturally homogeneous classrooms to assist students in the work of acquiring classroom discourses. This discussion is based on the observation of peer essay review groups, in writing classes with culturally diverse students, including some international students who have, prior to entering my writing class, participated in formal English as a Second Language programs (ESL). Student writers come to these peer groups to present their essays for substantive feedback, indicating the degree to which the writers are communicating clearly, appropriately, and forcefully. To the extent that individual members of the writer's audience are unable to comprehend particular culturally derived forms—typically idioms and syntactical and morphological constructs— the writer must work toward restatement (i.e., revision). The linguistic forms used must render the writer's cultural knowledge. One writer's restatement is usually assisted by another group member. The restatement seems to move inevitably toward the standard, since control over written, standard discourse conventions is a primary, taken-for-granted objective of the typical college composition course.

The request for restatement of an idea constitutes a routine verbal exchange in any writing group, regardless of the ethnic composition of the participants, when the writer's audience fails to get his or her intended meaning. In a group of students who do not share cultural presuppositions, but do share, to varying degrees, the discourse of the classroom, the presumed "target discourse" or academic code becomes a lingua franca, a common language, toward which the students move their language forms in order to be understood by people who do not share their linguistic background. Of at least equal importance in this apparent convergence toward the standard is the unavoidable and, to my mind, necessary retention of some recognizable features from the student's home discourse. For at least two reasons, standard English convergence—or mastery as we call it, from the point of view of the language learning process—is almost always incomplete. First of all, as ESL teachers have stressed to us, intractable features of the native language will intrude upon the surface of the second language. In addition, as most of us are aware, there appears to be a critical age for language learning; most observers indicate that after the beginning of adolescence, a second language can be learned to a large extent, but not without considerable difficulty. As a case in point, "almost everybody can remember how difficult it was to learn French at school. Even the best pupils had a slightly odd accent, and made numerous grammatical mistakes" (Aitchison, 1985, p. 93).

Of equal importance, though not nearly so well-known, is the degree to which individuals from linguistic and cultural practices that are not English or American may also utilize different rhetorical strategies in essay composing. Robert Kaplan (1972, pp. 296–302) explores a range of rhetorical patterns found in non-Western cultures as well as differences within the Western tradition. For example, French speakers, as opposed to English speakers, when explicating an idea or structuring written arguments, are less likely to follow the linear, Platonic-Aristotelian sequencing of ideas. This "Anglo-European" pattern, as Kaplan reminds us, is deductive or inductive, but generally a rhetorical unit that has a main idea or thesis followed or preceded by substantiating explanation, details, facts, and so on. Among the other cultural patterns observed in essay strategies were greater digressive possibilities among the French and indirection and circumlocution among Orientals (the term Kaplan uses to identify "Chinese and Korean, but not Japanese," p. 301). The issue here is that the challenge and promise of broad cultural diversity in the classroom goes much beyond the instructor's commitment to include in curricula works that heretofore have been absent. Once we recognize that our students enter the writing classroom with subtle, but significant culturally derived differences in the areas of writing sylistics and rhetorical strategies, added to obvious language differences in idioms and morphology, we must struggle with what I see as a unique responsibility. We must establish a climate of cultural interaction among students and between students and texts, so that linguistic constructions of identity will not be silenced, but augmented by the students' appropriation of classroom ways of using language.

Within the peer review writing group we are often witness to a negotiation that seems to exemplify the possibilities I have just suggested. Sometimes idioms, cultural references, such as those referring to indigenous places and practices, remain in the writer's text as he or she has initially presented them. At these times, both the writer and his or her group members determine that the surrounding linguistic context situates a culturally derived structure clearly enough so that others can get the meaning. The essay then remains close to the precision and honesty of the writer's voice. When the African American student has written forcefully about an inevitable consequence finally befalling someone who had seemingly avoided responsibility for negative behavior, that student writer does not have to go further to "translate" the black cultural aphorism: "God dont love ugly." The student may well insist that a powerful image is lost through standard English translation or even excessive interpretation. The peer group discussion that ensues in these instances is the metadiscourse, the talk about talk that is, in effect, a structured negotiation. The writer, in his or her desire to be heard and understood, is willing to make changes, but only to the point where his or her voice is still recognizable in its general and idiocultural specificity.

Herein lies the peculiar power and potential of the heterogeneous peer group. What I am calling a negotiation, the students' participation in a *metadiscourse*, is, in Bakhtinian terms, the inevitable consequence of heteroglossia. That is to say that each student comes to the group with a text, constructed to a large extent in "internally persuasive discourse . . . akin to retelling a text in one's own words, with one's own accents, gestures, modifications" (Bakhtin, 1981, p. 424). However, what follows is an inevitable and ongoing interaction of languages and the ideological realities they represent, with each language having the potential of influencing the other (p. 412).

I want to describe the workings of these writing-class peer review groups in order to clarify the ways in which the writer's cultural difference can be voiced and respected while the needs of the writer's audience and the structure of the classroom discourse continue to influence the written, linguistic presentation of each student.

As indicated earlier, the teacher must constitute the peer review group and present the students, through printed handouts and actual verbal modeling, with a format for responding to one another. The student who presents a group of peers with a draft of an essay would be the recipient of different kinds of responses, from straightforward identification of surface error to far more sophisticated and complex questions and answers regarding the relationship between juxtaposed ideas and the intended connection between clauses that are linked only tangentially.

While not the concern of this chapter, peer review groups, in addition to serving as a setting for intervention in the writing process, might also be assembled to provide students the opportunity to share answers to questions relating to a literary text or a social science concept. While I have regularly used peer review groups in my literature and anthropology classes, as well as my writing classes, for the purposes of this chapter I will confine my discussion to groups of the latter sort. The development of my practices with peer groups as described below developed over the course of more than 20 years.

In the early years when I first experimented with peer groups as a part of my pedagogy, I was careful to separate students who were friends outside of the classroom. This was intended to encourage a greater sense of community within the larger group. After a few of those early semesters, it occurred to me that ethnic, gender, class, and age diversity, to the extent that the class composition afforded this, would also enhance the workings of the group. At this time, I was simply concerned with providing students with the opportunity to interact positively with others, different from themselves. This was a concern to my mind with the affective domain of learning. It would be emotionally gratifying and enriching.

During these early years, I was only vaguely aware of the cognitive-linguistic dimension of this arrangement. While it was indeed significant that these students had the opportunity to interact with people from different backgrounds, I was soon to learn that the advantages and the challenges of this deliberate multicultural arrangement derived from the ways in which all students were prompted to construct and reconstruct ideas so that their ideas were only minimally reliant on cultural presuppositions communicated in the form of idioms, nonstandard English dialectal morphologies, and even culturally derived rhetorical strategies. That is, to the extent that the students in a group were unable to receive the intended message of the speaker/writer, that speaker/writer had to restate the point until he or she had reached a level of general comprehensibility. The students engaged in group process, it seems, were prompted to move their writing, unawares, toward what I have called a *lingua franca*, a common language that was divested of very specific, closed network cultural meanings that would foreclose on the comprehension of group participants who did not share the writer/speaker's cultural background. While one could not accurately identify this so-called *lingua franca* as neatly identifiable standard English, the closest descriptive label available for the common language is a semiformal standard that, for the most part, has been divested of nonstandard American English regional, social, or ethnic markers as well as unconventional morphological or idiomatic constructions that are often seen as second language interference features in the writing of students who have learned English as a second language.[2]

From these observations, I have been prompted to explore the ways in which the peer review group in a writing class, particularly, but in any substantive subject class as well, could encourage the development of standard, classroom discourse in students who have only partial acquisition and control of standard print code, or classroom discourse. The potential of the peer review group to encourage such refinement of classroom discourse seems to be dependent upon a number of conditions, the development of which would fall to the classroom instructor. The general tenor of the group would closely reflect the mutual author and audience responsibility for ownership of ideas, along the model set forth by Peter Elbow (1973) in the ground-breaking contribution to writing pedagogy, *Writing Without Teachers*. One of the most impressive accomplishments of this book is its clarity in demonstrating the ways in which a writer's audience can respond without appropriating the writing—that is, telling the author what he or she failed to do and telling him or her, authoritatively, what ought to be done.

Instead, peer reviewers are shown how they can respond in a number of ways, including the use of descriptive metaphors, such as "This paragraph marches forward; the second seems to crawl. The 'march' is easier to follow" (pp. 90–91). In this way the reader is taking the responsibility to show the writer how she is reacting to the writing, how it is affecting her. Similarly, the writer is instructed to avoid the temptation to defend and to explain. It will be most useful to him if he just acknowledges receipt of the response, perhaps making note of it. Ultimately, it is his responsibility to utilize the feedback in a way that is useful in revising the essay. Final revision decisions are his, and he will use or ignore the feedback as he sees fit. This general practice includes the sending of "I" rather that "you" messages, especially in the early stages of group work when individuals are just getting to know one another. This is generally a period of extra self-consciousness and insecurity. Most participants have had little or no experience giving and receiving feedback from their peers in the process of their composing activities.

In recent years, it seems my basic writing classes have had many more students than usual from very different cultural backgrounds. For example, I have recently had relatively small classes of up to 15 students.[3] In one such class I had one young man and one woman from Korea, one young man from Uganda, a young woman from Colombia, one from Taiwan, one young urban Puerto Rican woman, one suburban middle-class white woman, and three urban inner-city black men, two of whom were several years older than the rest of the students. While each of these students had considerable control over the conventions of standard discourse, each regularly incorporated culturally derived forms in essays. When others in the group were ready to respond to a particular essay, they quickly identified the idioms, the grammatical structures, and even the rhetorical strategies that either appeared inappropriate or were simply not easily followed by the audience. Language became a terrain of negotiation, where persons separated by cultural practices had to move toward standard forms, the only common ground, in order to satisfy the audience's need to understand the written piece.

The following examples come from the same assignment I made in two basic writing courses, taught the first semester of the school year, at the four-year state institution where I have worked since the early 1980s. Students in these classes are provided with instruction and practice in utilizing different voices and a range of rhetorical strategies, generally determined by particular objectives for a particular assignment that must reach an identifiable audience. That is, there is considerable discussion of the ways a personal, committed voice, for example, as opposed to a detached, discursive voice, might be more appropriate for one audience than another. In addition, there is on-going attention to conventional print code, in terms of both format and standard morphology or grammar. These mechanical or surface features of writing are usually addressed in the context of the student's own piece of writing; discussions and exercises may take place in the class or in one-on-one and small group tutorials outside of class.

Each of the following examples from student writing, which illustrate the particular words, idioms, or phrases that were questioned during the process of group peer review of essays, will be preceded by a brief background sketch of the reading subject who is presenting his or her essay. The first example come from an African American man in his mid-thirties, whom I am calling Harry. Harry grew up in a small, inner-city black enclave in southern New Jersey. He is generally forthright and exceedingly motivated, determined to put great distance between his current activities as a student and, in his words, "the outlaw activities of his youth." He is passionate about his new life as a student, his children, and his future in human services. Harry's excerpts and those that follow his come from essays written in response to a writing assignment on present-day spiritual practices. Students were asked to read an essay on New Age practices and interview one person who practiced an organized religion. They were to describe New Age as they had come to understand it through the reading and through classroom discussion, and to determine whether the individual whom they interviewed did in fact share the essay author's mostly negative opinion of what was perceived as New Age. Some of the students hypothesized that even those who belonged to traditional churches and practiced their religions actually participated in some of the activities associated with New Age, such as keeping crystals, burning incense while meditating, using herbal medicines, and the like. In short, students were going to determine whether the person they interviewed, a religious person in the conventional sense, expressed the same distrust of New Age practices as the author, Christopher Lasch (1993). In writing about the skepticism and disdain with which Lasch described New Age religious practices, Harry hastens to articulate, in a strong personal voice, his own interrogation of the fairness of the writer:

What's the difference between traditional religion and the New Age Movement? Both of them pray in their own way, and they both have some kind of faith in something that they don't see or hear. Both have symbols; if it is not a cross, it is a stone, or a star or something. How in the hell can any of those symbols do anything for anybody, scientifically?

The writer then continues:

I read the article "New Age Movement: No Effort, No Truth, No Solutions," and this essay is a very hard essay to write about, without hurting somebody's feelings. The article talks about New Age benefits, New Age faults, and Traditional Religion's benefits, but the writer, Christopher Lasch, did not mention traditional religion's faults, like all these traditional religions never had any.

Further on, he adds:

The Europeans used their traditional religions or their guns to take land from every race on this earth. The Europeans, too, felt their God was the best God for Humankind. "Believe in my God or die." Could Lasch be acting out of his own ethnicity or religion?

What of peer responses? While the Puerto Rican woman, the white American woman, and the Ugandan man in his group understood the sardonic tone and the historical allusions, the Korean woman, who had been in this country only about four years, was not sure what the writer meant when he asked if Lasch were "acting out of his own ethnicity." After some discussion, the Puerto Rican woman and the white woman, who both had been enculturated in this society and had first-hand familiarity with its racial conflict, encouraged Harry to elaborate so that his meaning would be accessible to all his readers. Hence Harry decided to explain further:

Could Lasch be acting out of his own ethnicity or religion? Is he making judgments because he comes from a privileged group? Or could Lasch have been so much of a Pentecostal [one who believes that the faithful get filled with the Holy Ghost as a sign of their being saved] that he is close-minded?

The reader of this essay might well question why and how have the student-writer's additions made his point clearer. It is in an example like this one that we see the way in which student negotiation determines the ultimate point of clarity, rather than any arbitrary measure of right, or sufficiency. The listeners typically ask, "Could you put something else in there. I get it, basically, but not completely." The writer then says, "What if I say . . . ," and the group members might approve, disapprove, or give an example, "Could you say . . . ?" which might be accepted as is, modified, or discarded by the author. The point here is that ultimately the writer is in control, but he is always reminded that he has an audience to reach, and everyone in that audience does not share the cultural experiences that inform his thinking and writing. It is also of critical importance that we call attention to the author's retention of his black, cultural signifying practice, which is the indirect calling into question of Lasch's underlying motivations in writing the article. While Harry has been influenced by the needs of his audience, he has also retained his own "internally persuasive" discourse.

The next example comes from an essay on the same topic. The writer is a young woman from Taiwan, who has studied in this country for less than five years. She is forthright and assertive in both her oral and written voices. She usually brings a quirky, bold humor to the group, which is appreciated by everyone, in spite of the fact that her spoken English is sometimes halting. Her peer review group consisted of a young African American woman, a young Dutch woman who was in her first semester in America (direct from Holland), a young Puerto Rican woman, and a young white man. Lil speaks English slowly, carefully picking out her words, automonitoring and correcting. She is as deliberate and scrutinizing in her writing. In addition to her peer group work, she routinely spent many hours a week in the college's writing center, working with tutors who have specific experience with ESL students. The essay revisions facilitated by the peer group members, therefore, were further refined through this tutorial work. What follows now is an excerpt from the writer's draft, which she brought to the group for intervention:

Lasch described New Age movement is no effect, no truth and no solutions. A lot of people may not have too many rules to control their lives.

Group members wanted to know whether this writer meant, in the second sentence, that they didn't have the rules because they were not available to them or they just didn't want the rules. "Why don't they have rules in their lives?" Lil was asked. Her response is in her revision. In addition, her revision reveals correction of the nonstandard English morphologies in the first sentence.

According to Lasch, New Age Movement has no discipline, takes advantages of people, and fails to help people. Some people may not need the traditional religion's rules to control their lives. Without this religious discipline, it could make more people happier.

While the writer has not edited her writing to standard English perfection (we can see native language interference in a number of places), she has maintained her intended meaning and the force of her own subtle interrogation of the author, while making the passage more comprehensible to other readers. Those who regard the student's revisions with lingering concern over her failure to correct *all* grammatical features must keep in mind that we defeat our own purposes if we mark more error patterns than a student can master in the process of writing one essay. I believe with Donald Knapp (1972, p. 219) and others who specialize in ESL instruction (as I do not) that it is of little value to ask students to master more than two or three mistake patterns per week, as it only serves to discourage the student who is overwhelmed by what is perceived as the enormity of his or her error.

James Gee (1990) is particularly insightful in his explication of the complexity and sensitivity of the process of helping students to acquire literacy in school discourses. First of all, he cautions us after the insights of others, such as the Scollons who studied Athabaskan Indian language practices and Shirley Brice Heath who did monumental work in the Piedmont Carolinas, that

discourse practices are always embedded in the particular world view of particular social groups; they are tied to a set of values and norms. In apprenticing to new social practices, a student is acquiring a new identitiy, one that at various points may conflict with her initial enculturation and socialization, and with the identities connected to other social practices in which she engages. (p. 67)

Our work then is inherently paradoxical as we know that while language is a powerful gatekeeper, learning the discourse of public power will not suddenly remove all the other barriers to equal opportunity and access for marginalized groups. Moreover, we do little if we fail to recognize the critical sustaining power and inherent value of home discourses. There are classroom practices, I have argued, that provide opportunities for students to talk about talk, engaging in a "metadiscourse of difference." They are aided, as Gee would say, by teachers in "expanded roles as school-based literate persons" (p. 68), who guide them through the kind of explaining, reasoning, and questioning activities on an adult level that approximate what the child born into these standard English practices does in the early acquisition process. I hope to have gone a stop further, however, to suggest that most students are willing apprentices in the study and practice of standard discourses, especially when their home discourses or native languages are counted for the valued and valuable currency that they are. Our students are perhaps more aware than we of the possibility that, in spite of their willingness to learn standard discourse practices, they still require spaces for their cultural voice in the academic classroom. Nonstandard rhetorical strategies, such as narration and circumlocution or indirection, along with Platonic-Aristotelian linear thinking/writing, might be needed to truly represent our culturally diverse ways of making meaning.

To suggest that there is no thoroughly unitary voice of America, and that we can always already hear the full range of competing and harmonizing discourses, indicates that across the battleground of the *culture wars* we will have to, in spite of intractable resistances, regard the inevitable but uneasy truce of ongoing dialogue. When we invoke the metaphor of *war*, in discussions of cultural diversity, we are foregrounding a fundamental problem that seems only to be intensifying in contemporary American culture, most visibly in academic communities. The power of metaphor-making lies in the metaphor's multivalence; in the case of culture wars, the competing values and ideologies and their representative cultural by-products or artifacts challenge each other from opposing camps. One of the most salient features of the metaphor, the battleground, suggests that when and if the din of the conflict quiets, we will be left with one or several potential winners on the one hand and a roster of casualties on the other. The image of war necessitates enemies and allies, presumably intent upon, at best, obliterating the other, at the very least, rendering competitors impotent and silent. We may, however, reject the polemicism inherent in the metaphor and lead it away from victory on the one hand and loss on the other. Instead, in the current contest for ideological and cultural representation, we must move toward a solution that is more fruitful and more humane and, I would like to think, already in process.

NOTES

1. In this context, I am thinking of discourse as more than just talk—that is, as specific and distinct, culturally constructed fields of representation and ways of being in the world. James Gee (1990, p.143) comments aptly on this broader sense of discourse:

A discourse is a socially accepted association among ways of using language, of thinking, feeling, believing, valuing and of acting that can be used to identify oneself as a member of a socially meaningful group or "social network," or to signal (that one is playing) a socially meaningful "role."

2. In spite of my contention that the resulting discourse within the group has moved away from culturally derived forms, I would suggest here, as I have argued elsewhere (Nelson, 1991), that the written voice inevitably carries some cultural markings. Teachers should be sensitive to the ways in which occasional idioms or lexemes, removed from the standard, might be important to preserve, because attempts to translate them might deprive a composition of the specificity of the writer's intended meaning. In cases where student writers make such determination, it should be clear to the teacher as well as other members of the reading audience that the culturally derived idiom is not error, but rhetorical strategy; that is, the reader must be reasonably confidant that the writer has consciously chosen the nonstandard form for its emblematic significance or for some other rhetorical purpose.

3. Although the classes to which I refer had about 15 students, the maximum number enrolled in the basic writing class at my institution is 25. My classes, upon which this discussion focuses, are more nearly homogeneous than the other basic writing sections in any given semester. The students in my classes were identified through entrance testing to be the most at risk of failing to meet the rigors of college-level writing. The numbers in classes of this kind, therefore, reflect the numbers of those so identified at the time; that is, if a greater number "tested in," in any given semester, the classes could theoretically go up to 25 students.

REFERENCES

Aitchison, Jean. 1985. "Predestinate Grooves: Is There a Preordained Language 'Program'?" In V. P. Clark, P. A. Eschholz, and A. F. Rosa, eds., *Language: Introductory Readings*. New York: St. Martin's Press.

Bakhtin, M. M. 1981. *The Dialogic Imagination*, Michael Holquist, ed., C. Emerson and M. Holquist, trans. Austin: University of Texas Press.

Bridwell-Bowles, Lillian. 1992. "Discourse and Diversity: Experimental Writing Within the Academy." *College Composition and Communication*, Vol. 43, No. 3, October, pp. 349–368.

Elbow, Peter. 1973. *Writing Without Teachers*. New York: Oxford University Press.

Freire, Paulo. 1972. *Pedagogy of the Oppressed*. Myra Berman Ramos, trans. New York: Herder and Herder.

Gates, Henry Louis, Jr. 1992. *Loose Canons: Notes on the Culture Wars*. New York: Oxford University Press.

Gee, James. 1990. *Social Linguistics and Literacies: Ideology in Discourses*. New York: The Falmer Press.

Hartwell, Patrick. 1982. *Open to Language*. New York: Oxford University Press.

hooks, bell (Gloria Watkins). 1989. *Talking Back, Thinking Feminist, Thinking Black*. Boston: South End Press.

Kaplan, Robert B. 1972. "Cultural Thought Patterns in Inter-Cultural Education." In H. B. Allen and R. N. Campbell, eds., *Teaching English as a Second Language*, 2nd ed. New York: McGraw-Hill, pp. 294–309.

Knapp, Donald. 1972. "A Focused, Efficient Method to Relate Composition Correction to Teaching Aims." In H. Allen and R. N. Campbell, eds., *Teaching English as a Second Language*. New York: McGraw-Hill.

Lasch, Christopher. 1993. "The New Age Movement: No Effort, No Truth, No Solutions." In R. Atwan, ed., *Our Times/3*. New York: St. Martin's Press, pp. 245–252.

Nelson, Linda Williamson. 1990. "Codeswitching in the Oral Life Narratives of African American Women: Challenges to Linguistic Hegemony." *Journal of Education*, Vol. 172, No. 3, pp. 142–155.

———. 1991. "On Writing My Way Home: Finding My Authentic Self Within the Academy." In M. Schwartz, ed., *Writer's Craft, Teacher's Art: Teaching What We Know.* New York: Boynton Cook.

The Cultural Ethos of the Academy: Potentials and Perils for Multicultural Education Reform

Geneva Gay and Wanda Fox

Since the inception of demands for teacher education curricula to incorporate more ethnic and cultural diversity, quite a bit has been written about the best way to achieve the desired results. By far the greatest emphasis in these proposals has been on changing the content of courses and programs of study, while the instructional process itself has been virtually ignored. In some ways this is not surprising, given the normative pedagogical standards and cultural ethos of academe. However, it does raise a question about whether this emphasis is congruent with the major theoretical tenets, priorities, and directions of multicultural education. If it is not, then what new perspectives and paradigms need to be added to reform strategies to bridge this gap, and thereby to improve the likelihood that multicultural education in colleges and universities will be achievable? These questions are explored in this chapter and some possible answers are suggested for them.

Three major topics are developed. The first is a conceptual framework that establishes some theoretical parameters for implementing effective multicultural programs. The second topic is salient features of the ethos of the academy, including values, structures, expectations, and procedures that constitute the institutional culture of colleges and universities. The chapter concludes with a discussion of reform strategies that can make the implementation of multicultural education in academe more viable.

CONCEPTUAL FRAMEWORK

The premises underlying these discussions derive from four major concepts and themes woven throughout the theory and philosophy of multicultural education. One of them is the importance of contextual and developmental appropriateness in making decisions about educational reforms to promote ethnic and cultural diversity. This means that changes are most effective when they are informed by and respond directly to the details of specific ecological settings. An educational ecology encompasses the relationships between formal institutional policies, protocols, and practices; informal customs, traditions, and expectations; and the values and beliefs of the individuals who inhabit these environments. Consequently, particular multicultural education initiatives should vary according to the places, times, audiences, and purposes for which they are intended.

Another recurrent theme in multicultural education theory is that its implementation requires systemic and systematic change. Effective teaching about and for cultural diversity is characterized by purposeful planning, a regularity of occurrence, and a presence in all dimensions of the educational process, as well as in all aspects of the educational institution. It is for all students, subjects, and educational settings. As S. Nieto (1992, p. 213) explains, because multicultural education is "about all people, it is also for all people, regardless of their ethnicity, language, religion, gender, race, or class." While curriculum content that reflects the contributions of a variety of ethnic and cultural groups is essential to this mandate, it is not sufficient. Incorporating cultural diversity into other elements of the educational enterprise, such as instructional strategies, learning climate, knowledge construction, research paradigms and methodologies, administrative styles, and assessment procedures are of equal importance. Such an "infusion ideology" acknowledges the cultural plurality of the United States and insists that this reality should be reflected in all dimensions of education (Banks, 1994).

Closely related to themes of contextual and holistic changes is the integral role of personal values, beliefs, and life experiences in teaching and learning processes. Multicultural education is grounded more in a way of thinking, being, and behaving than it is in a distinguishable body of content to be transmitted to students. At its philosophical center is the fact that human beings are incredibly diverse, that the expressive manifestations of humanity are determined by cultural socialization, and that teaching and learning are human endeavors that occur in given cultural contexts. Students and teachers bring to the instructional process their own complex cultural systems that affect how they think, know, learn, believe, communicate, and relate (Shade, 1989). Multicultural education accepts this diversity and acknowledges that since both knowledge and humanity are cultural creations, they can never be totally objective, neutral, infallible, absolute, complete, or universal. Therefore, the educational process should be perceived as a constant quest for human betterment that is characterized by critique, tentative solutions, reflections, multiple perspectives, and knowledge reconstructions. Multicultural education adds the lens of ethnic and cultural pluralism to these processes.

The fourth and overriding theme is that at its essence, multicultural education is transformative and revolutionary. It seeks to change some of the fundamental beliefs, assumptions, and values U.S. society holds about ethnic and cultural diversity. It replaces old social standards of Eurocentric cultural assimilation and homogeneity with new ones of cultural plurality and heterogeneity. Rather than promoting a competitive hierarchy of plurality in which European-American norms predominate, multicultural education advocates cooperative plurality without any hierarchical domination among the different cultures and groups that comprise the United States. It directly confronts the fact that the United States is a racist society with a long history of white supremacy and Eurocentric cultural hegemony, and is committed to creating a social transformation (Bennett, 1990).

A transformative approach to multicultural education reconceptualizes the foundational principles of U.S. education within the context of cultural diversity. It creates multicultural canons; teaches students to be reflective, critical thinkers and decision makers; presents knowledge as a social construction; and is committed to achieving social equity and justice for all citizens (Banks, 1994; Gay, 1994; Suzuki, 1984). This emphasis concentrates on what B. B. Tye (1987) calls the deep structures of educational institutions. By "deep structures" she means the value assumptions of mainstream culture. For example, the prominence given to individual competition in academics is analogous to the capitalistic imperatives of market demands, entrepreneurship, and the notion that the best are winners. Multicultural education questions and transforms these basic value assumptions. C. E. Sleeter and C. A. Grant (1994) characterize such emphases on changing the essential core of schooling to reflect cultural diversity as education that is multicultural and social reconstructionist.

This kind of education is a form of personal empowerment in which learning becomes a basis for challenging inequitable and unjust social practices that disadvantage some groups while privileging others. It also teaches students from all ethnic, social, and cultural groups about knowledge as a tool of power and emancipation; that their histories and experiences are valid and make a difference; and that what they say and do are a significant part of the struggle to make the nation and world better places to live for everyone (Giroux, 1993; Sleeter, 1991). Once the paradigmatic shift from emphasizing cultural assimilation and academic passivity to cultural pluralism and social activism is implemented, it will constitute a social revolution because it creates major changes in fundamental educational values, beliefs, structures, and practices.

We will return to the four themes—contextual and developmental appropriateness; systemic and systematic change; the integral role of personal values, beliefs, and life experiences in teaching and learning processes; and the transformative and revolutionary nature of multicultural education—later in this chapter when we suggest reform strategies for effectively achieving multicultural education within academe, following a discussion of key elements within the ethos of academia that impede their implementation.

CULTURAL ETHOS OF THE ACADEMY

Traditionally, colleges and universities have been thought of as places where students and teachers engage in the open and uninhibited exploration of ideas and where the knowledge and thought generated from research and scholarship are subjected to careful critique to determine their rigor and validity. R. F. Goheen (1969, pp. 22–23) adds that the university is "a place where people are assembled to press the search for truth, the adventure of ideas, as teachers and learners, freely and without fetters of dogma or prescription . . . [and where] students learn to do their own thinking, their own reflecting." These notions create a mental image of students and professors engaged in vibrant, interactive, and stimulating dialogues where all claims of truth are thoroughly scrutinized. They portray universities as places where the prevailing practice is to be critical of old ideas, skeptical of present wisdom, passionate about the discovery of new knowledge, and committed to the spirit of free inquiry. In reality, quite the reverse is true.

In fact, most university classrooms, including those in colleges of education, are notoriously devoid of engaging dialogue, intellectual curiosity, questioning exploration, and active student participation. E. L. Boyer's (1987) study of undergraduate education in 29 colleges and universities confirms these assertions, corroborated in findings by P. Shore (1992), V. B. Smith and A. R. Bernstein (1979), and R. D. Simpson and S. H. Frost (1993). Boyer (1987) reported a persistent tension between conformity and creativity in the classroom. Faculty members repeatedly complained about the passivity of students, "whose interests are stirred only when reminded that the material being presented will be covered on a test" (pp. 4-5). In too many classes there was an absence of vigorous intellectual exchange, a condition for which Boyer and his colleagues attribute responsibility to both faculty and students.

The fact that students contribute to the passive and staid climate of college classrooms comes as no surprise when one considers the characteristics of the structures, climates, processes, and dynamics of the K–12 educational system, as described by J. I. Goodlad (1984) in his study *A Place Called School*. The students most likely to "succeed" and go on to college often are those who have been most effectively socialized at the secondary level. Unfortunately, Goodlad's compelling portraiture of life in the secondary classroom includes the following features that are also widely practiced at the college level:

- The domination of the teacher in determining the content, tone, and conduct of instruction. This domination is characterized by teachers standing or sitting in the front of the classroom explaining or lecturing, and having unilateral control over decisions about what, when, where, and which students will learn.

- Students engaged in a narrow range of passive learning activities such as listening, preparing assignments, taking notes, and tests.

- An emotive tone to human relations that is neither harsh, abrasive, and punitive, nor warm, enthusiastic, and joyful.

- Large, whole group instruction.

- Students becoming increasingly more compliant and accepting of teacher authority as the grades increase, instead of assuming independent decision-making roles in their own education.

- An instructional environment that is constrained and constraining.

- Individual students working and achieving alone in large group settings.

- Students who are passively content with the classroom life they experience.

Goodlad concludes that this combination of attributes and circumstances of life in the classroom "conspires to limit the school's role in the humanization of knowledge" (p. 126).

At the university level, the ongoing socialization of students to a passive, teacher-dominated environment is further intensified by the hierarchical social class and academic divisions that typically exist between students and professors, which do not allow them to have equal status or mutually supportive and co-operative intellectual relationships. Consequently, students become subservient to unquestionable ideas of expert scholars in the classroom and in their fields of study. These experts are presented as icons of authority to be idolized and imitated. Too often, students spend most of their time memorizing and regurgitating the knowledge that these experts have produced without ever questioning or critiquing it. The rare students who dare to question too often are soon silenced by a system of sanctions governed by unspoken, yet clearly understood, expectations. Among these are attitudes of instructors that it is presumptuous of novices to question experts, and attitudes of other students who believe that one who questions too much is interfering with their quality time with professors. The latter attitude may be expressed as "I took this class to listen to the professor, not other students."

Academic relationships of this sort are not conducive to the best quality education. "To be vital, to produce genuine thinking and creative habits of mind, education . . . requires opportunities of give-and-take, in some degree of intimacy between the student as an individual and teachers who themselves exhibit a spirit of inquiry, of rational deliberation, of intellectual creativity, of honest judgment" (Goheen, 1969, p. 88). However, if faculty and students do not see themselves as being closely linked in a common cause venture, if students view professors as distant and unapproachable, and their instructional material as irrelevant and uninteresting, if the classroom is charged with tension and intimidation, then learning effectiveness is minimized, and the process becomes merely a series of uninspired rituals and routines (Boyer, 1987).

Another pervasive element of the ethos of the academy is evident in the teaching style that predominates. Lecturing is sacrosanct. Information is presented by instructors and passively received by students. Too little incentive and opportunity are provided for students to question ideas, challenge positions, clarify points, explore their doubts, introduce new assumptions and alternative perspectives, and critique each others' as well as their professors' contributions (Boyer, 1987). Deviations from this format are exceptional and isolated. It is so deeply ingrained in notions about what are correct college customs that one who does not lecture is often suspect of not being adequately prepared, sufficiently scholarly, and not really teaching.

Several other powerful messages are implicit in the virtually exclusive use of lecturing as a teaching style. A central message is that knowledge is something that one person can give to another, as opposed to something that is constructed by each individual in a process mediated by culture, values, and life experience (Banks, 1993). Even if one believes that knowledge can be directly transmitted from one person to another, the lecture method of teaching assumes that such knowledge is inherently interesting and motivating. Therefore, all teachers need to do is present information to students and that will be sufficient for them to learn. A closely related third message is the utmost importance of knowledge. Because knowledge is more significant than those who consume it, the primary obligation of instructors is to transmit it in its purest form, and to preserve its sanctity. Thus, a teaching style is employed that minimizes student engagement with the information being presented. Furthermore, exclusive use of lecturing implies that all students learn in the same way, since lecturing does not allow for any alternative learning styles.

Teaching styles are powerful forces within academe. On many campuses, the impact of teacher-dominated, hierarchical classrooms is just one more factor that reinforces the European-American dominance of the entire U.S. society, including higher education. A case in point is the battle over the canon. Institutional discourse, as manifested in policy guidelines, social protocols, and curriculum designs, continues to perpetuate the idea that all standards of intellectual quality derive from Eurocentric cultural origins. If universities were indeed as open to new ideas and academic freedom as the mythology claims, the notion that literary quality and academic knowledge are socially constructed and culturally determined would be a given, and not subject to debate. Knowledge and pedagogical canons that were not by nature culturally pluralistic would be intolerable, since they would violate this normative expectation.

The conforming, conservative, Eurocentric features of the ethos of the academy are further evident in the response to Ethnic and Women's Studies programs and scholarship. The persistent questions about the legitimacy of these initiatives, despite an impressive body of supportive scholarship, suggest that the academy is not open to ideas and interpretations that challenge its prevailing paradigms. This disposition is conveyed further through the scathing attacks on the scholarly merits of the research of ethnic and female scholars who study their own groups' issues, cultures, histories, and experiences. The critics view Women's or Ethnic

Studies programs as feminist or ethnic group scholarship, and other related multicultural efforts as not being serious scholarship and deserving of a significant place in the academy's system of programs and values. According to the critics, they do not meet acceptable (meaning Eurocentric) standards of research rigor. These and other multicultural education efforts are dismissed as merely politically correct propaganda created by special interest groups, and not to be confused with serious scholarship. The works of Arthur Schlesinger, Jr. (1992) and Dinish D'Souza (1991) are illustrative of these critiques.

In keeping with the hierarchical structure of academe, such attacks have a strong gatekeeping effect. Individuals who wish to become part of the inner sanctum of the professorate are too often intimidated into making the necessary concessions and conforming to the status-quo expectations. If their highly respected and accomplished colleagues, who also have decision-making power over their job tenure and promotions, deem their research, scholarship, and teaching interests insignificant, what else can one do but concede? Those individuals who do not concede to these pressures are relegated to function largely on the periphery of academe, relative to positions of authority, respect, and influence. A few exceptions may be allowed full-fledged membership into the club to demonstrate the academy's tolerance and liberalism. In effect, their presence is mere tokenism, and does nothing to deny just how powerful pressures for conformity are in colleges and universities. These attitudes and behaviors are examples of the deeply entrenched hierarchical caste structure that exists in the academy, which continues to privilege those individuals, ideas, and practices already in positions of power and influence. It perpetuates a dangerous kind of cultural and intellectual provincialism that is counterproductive to the potentials of multicultural education.

In addition to conformity and conservatism, social passivity is a prominent feature of the ethos of the academy. Even when social issues are subjected to critique and analyses in the classroom, this tends to be a theoretical and academic exercise. Rarely are college campuses sites of social consciousness and political activism that are fueled and directed by classroom discourse activities. When social activism does happen, such as protests against the Vietnam War, Desert Storm, sexism, racism, and demands for multicultural education, the initiatives almost exclusively come from outside formal programs of study. Thus social activism in the academy tends to be ad hoc, informal, and crisis-driven rather than a regularly promoted and valued element of college culture. When there are no pressing national or international events occurring, college campuses drift quickly back into their normative pattern of social apathy, moral abdication, and political inactivity. These tendencies have significant implications for understanding the current status of multiculturalism in higher education, and for designing future reform strategies for a movement that is highly social, political, ethical, humanistic, and reconstructive.

The strong value of scientism, an additional feature that permeates the entire structure and dynamics of the academy, is responsible for cultivating some of the depersonalization, lack of human investment, and social distancing that exist on college campuses. The importance scientism attaches to objective, rational, factual, and analytical methods of inquiry and explanation determines the character of research, scholarship, teaching, and the interpersonal relationships among students and instructors. It generates a kind of dispassionate and impersonal persona that pervades the entire institutional climate, and generates the aura Goodlad (1984) observed in K–12 schools as "emotional flatness" and "affective neutrality." Consequently, students rarely engage with each other in cooperative academic efforts; a kind of religiosity is attached to "empirical data," which excludes any possibility of its fallibility; relationships between students and professors are infrequent and restricted to formalities associated with class requirements; and a tone of austerity prevails. The "personal and the personalized," the passionate and compassionate seem to have no place of significance in the academy.

A graphic illustration of these dispassionate, impersonal, and "scientific" elements of the ethos of the academy is evident in rewards attached to research. Researchers with positivist and empiricist orientations often are given higher accolades of achievement for the technical quality of their discoveries without any regard for their moral, ethical, and social consequences. Yet individuals who study social issues and events in which they have a personal vested interest—such as African American, Mexican American, or Native American sociologists studying racism—are suspect because of the presumption of inherent subjective bias. Research that is not experimental, quantitative, and data-based is still viewed rather skeptically with respect to its quality and value, despite the increasing frequency and recognition given to qualitative studies.

Finally, among the most telling symbols of the ethos of the academy, and of particular significance in considerations about multiculturalism in higher education, has to do with personnel. The disproportionate underrepresentation of students and professors of color at most universities suggests something about these institutions' commitments to equality of opportunities and power sharing. Ethnic and cultural diversity simply is not a distinguishing characteristic of most colleges and universities. The numbers are too few and their placement in the institutional chain of command, power, and authority is not enough to constitute a critical mass of influence. This is a pervasive and compelling reality regardless of the unit of analysis used, whether it be student enrollment, faculty representation, administrative positions, curriculum content, resource allocations, policy regulations, or cocurricular activities.

The principles and practices we have just described create a specific institutional character, climate, spirit, and culture that constitute the ethos and ambiance of educational environments. Unfortunately, many of these characteristics are not compatible with the attributes and envisioned goals of multicultural education. However, implementation of multicultural education has the potential to reverse these trends, to open new vistas of personal, intellectual, and moral explorations, to revitalize social consciousness, and to make the purpose of education come closer to realizing its commitment to individual enrichment and social betterment.

In a given college or university situation, an important first step toward improving the process of implementing multicultural education is to examine and seek to understand the particular nature of this ethos, and then to design intervention strategies accordingly. This approach is consistent with the multicultural premise that stresses the importance of contextual and developmental appropriateness in making decisions about educational reforms to promote ethnic and cultural diversity. In the next section we will suggest possible points of entry for making multicultural education in institutions of higher education more effective.

REFORM STRATEGIES

Multicultural education in colleges and universities should have a dual-directional approach, with one focus being infusion and the other transformation. The infusion strategies would concentrate on embedding a multicultural presence and perspective into all dimensions of existing institutional enterprises, through revisions in curriculum content, instructional strategies, hiring practices, administrative procedures, and other institutional functions. Transformative strategies address more fundamental value assumptions and organizational climate of colleges and universities with respect to ethnic and cultural diversity. Transformative strategies focus on changing values and perspectives of the individuals and groups involved with higher education, while infusion strategies are directed at current structures and practices. Both emphases are needed and should exist in tandem with each other for two reasons. First, in the foreseeable future there is not likely to be enough deep, multicultural change in the existing structures of colleges and universities using infusion strategies to make a significant difference. It is uncertain whether they have the will or skill to multiculturalize their existing cultures, climates, programs, and structures. Yet the effort must be made. Second, the need for multiculturalism in the academy is so imperative that we cannot afford to wait for internal reform to occur. Pressures must be exerted to transform the academy by replacing existing practices with ones that are more culturally pluralistic.

Three types of reforms must take place simultaneously to achieve these goals, involving personnel, institutional development, and curriculum and instructional change. In order to be effective, efforts in all three of these areas need to be linked to the multicultural principles described earlier: they should be made in a contextually and developmentally appropriate way; they should be systemic and systematic in nature; they should recognize the integral role of personal values, beliefs, and life experiences in all teaching and learning processes; and they should be characterized by transformative, revolutionary changes that build toward a more inclusive educational community as well as a more just, equitable, and representative society as a whole.

Personnel

The hiring of more multicultural instructors and administrators is imperative. There is no way that multicultural education can exist in the academy without adequate personnel to support it. However, who these personnel are and the hiring practices used to acquire them need to be radically redefined. Currently, colleges and universities too often operate on the assumption that multiculturalism is the responsibility of only instructors of color. This assumption is fallacious and dangerously biased. First of all, membership in an underrepresented ethnic or racial group does not guarantee affiliation with the group or academic expertise in multicultural issues. Another problem with this assumption is that it exempts white faculty and absolves them of responsibility for implementing multicultural education. Professors of color who have expertise in multiculturalism cannot and should not be expected to do the job alone. We cannot earnestly move toward a multicultural, nonracist society until Eurocentric predominance is recognized and proactively addressed, particularly by European Americans. Most individuals in the academy would staunchly identify themselves as being nonracist. However, cultural and institutional racism persist (Scheurich, 1993; Sleeter, 1993, 1994). As B. P. Bowser, G. S. Auletta, and T. Jones (1993, p. 84) explain:

Redefining our communities of interest to include our participation in both our ethnic-specific community and new inclusive educational community is necessary for all of us.

However, because of the historic and present-day role of European Americans in excluding people of color from education institutions, a particular burden is placed on those of us who are European American. Those of us who are people of color have less power in this society and in education than do European Americans, but we are not powerless and cannot be excused from working to break down the barriers that exclude us.

Furthermore, the pool of ethnic minority candidates for college administrative and teaching positions is shrinking, and there will not be enough available in the near future to make a significant difference. The fact of the matter is that college faculties are and will continue to be predominantly white European Americans. Future hirings and promotions should be contingent upon all candidates from whatever ethnic groups and cultural backgrounds demonstrating multicultural sensitivity, knowledge, skills, convictions, and commitments. The addition of more ethnically diverse faculty members is an infusion strategy, while development opportunities and hiring and promotion practices that emphasize multicultural competence are transformative.

Another transformative way to create a multicultural faculty is through televised teaching and job exchanges in sister-campus programs. Conventional hiring practices where appointments to faculty positions are exclusive to a single institution and residential may have to be changed to more innovative arrangements. One possibility is to make use of technological capabilities to diversify existing curriculum programs and instructional personnel by developing a series of televised or video courses taught by ethnically and culturally diverse individuals. These courses could be in-residence at the hiring campus, videotaped, and then presented in the regular schedule of classes with a local professor or teaching assistant (in a team-teaching arrangement) serving as the course facilitator. The presentation of these courses could be further enhanced by using teleconferencing, interactive video, and distance learning capabilities for students to have personal contact with the televised instructors. We have the technology to achieve this kind of imaginative staffing, and it is financially feasible. Over a relatively short period of time, colleges and universities could develop an impressive series of televised multicultural courses and a highly diverse ethnic presence among their instructional staff. These resources could even be exchanged across campuses.

The possibilities of this hiring strategy are virtually limitless. It has the potential to relieve the stress of not being able to have a number of ethnically diverse faculty and multicultural programs in residence. Individuals who are unable or unwilling to change the location of their residence may be willing to teach televised classes for other institutions. Thus, one who is in residence at a university in California may also be a televised instructor for another institution in New York, Maine, Florida, or Wisconsin. Furthermore, this innovation could allow colleges and universities to access the expertise of individuals who are not traditional academicians, such as performers, businesspersons, writers, social activists, and filmmakers. The presentations of several different individuals in different careers on a common theme could be packaged together to form a single televised course. For example, a televised course on "Combating Racism" might combine the perspectives of a movie or television celebrity, a corporate manager, a novelist, a federal judge, and a labor organizer from different parts of the country and time periods. Televised courses could also add exciting international dimensions to the curricula and faculties of colleges and universities that are not affordable otherwise. Thus, students could easily have access to the perspectives and experiences of high-profile individuals in other countries who represent and are engaged in multicultural issues.

A less radical but equally powerful way to diversify college faculties and curricula is through exchange programs between sister schools. Predominantly white institutions might establish sister-campus relationships with predominantly ethnic minority colleges and universities, such as historically black institutions of higher education and Native American colleges. Arrangements could be made for the employment of faculties and enrollment of students in each of the sister campuses to be reciprocal, and for there to be regularized exchanges between them. At any given point in time a certain percentage of the faculty from the respective campuses would exchanges places with each other. Thus, an African American professor from Hampton University would trade places with his or her counterpart at the University of Iowa, if these two universities were sister schools. Students could travel back and forth between campuses without losing credits or being financially constrained. They could continue to meet all of the registration requirements of their home campus, but take the course instruction at the sister campus. An additional stipulation could be made that a specified amount of time, such as a semester or year, of all students' undergraduate programs must be spent at one of the sister campuses. This idea of multicultural student and faculty exchanges is not very far afield from some existing exchange programs in foreign language that use a semester or year abroad experience. The focus, location, and magnitude are different, but the intent is similar—that is, to enrich theoretical learning by practical immersion experiences. Thus, students' learning about cultural diversity would be enhanced by living and learning in culturally different settings.

Institutional Development

Because institutional values are embedded in and transmitted through imagery and symbols, colleges and universities need to create a system of images that convey their commitments to multiculturalism. A central element of this initiative should be the creation of a top-level, fully funded administrative position (possibly a vice president for institutional development) with line authority for developing and conveying a commitment to multiculturalism. This position should be similar in significance to a vice president for academic affairs. The officer and his or her staff should be responsible for developing, articulating, and disseminating the institution's commitments and developments in cultural diversity. The central function of this office would be to develop and undergird multicultural development efforts for students, faculty, and staff. Such efforts would focus on transformative issues related to personal values, life experiences, and beliefs about the current structure of U.S. society and foundational strategies for social change toward a more pluralistic, culturally cooperative (versus competitive and hierarchical) society.

In addition, this office for institutional development could undertake infusion-oriented strategies to revise current institutional structures. It might pursue several different activities to achieve this purpose: (1) developing media campaigns to promote the institution's cultural diversity values and actions; (2) creating a system of awards and recognitions for stellar achievements in multiculturalism by students, professors, and academic and administrative units; (3) presenting regular "state of the institution reports" on developments in multiculturalism; (4) creating a system of symbols that represent the institution's vested interests in multiculturalism, such as logos, mottoes, slogans, and pennants; and (5) administrating a distinguished professorial chair in multiculturalism. This office should be assisted by a multicultural policy body, with the same stature and authority of a faculty senate or universitywide curriculum committee, empowered to make binding decisions about multicultural issues for the entire campus.

Curriculum and Instructional Change

Several different curriculum and instructional changes also are necessary if multicultural education is to become firmly entrenched in the culture and ethos of the academy. Organizationally, these must include infusion efforts that are structurally similar to patterns commonly used by colleges and universities as well as provide some transformative alternatives. Within the university setting, it is especially important to enact such changes in teacher preparation programs because they have particular influence on current and long-term educational practices. The students in these programs will return to K–12 classrooms and other educational settings as teachers. Depending on the types of curriculum and instructional processes these future teachers experience in college, and beliefs they develop about engaged teaching and learning, they either will become educators who perpetuate the status quo or ones who work to change and improve the entire educational system.

Minimally, some formal instruction in ethnic and cultural diversity should be part of the universitywide or general, as well as specialization, core requirements for all students. By including multiculturalism in core requirements it will be impossible for any student to avoid exposure to it. Furthermore, this is a powerful signal of the institution's position on the importance of cultural diversity in the education of college students. These core requirements may be in the form of separate courses, as well as elements woven into other general education foundational courses. For example, students from across the university might enroll in a course on "ethnic and cultural diversity in the United States." They may also learn about cultural diversity issues and experiences in such courses as "speech and communications," "Western civilization," "American literature," "introduction to sociology," and "principles of human growth and development."

Curricular provisions also should be made for students to study cultural diversity within their specialty area. For example, programs of study for education students should include a specific course addressing the impacts of diversity on teaching and learning, with application of these principles further developed in subsequent methods and practicum experience courses. Offering both introductory survey courses and specialized degree options is an infusion approach consistent with curricular structures common in colleges and universities.

The availability of courses in cultural diversity is essential to multiculturalizing the curricula of the academy but this is not sufficient. Such courses should be complemented with reform strategies that focus on the kind of instruction that occurs within all types of courses. As methodology, multicultural education is an orientation to teaching and learning in ways that are more responsive to the cultures, experiences, contributions, and characteristics of the wide variety of ethnic, social, and racial groups that comprise the United States. It has content, process, and context dimensions, and involves classroom policies, programs, practices, and procedures. As H. Hernandez (1989, p. 15) explains,

multicultural education emphasizes the interrelationship of process and content. The one represents the substance of curriculum and instruction; the other, the contexts and processes involved in its transmission. Without addressing both dimensions, any specific approach teachers select is incomplete and inadequate. To deal with content alone ignores the "hidden curriculum" enacted in classrooms on a daily basis; to overlook the "intended curriculum" denies the subject matter that is the focal point of classroom life.

Consequently, issues such as establishing compatibility between teaching and learning styles, affirming the life experiences of ethnically diverse students, and giving voice to multiple sociocultural realities should receive as much priority as providing specific multicultural information related to various disciplines.

Another process feature of multicultural education is the strong emphasis it places on affective learning and personal involvement. Students should be encouraged to become personally vested in the pursuit of freedom, equality, and justice for all groups, and especially those who historically have been marginalized because of race, gender, class, language, and religion. This involvement should be promoted at many different levels, including knowledge acquisition, moral commitment, and social action. It is not enough for students to merely learn a body of facts about cultural diversity; they must understand the personal and social value of this knowledge, personally internalize it, and act upon it to improve the quality of their own and others' lives. Because multicultural content is inherently emotive, personal, conflictual, involving, and transformative, teaching strategies applied to it should be action- and affectively oriented, interactive, personalized, and cooperative; should legitimize the voices, perspectives, and experiences of different ethnic and cultural groups; and should give students many opportunities to examine their feelings and emotions about culturally pluralistic issues (Banks, 1994).

However, due to claims of academic freedom, it may be particularly difficult to negotiate changes for the kind of instruction that should take place. Evaluations may prove to be a useful point of entry. Most colleges have some system of student evaluation of courses and professors, and increasingly peer evaluations are employed as part of tenure, promotions, and merit pay reviews of faculty. These evaluations should be revised to incorporate elements of cultural diversity so that the quality of classroom instruction is assessed on how well it deals with multiculturalism. Therefore, faculty development opportunities and subsequent evaluations of classroom instruction and interactions should examine such variables as: the presence and appropriateness of multicultural examples and experiences used in instruction; variability in teaching styles sensitive to different ethnic and cultural learning styles; multicultural expectations transmitted to students regarding assignments and related activities; the use of assignments dealing with multicultural issues; the extent to which students are invited and encouraged to think critically, reflectively, ethically, and morally about different conceptions of knowledge and multicultural issues; the use of cross-ethnic cooperative learning groups; the regularity and centrality of multiculturalism in the content, context, and processes of instruction; and the extent to which students are taught to be socially responsive in their personal and professional lives.

Various kinds of incentives should also be used to entice instructors to become involved and reward their accomplishments in multicultural education. Existing practices of granting awards for outstanding teaching can be extended to the domain of multiculturalism. Internal competitive grants can be given for exceptional multicultural accomplishments in research, community service, or curriculum development.

A final, transformative strategy for implementing multiculturalism that has both curriculum and institutional development ramifications would be to create an entirely new academic unit. Universities could create a college of multicultural studies to design and administer programs dealing with ethnic and cultural diversity. This college could function similar to colleges of general studies or undergraduate education. All students would begin their college careers by enrolling for the first year in the college of multicultural studies. This one-year course of study could include general subjects taught from a multicultural perspective, specific issues and topics about ethnic and cultural diversity, and a practicum experience where students participate in some real-life multicultural situations. Students would have to successfully complete this course of study before they could proceed with their other studies.

CONCLUSION

Throughout the theory, research, and scholarship on multicultural education, there are recurrent themes that it is for and about everyone, that its effectiveness is contingent on systemic and deeply embedded institutional change, and that our future vitality as individuals and a nation depends on the validation of cultural diversity. Because ethnicity and culture are endemic to humanity, they can never be totally eradicated short of annihilating humankind. Individuals are healthier and society enriched by cultivating their ethnic, cultural, and personal diversities. A nation built on these beliefs will come closer to fulfilling the democratic imperatives of equality and justice for everyone than one based on the former model, which tried to make ethnically different people into imitations of European Americans.

When these ideals are applied to colleges and universities, certain standard features of their institutional cultures and structures are readily apparent that need to be infused with or transformed by multiculturalism. These include the administrative and instructional personnel, the institutional climate and values, and the patterns of curriculum and instruction. Whether the focus of multiculturalism is infusion or transformation, the degree to which it is successful will be a reflection of the extent to which its substance, structure, and discursive practices are informed by and responsive to these institutional characteristics. Therefore, a feasible way to begin the process of multicultural reform in colleges and universities is with a thorough understanding of their cultural ethos, and an identification of its points of conflict and compatibility with principles and practices of multicultural education. Then, reform strategies specific to these diagnoses should be designed. Such an approach personifies the principle of ecological and developmental appropriateness in planning and implementing institutional and social change. Its application will improve the overall quality and effectiveness of multicultural education in teacher preparation programs as well as in the academy as a whole.

REFERENCES

Banks, J. A. 1993. "The Canon Debate, Knowledge Construction, and Multicultural Education." *Educational Researcher*, 22(5): 4–14.

————. 1994. *An Introduction to Multicultural Education.* Boston: Allyn and Bacon.

Bennett, C. I. 1990. *Comprehensive Multicultural Education: Theory and Practice.* Boston: Allyn and Bacon.

Bowser, B. P.; Auletta, G. S.; and Jones, T. 1993. *Confronting Diversity Issues on Campus.* Newbury Park, CA: Sage.

Boyer, E. L. 1987. *College: The Undergraduate Experience in America.* New York: Harper and Row.

D'Souza, D. 1991. *Illiberal Education: The Politics of Race and Sex on Campus.* New York: Free Press.

Gay, G. 1994. "At the Essence of Learning: Multicultural Education." West Lafayette, IN: Kappa Delta Pi.

Giroux, H. A. 1993. *Living Dangerously: Multiculturalism and the Politics of Difference.* New York: Peter Lang.

Goheen, R. F. 1969. *The Nature of a University.* Princeton, NJ: Princeton University Press.

Goodlad, J. I. 1984. *A Place Called School: Prospects for the Future.* New York: McGraw-Hill.

Hernandez, H. 1989. *Multicultural Education: A Teacher's Guide to Content and Process.* Columbus, OH: Merrill.

Nieto, S. 1992. *Affirming Diversity: The Sociopolitical Context of Multicultural Education.* New York: Longman.

Scheurich, J. J. 1993. "Toward a White Discourse on White Racism." *Educational Researcher*, 22(8): 5–10.

Schlesinger, A. M. Jr. 1992. *The Disuniting of America: Reflections on a Multicultural Society.* New York: W. W. Norton.

Shade, B.J.R. 1989. *Culture, Style, and the Educative Process.* Springfield, IL: Charles C. Thomas.

Shore, P. 1992. *The Myth of the University: Ideal and Reality in Higher Education.* New York: University Press of America.

Simpson, R. D. and Frost, S. H. 1993. *Inside College: Undergraduate Education for the Future.* New York: Insight Books, Plenum Press.

Sleeter, C. E., ed.. 1991. *Empowerment Through Multicultural Education.* Albany: State University of New York Press.

Sleeter, C. E. 1993. "Advancing a White Discourse: A Response to Scheurich." *Educational Researcher*, 22(8): 13–15.

————. 1994. "White Racism." *Multicultural Education*, 1(4): 5–8, 39.

Sleeter, C. E. and Grant, C. A. 1994. *Making Choices for Multicultural Education: Five Approaches to Race, Class, and Gender*, 2nd ed. Columbus, OH: Merrill.

Smith, V. B. and Bernstein, A. R. 1979. *The Impersonal Campus: Learning and Development.* San Francisco: Jossey-Bass.

Suzuki, B. H. 1984. "Curriculum Transformation for Multicultural Education." *Education and Urban Society,* 16: 294–322.

Tye, B. B. 1987. "The Deep Structure of Schooling." *Phi Delta Kappan*, 69: 281–283.

Index

About the Contributors

NEVILLE ALEXANDER is Executive Secretary of the Health, Education and Welfare Society of South Africa (HEWSSA Trust), and Director of the Project for the Study of Alternative Education in South Africa at the University of Cape Town. He is the author of *Sow the Wind* (1985), *Education and the Struggle for National Liberation in South Africa* (1990), and *Some Are More Equal Than Others: Essays on the Transition in South Africa* (1993).

WARD CHURCHILL is Associate Professor of American Indian Studies and Communication with the Center for the Study of Ethnicity and Race in America at the University of Colorado-Boulder. He is a regular columnist for *Z* magazine and editor of the journal *New Studies on the Left*. He is Co-Director of the American Indian Movement in Colorado, Vice-President of the American Indian Anti-Defamation Council, and nation spokesperson for the Leonard Peltier Defense Committee. Ward has published extensively on issues related to American Indians, including *Fantasies of the Master Race: Cinema and the Colonization of American Indians* (1992) and *The COINTELPRO Papers: Documents from the FBI's Secret Wars against Dissent in the United States* (with Jim Vander Wall) (1990).

PRISCILLA LUJAN FALCÓN is a Professor of History and Mexican Studies at Adams College in Alamosa, Colorado. She is very active in the land struggle of Mexicans in the Southwest, and has worked for numerous years in the effort to defeat the English Only Movement. She has published various articles and chapters on bilingual education, history, and the experience of Mexicans in the United States.

WANDA FOX is an Assistant Professor in Curriculum and Instruction at Purdue University. She teaches a course in multicultural education and has been actively involved in developing a new multicultural education course for undergraduates in teacher education. She is also the coordinator for the Consumer and Family Sciences Education Program, which primarily prepares secondary teachers.

GENEVA GAY is Professor of Education, Curriculum and Multicultural Education at the University of Washington-Seattle. She coedited *Expressively Black: The Cultural Basis of Ethnic Identity* (Praeger 1982). Her works on multiculturalism include articles in journals such as *Phi Delta Kappan* and *Contemporary Education.*

SANDRA JACKSON is Associate Professor, Secondary Education and Curriculum, at DePaul University in Chicago. She has contributed chapters to *Developing Multicultural Curriculum for Teacher Education*, edited by Christine Sleeter and Joseph Larkin (1994) and *Education in Sub Saharan Africa*, edited by Cynthia Sunal (1995). She is currently working on an examination of curriculum and deliberation in higher education.

MARIE ANNETTE JAIMES * **GUERRERO** is a Visiting Professor at Arizona State University, School of Justice Studies, in the American Indian Justice Studies Certificate Program. She is the editor of and contributor to *The State of Native America: Genocide, Colonization and Resistance* (1992), and has written on Native Americans as indigenous peoples and on issues of race/racism, class, ethnicity, and gender and sexism.

FÉLIX MASUD-PILOTO is Associate Professor of History and Latin American/ Latino Studies at DePaul University in Chicago, where he is also the director of the Center for Latino Research. He has published numerous articles on Latinos in the United States and is author of *With Open Arms: Cuban Migration to the United States* (1988).

CAMERON McCARTHY is Associate Professor of Education and Human Development at the University of Illinois in Urbana-Champaign. He is the author of *Race and Curriculum* (1990) and co-editor of *Race, Identity and Representation in Education* (1993).

LINDA WILLIAMSON NELSON is Associate Professor of Anthropological Linguistics and Writing at Stockton College in Pomona, New Jersey. Her scholarly work addresses writing, rhetoric, speech codes, and classroom discourse. She has written articles for *Boston University Journal of Education* and has contributed chapters to *Unrelated Kin: Ethnic Identity and Gender in Women's Personal Narratives*

(1995), edited by G. Etter-Lewis and M. Foster (1994) and *Writers Craft, Teacher's Art: Teaching What We Know* (1991), edited by M. Schwartz.

IMARI ABUBAKARI OBADELE is Associate Professor of Political Science and African Studies at Prairie View A&M University in Cypress, Texas. He has over 30 years of experience with the struggles of Afrikans in the United States and has published extensively on educational issues related to the Afrikan experience, including *America: The Nation-State* (1990), and *Foundations of the Black Nations* (1975).

TERENCE O'CONNOR is Associate Professor of Education at Indiana State University and has written widely on issues related to educational reform, curriculum change, teaching, multiculturalism, and pedagogies of difference. He has contributed to the *Journal of Education.*

JOSÉ SOLÍS is Assistant Professor at DePaul University in Chicago, where he teaches educational foundations and liberal arts studies, including feminism and women of color. He is coeditor of *Foundations of Educational Policy in the United States* (1989) and author of *Public School Reform in Puerto Rico: Sustaining Colonial Models of Development* (Greenwood, 1993). He is currently working on a history of Puerto Ricans in the Puerto Rican public school system under U.S. colonialism.

LOURDES TORRES is Professor of Spanish Linguistics in the Department of Spanish and Italian at the University of Kentucky-Lexington. She has published in different areas related to U.S. Latina/o literature and issues related to Latinas and language. She coedited *Third World Women and the Politics of Feminism* (1991).

ARLETTE INGRAM WILLIS is Assistant Professor of Education, University of Illinois at Urbana-Champaign. She teaches courses in secondary reading methods, multicultural literature, and trends and issues in reading research. Her publications focus on the history of reading research in the United States, literacy, multicultural literature for secondary students, and multicultural education for preservice teacher educators.

ISBN 0-89789-415-4

90000>

EAN

9 780897 894159

HARDCOVER BAR CODE